THE HAITIAN ECONOMY: MAN, LAND AND MARKETS

The Haitian Economy
Man, Land and Markets

Mats Lundahl

ST. MARTIN'S PRESS   NEW YORK

Library of Congress Cataloging in Publication Data

Lundahl, Mats, 1946-   .
    The Haitian economy.

    Includes index.
    1. Haiti – Economic conditions – 1971-   .
2. Peasantry – Haiti. 3. Agriculture – Haiti. 4. Poor –
Haiti. I. Title.
HC153.L86   1983   330.97294'06   83-13852
ISBN 0-312-35661-7

CONTENTS

PREFACE

The essays contained in the present book deal with a number of themes related to my previous book *Peasants and Poverty: A Study of Haiti*. Together, they constitute a kind of companion volume to that book. On the one hand they single out some of the questions analyzed in *Peasants and Poverty* for special treatment, while on the other they examine certain related issues that were not dealt with in that volume.

Most of the essays have been published in journals. These are reprinted by permission. The original source appears after the title of each essay. Three essays are completely new: 'Haitian Migration to the Dominican Republic', 'Imperfect Competition in Haitian Coffee Marketing' and 'Co-operative Structures in the Haitian Economy'.

Financial support for this publication has been received from SAREC. Alan Harkess has corrected most of my English and has in addition translated the first essay, 'Haiti's Dilemma', from Swedish. Ulla Olofsson and Ann Sjöstrand have typed most of the manuscripts. Agnetta Kretz has drawn all diagrams. Two essays, 'Haitian Migration to the Dominican Republic' and 'Price Series Correlation and Market Integration: Some Evidence from Haiti', have been written together with fellow researchers: Rosemary Vargas and Erling Petersson, respectively. Both have given their permission for publication in the present volume. For all this, and for the constructive comments of friends and colleagues who have been plagued by my writings (acknowledged in connection with each separate essay), I am most grateful. Any outright mistakes and curious reasoning that remain are my own responsibility.

Mats Lundahl
Lund

INTRODUCTION

One way or another, the essays in the present volume all relate to the poverty of Haiti and to the failure of the Haitian economy to develop. In particular, they are concerned with the stagnation of the country's most important sector: peasant agriculture.

Haiti is the only Latin American country that falls outside the 'middle-income' category in the World Bank classification of less developed countries, ranking at par with Pakistan, Tanzania and mainland China in the 'low-income' group, with a per capita income of only US$260 in 1979.[1] Viewed in a static perspective, the Haitian economy does not appear in a very favorable light.

In a dynamic perspective, the situation appears even worse. The standard of living of the average Haitian has failed to improve over the past few decades. (If anything, it has declined for large segments of the population.) From 1955 to 1975, Haiti's real GDP increased at a yearly rate of only 1.7 per cent, and at the same time, the population grew by 1.6 per cent per annum.[2] Thereafter, only marginal improvements have taken place, and these improvements do not show any signs of being of the lasting kind. According to the *Institut Haïtien de Statistique*, during the seventies as a whole, the real GDP increased by 2.4 per cent per year.[3] However, the growth of the population during the same period is believed to have been of the order of 1.7 per cent per annum.[4] Furthermore, the rate of growth is highly unstable. Thus, in 1979, real GDP per capita fell by 0.3 per cent. The following year, it increased by 5.3 per cent, while the most recent estimates for 1981 indicate complete stagnation.[5]

Although a considerable degree of uncertainty surrounds these figures, they undoubtedly convey a very real message. The Haitian economy is stagnant. It tends to generate a strong pressure on the population to migrate, away from a society and an economy which seems to offer no other alternative than a stagnating or declining standard of living. Almost any other alternative would seem preferable, however uncertain and unattractive it may appear to the outside observer.

Virtually the only bright spot in the economy during the past decade has been the growth of the light assembly industries, which in 1980 employed a total of 60,000 people — mainly women — and which accounted for 16 per cent of the country's exports. No less than one quarter of the population of the capital, Port-au-Prince, is believed to be supported by the wages generated by these factories.[6]

In other respects, the economy has remained in the doldrums. Most significantly, the agricultural sector has proved incapable of expanding output fast enough to meet the increased demand for food. Nutritional studies point towards a declining calorie intake in rural areas, and urban districts, notably the capital, have become increasingly dependent on wheat imports.[7]

The failure of the agricultural sector to provide an adequate nutritional standard for the population is only one of the two sides of the productivity problem of that sector. The other side is that with time it is becoming even more difficult to make a living in the countryside. When rural per capita incomes cannot be sustained, a heavy migration 'push' is created. On the one hand, the exodus from the rural areas is directed towards the capital and, on the other, towards emigration. In the mid-seventies, Port-au-Prince was a city with a population of approximately 500,000. Today, the figure is believed to be around one million. The results of this influx are easily visible: mushrooming slum areas with extremely high open or disguised unemployment rates. The alternative is to leave the country, temporarily or permanently, i.e. mainly to cut sugarcane in the Dominican Republic under onerous conditions or to become a boat refugee trying to reach the United States.

Interpretations of Haiti

The first four essays deal with the question of the interpretation of Haiti's underdevelopment. 'Haiti's Dilemma' provides a summary of my own (1979) view, i.e. the argument advanced in *Peasants and Poverty*.[8] The argument is divided into three main strands. At the center is the physical destruction of the soil, caused by the tree-felling and the agricultural activities of man. As the population grows, more trees have to be cut, to provide wood and fuel. At the same time a process where labor-intensive cultivation takes the place of land-intensive activities is set in motion. Unfortunately, with the existing Haitian technology, this process is also one of increasing soil erosion which in a spiral fashion tends to undermine the productive capacity of the agricultural sector.

This process of destruction has been allowed to continue without intervention for centuries. Most notably, Haitian governments have never provided any assistance to speak of in any of the fields related to agricultural development. Possessed by a mentality that has held the peasants to exist for the sake of government, rather than vice versa, the politicians in power have taxed the agricultural sector without providing any help in solving its problems.

Hence, the core of Haitian underdevelopment is to be found in the interaction of economic, physical and political factors. The use of increasingly labor-intensive techniques in agriculture has led to a gradual deterioration of the natural resource base on which the peasants have to rely for their subsistence. The politicians, in turn, have done next to nothing to change this state of affairs. The interests of the peasants have been completely subordinate to the predominantly private interests of the Port-au-Prince politicians.

'Two Interpretations of the Haitian Reality: Critique of a Critic' is a response to a long review, by Giovanni Caprio, of *Peasants and Poverty*.[9] In this review, Caprio argued that my approach to the study of Haitian underdevelopment was hampered by the lack of a historical perspective and by the failure to incorporate the impact of the workings of the capitalist world economy into the analysis. He also reacted against my use of neoclassical economic theory in parts of the book, recommending that it should be replaced by a dialectical approach.

In my response to Caprio, I reject all of these propositions. The book does contain a historical perspective, especially in the section dealing with government passivity, a feature which in this case could hardly be understood without a firm grasp of the historical events that created this passivity. Likewise, an analysis of the impact of the international economy is also a part of my study, although it is not conducted in terms of the perspective called for by Caprio. International factors are most evident in the discussion of peasant production decisions, foreign indebtedness and, of course, the American occupation. Nevertheless, the most important causes of underdevelopment, in the Haitian case, are domestic ones, causes that are intimately connected with the way the domestic economy and domestic politics work.

The question of how present-day Haiti should best be analyzed and understood also constitutes the main theme of the next two essays, where the historical perspective is explicitly brought into the foreground. 'Haitian Underdevelopment in a Historical Perspective' examines five recent interpretations, by five different authors, of Haiti's plight. The first of these interpretations, by Wolf Donner, concentrates on the physical soil destruction process and on the question of why the Haitian peasants do not adopt techniques which allow for the conservation of the soil for the benefit of future generations and on the consequences of this for the agricultural sector. Two other authors, Giovanni Caprio and Benoît Joachim, who attempt to interpret Haiti's problems with the aid of the standard Marxist framework, based on dialectics and historical materialism, conclude that to a very large extent, international capitalism is responsible for what has taken place in Haiti from the first colonization by the Spaniards up to the present day. Their arguments are discussed, criticized and compared with another interpretation of Haitian history, by David Nicholls, which runs in terms of ideas of color and race. Finally, an examination is made of the imaginative solution of Haiti's problems offered by Jean Jacques Honorat, which partly rests on cutting commercial and other ties with Western developed economies and partly on a perceived difference in analysis and rationality between Haitians on the one hand and Europeans or Americans on the other.

The last essay in the first part, 'Written in Blood. The Story of the Haitian People 1492-1971', consists of a review of the most voluminous work on Haitian history to appear for a long time, by Robert Debs Heinl, former head of the US Marine Corps training mission to Haiti in the late fifties and beginning of the sixties, and his wife, a book which unfortunately has little to offer to those who are not primarily interested in the events themselves but in the forces and mechanisms which gave rise to them.

Man and Land

The Haitian agricultural sector operates under severe population pressure. Every year, a smaller arable land area must feed a larger population. The increasing pressure on the land, in turn, has given rise to a number of secondary changes. Some of the latter are designed to offset or mitigate the impact of the primary change.[10] Others are of a different nature. However, what is common to them all is that they affect the operation of the agricultural sector.

Among the most important population-induced changes are those that relate to property rights in agriculture, discussed in two essays in the present volume. The first one, 'Population Pressure and Agrarian Property Rights in Haiti', takes a long-run perspective. The design of property rights in the agricultural sector, not only in land, but also in men, has always been strongly dependent on the relative supply of men and land. The plantation system of colonial Saint-Domingue, for example, can be interpreted in these terms. When the slavery-based plantation system was created, the European demand for sugar was high and land was plentiful, but after the extermination of the indigenous population of Hispaniola, labor was lacking. To solve this problem, slavery had to be introduced.

Demographic changes also had an impact on agrarian property rights during the nineteenth century. The disintegration of the plantation system was to a large extent the result of the demographic decline that had taken place as a result of the wars of liberation. Once again, land was abundant in relation to labor. However, there was no authority that was strong enough to preserve the plantation system. Haiti became a peasant nation where family owned and operated farms became the predominant units. This form of agrarian property rights has persisted to the present day.

'Intergenerational Sharecropping in Haiti: A Re-interpretation of the Murray Thesis' deals with a particular aspect of the changes in property rights. In his thesis on population growth and land tenure in Haiti, Gerald Murray makes the observation that intra-family property rights in land appear to have undergone a change over the past couple of generations. Whereas formerly, sons used to be given a pre-inheritance grant of one-fourth of a *carreau*,[11] today, according to Murray, the first access route to land is via (filial or non-filial) sharecropping.

Murray interprets this change in property rights as a device for mobilizing labor. The alternative interpretation offered in my essay takes population growth as its point of departure. When the population increases and the arable area shrinks this is likely to lead to a renegotiation of lease contracts in the land market. The price of land will go up in terms of labor. This change, which can be traced in Murray's field data, is likely to take place regardless of whether the contracts in question are share contracts or entail pre-inheritance grants. From the point of view of labor mobilization, the former type of contract is not likely to do any better than the latter. Both types have coexisted for a long time. Viewed in this light, it may well be that the question of sharecropping versus other types of tenure is a superficial one, at least in the context of population growth. To explain the incidence of sharecropping other theories may have to be invoked.

Population growth in an agrarian society *ceteris paribus* leads to declining incomes. Following an excessive decline in income, mechanisms are triggered which tend to restore the old income levels or at least to act as a brake on the downward movement. One of the most obvious of these mechanisms is out-migration. Migratory currents have played, and continue to play, an important role in Haiti for alleviating the pressure on the land. Two of the present essays are devoted to a discussion of emigration from the country. Although the 'boat people' who currently try to make for the United States receive most of the attention, at least outside Haiti itself, other routes have historically been more important.

The first one led to Cuba. 'A Note on Haitian Migration to Cuba, 1890-1934' analyzes how, around the turn of the century, the expansion of the Cuban sugar industry gave rise to an exodus of Haitians towards the neighboring island. As a result of the wars fought in Cuba from 1895 onwards, the domestic labor supply was held at a low level. When the sugar industry began its expansion, labor had to be imported from abroad, notably from Haiti.

In Haiti, labor was abundant. Land was becoming increasingly scarce by the end of the last century, and the Haitians responded eagerly when given an opportunity to move in response to higher wages. In spite of difficult living conditions in Cuba, hundreds of thousands of cane-cutters left Haiti for Cuba between 1913 and 1931.

With the onset of the depression, the prices of primary products fell. At this time, population growth had also restored the Cuban labor force to a level where it was felt that the Haitians were no longer needed. Repatriation of Haitians was soon begun. Today, the migration from Haiti to Cuba is an event which belongs to the past. The Haitians who remain in Cuba are virtually all old men who came as sugar-cutters when they were young.

The second essay on emigration, written jointly with Rosemary Vargas, 'Haitian Migration to the Dominican Republic', discusses the size and determinants of the migratory currents across the border in Hispaniola, in a historical perspective. The first migrants were *marrons*, runaway slaves, who escaped to the Spanish side of the island during the colonial period, hoping for better treatment there, a wish that often came true. After Haiti's independence from France, in 1804, emigration took on a different character. The Haitian occupation of the Spanish part of Hispaniola and the subsequent invasion attempts produced a demographic vacuum in the border areas on the Spanish side — a vacuum that was soon filled by Haitians.

The third flow of migration, which still continues, was derived from sugar. Towards the end of the past century American and other foreign interests began to establish sugar plantations and *ingenios* in the Dominican Republic and the lack of sufficient domestic labor induced immigration by Haitians. As sugar cultivation gradually became the dominant activity on the Dominican side of the border, migration was little by little turned into a direct concern for the Haitian government. In the fifties an agreement was signed with the Dominican government which formalized the traffic. In 1980, some 200,000 Haitians are believed to have been residing, temporarily or permanently, in the Dominican Republic.

They live and work there under conditions which have been compared by some observers to slavery and are held in utter contempt by large segments of the Dominican population. Still, the Haitians keep moving into the eastern part of the island. After all, expected earnings are higher in Dominican *ingenios* than on low-productive Haitian farms.

Space and Markets

Internal and external migration can be discussed from yet another aspect: the spatial and regional one. The next essay, 'The State of Spatial Economic Research on Haiti: A Selective Survey', deals precisely with this facet of Haitian economic life.

Most of the time, economic analyses treat Haiti as if its territorial extension were negligible. Frequently, but not always, this is a good approximation. However, little work has been done on spatial and regional problems. The different regions are not even sufficiently described, although a beginning has been made, not least in connection with practical planning and development efforts. However, analytical works are by and large lacking. It is only in connection with the discussion of income distribution that regional differences and their impact have been singled out.[12]

The second important part of the spatial economy of Haiti is the flows of migration, both internal and external. Although internal migration has been a striking feature of modern Haiti for several decades, systematic investigation of this phenomenon was not begun until the mid-1960s. Nevertheless, much remains to be done.[13] When the survey was written, the existing state of knowledge regarding external migration was very incomplete. By and large it was limited to the flows towards Cuba and the Dominican Republic. Today, the flow of migrants to the Bahamas and to the United States have received well-deserved attention.[14]

The third and last area dealt with in the survey is the marketing system for agricultural produce. This is one of the better researched spatial aspects. Investigation was pioneered by Sidney Mintz and Paul

Moral in the 1950s, and during the first half of the seventies, a team headed by Jerry La Gra, under the auspices of the *Institut Interaméricain des Sciences Agricoles* (IICA), did an excellent job in mapping the entire internal marketing system and discussing how it functioned.

Whether the marketing of agricultural export and food crops takes place in a competitive fashion or not has been a matter of almost perennial dispute among the students of the Haitian economy. 'Imperfect Competition in Haitian Coffee Marketing' examines the case of coffee, or to be more specific, the evidence put forward by Christian Girault in his recent book on coffee growing and marketing in Haiti.

Girault argues that competition is severely limited at all levels of the marketing process. As far as exporters are concerned, he is undoubtedly correct. Their number is small and the industry is strictly controlled by their association. By means of fixing prices and quotas it is ensured that competition, which was fairly intense in the 1950s, does not lead to an undesirable number of exits from the market.

On the *spéculateur* level, matters are not so clear. The *spéculateurs* buy from the peasants and sell to the exporters. Their number is much greater than that of exporters which, in turn, makes collusion a much more difficult matter, a conclusion that seems to be borne out by the available figures for profit margins. It could, of course, be the case, as Girault argues, that the *spéculateurs* prefer instead to squeeze the peasants via advances against the future crop. However, the scanty evidence available does not seem to support this argument.

Competition is much more intense in the marketing system for food crops. This fact is the point of departure for 'Price Series Correlation and Market Integration: Some Evidence from Haiti', written jointly with Erling Petersson, where the interpretation of correlation coefficients between price series from different markets as a measure of market integration and efficiency is discussed.

This technique has been used quite frequently in studies of market efficiency. The method has, however, often been criticized. In particular, it has been maintained that unadjusted price series may contain common underlying trends and seasonal variations that tend to give rise to spurious correlation, so that markets appear to be well integrated even when goods do not move smoothly between market-places in response to price differentials. A suggested remedy has been to regroup the data into series for each month, to remove the seasonal element, and to correlate the residuals that remain, having also taken account of the trends contained in these series. However, as the essay shows, not even this method appears to be reliable when trade patterns are complex.

Change and Stagnation

Compared with the situation half a century or a century ago, Haiti's economy presents a mixture of stagnation and adaptation to change. Very many nineteenth-century patterns can still be found. Others have undergone changes when the framework within which the economy has to operate has changed. The last three essays all deal with stagnation, adaptation and obstacles to change.

'Co-operative Structures in the Haitian Economy' discusses the characteristics of three important co-operative elements in Haitian peasant society: the *lakou*, the *coumbite* and the *sangue*. The *lakou* system, which arose when the plantation economy was dissolved, refers to the traditional extended family and its common physical residence. It represented the social insurance network of the traditional society on which its members could fall back in times of need. The most important work in a *lakou* was performed with the aid of a labor team, the *coumbite*, which was organized on a co-operative basis and which contributed to making a most efficient use of the available labor. The *sangue*, finally, is a spontaneously formed rotating credit organization.

With time, the *lakou* has more or less disappeared, and the *coumbite* has had to adapt to harsher economic realities. The growth of the population caused the former change; increasing poverty led to the latter. This has put the peasants in a more precarious position than before. They live closer to the subsistence level today than a century ago and the traditional defense against deprivation has more or less disappeared.

However, it may be contended that both the extended family, albeit in a different way, and the *sangue* in a sense represent two of the most important insurance devices today. The *sangue* competes successfully with the undeveloped formal banking system and is not infrequently used for financing migration ventures, i.e. to alleviate the population pressure. The latter is true also for the extended family, or what remains of it. In addition, relatives — often fairly distant ones — are expected to help the migrants when they arrive at their new destinations.

Thus, it is possible to argue that the traditional co-operative structures could constitute valuable elements in development programs.

However, this is a doubtful proposition. The reason is not that the structures do not work. Rather, they work too well in the sense that, for reasons to which we will soon return, they may provoke 'negative' interference from the political administration.

'Obstacles to Technological Change in Haitian Peasant Agriculture' gives a summary view of why the Haitian agricultural technology has remained stagnant for more than a century. This is a complex issue, where a large number of factors intervene. Some are of a largely physical nature, such as the characteristics of agricultural production itself and the rugged topography of the country. Of greater importance, however, are the economic factors. The cheapness of labor in relation to capital, for example, tends to preclude capital-using innovations of the 'Green Revolution' type. Indivisibilities and complementarities in production, in turn, enhance these difficulties, especially if money has to be borrowed to finance the ventures. The growth of the population may have contributed to keep savings and investment at a low level. Risks of various kinds, especially those related to the trial of novel techniques in the local environment, make the peasants less prone to leave their old ways. The low general level of education and the difficulties of obtaining information regarding appropriate new technologies complete the picture.

Consequently, an obvious question is whether the government has tried to change this situation. The final essay, 'Politics, Peasants, Government and Technological Change in Haitian Agriculture', discusses why this has not been the case. The Haitian peasantry came into existence following the redistribution of state lands begun in 1809. During this process, the peasants became increasingly separated from politics, which became an affair for small cliques contending for power mainly to further their own private interests. At the same time, the peasants were left to eke out their own existence without any positive encouragement from the administrations. The gap between the ruling elite and the peasant masses is enormously wide, as Haiti's history eloquently proves. The government has contented itself with taxing the peasants without providing any assistance, and the peasants, in turn, have an immense mistrust of the *autorités*.

Various authors have attempted to devise development strategies which do not rely on the government but which instead try to get around it. Some of these strategies have also proved to be reasonably successful when tried on a small scale. The problem with all of them, however, is that as soon as they become more ambitious, the risk becomes so high that the government steps in and either puts an end to the projects or takes them over and corrupts them. At least since the early 1820s no Haitian government has sincerely tried to develop the economy. The welfare of the masses has been completely subjugated to the private interests of the ruling cliques.

Notes

1. World Bank (1981:1), p. 134
2. World Bank (1976), p. 6, *Institut Haïtien de Statistique* (n.d.).
3. World Bank (1981:2), p. 5.
4. Ibid.
5. Ibid.
6. Agency for International Development (1982), p. 7.
7. Ibid., p. 31.
8. Lundahl (1979).
9. Caprio (1979), reprinted in *Conjonction* (Caprio, 1982:1), where his rejoinder to the present essay also appears (Caprio, 1982:2).
10. A detailed discussion of these matters is found in Lundahl (1982).
11. 1 *carreau* = 1.29 hectares.
12. An atlas of Haiti is in the process of being completed by a team headed by Christian Girault at the *Centre d'Etudes de Géographie Tropicale* in Talence.
13. When the survey was written, the works of Locher (1978) and Ahlers (1979) were unknown to me. Both are highly commendable.
14. See Buchanan (1982), Stepick (1982), Stepick *et al*. (1982), for migration to the United States and Marshall (1979) for migration to the Bahamas.

Bibliography

Agency for International Development. *Country Development Strategy Statement, FY 1984, Haiti*. Mimeo, Washington, DC, 1982
Ahlers, Theodore H. 'A Microeconomic Analysis of Rural-Urban Migration in Haiti', PhD Thesis, Fletcher School of Law and Diplomacy, Medford, 1979
Buchanan, Susan. 'Haitian Emigration: The Perspective from South Florida and Haiti', in Agency for International Development. *Country Development Strategy Statement. Annexes, FY 1984, Haiti*. Mimeo, Washington, DC, 1982
Caprio, Giovanni. 'Un livre de Mats Lundahl: Les paysans et la pauvreté: Une étude sur Haïti', *Le Nouveau Monde*, Supplément du Dimanche, 5 août 1979
Caprio, Giovanni. 'Les paysans et la pauvreté, une étude sur Haïti', *Conjonction*, no. 152, 1982:1
Caprio, Giovanni. 'Réponse à Mats Lundahl', *Conjonction*, no. 152, 1982:2
Institut Haïtien de Statistique. *Projection de la population totale d'Haiti de 1950-1986*. Mimeo, Port-au-Prince, no date
Locher, Uli. 'The Fate of Migrants in Urban Haiti – A Survey of Three Port-au-Prince Neighborhoods', PhD Thesis, Yale University, New Haven, 1978
Lundahl, Mats. *Peasants and Poverty: A Study of Haiti*. London, 1979
Lundahl, Mats. 'Peasant Strategies for Dealing with Increasing Population Pressure: The Case of Haiti', in Claes Brundenius and Mats Lundahl (eds.). *Development Strategies and Basic Needs in Latin America. Challenges for the 1980s*. Boulder, 1982
Marshall, Dawn. *The Haitian Problem: Illegal Migration to the Bahamas*. Mona, 1979

Stepick, Alex. 'Haitian Boat People: Both Economic and Political Refugees', *Law and Contemporary Problems*, vol. 45, 1982

Stepick, Alex, with Tom Brott, Dan Clapp, Donna Cook, Julie Doan and Jockesta Megie. 'The Roots of Haitian Migration', paper presented to the Wingspread Symposium on Haiti: Present State and Future Prospects, Racine, 23-26 September 1982

World Bank. *Current Economic Position and Prospects for Haiti.* Washington, DC, 1976

World Bank. *World Development Report 1981.* New York, 1981:1

World Bank. *Memorandum on the Haitian Economy*, Washington, DC, 1981:2

I. INTERPRETATIONS OF HAITI

1 HAITI'S DILEMMA*

Haiti is a country which is usually considered to have certain highly distinctive features in comparison with other Latin American nations. Almost all Haitians are black; a legacy from the French import of African slaves during the colonial period. The white element in the population is negligible. The country became independent as early as 1804, long before the rest of Latin America. It has subsequently managed its own affairs with the exception of the American occupation 1915-34. The language of the country is neither Spanish nor Portuguese but the vernacular is Creole, which is a mixture of French and different African languages; the official language is French. The economy is based upon peasant-owned smallholdings rather than vast latifundios or plantations. There is little industry in Haiti.

In spite of all these peculiarities, Haiti is nevertheless an interesting study for development economists. Viewed as a *problem area*, the country has much to offer the observer. Moreover, many of its experiences are likely to be of relevance to a number of other economies with similar concerns. Haiti is by far the poorest country in the Western hemisphere. Indeed, it is one of the poorest countries in the world. Most of the symptoms that are usually associated with underdevelopment are found in a relatively pure form in the Haitian economy. In particular, it is possible from this perspective to compare Haiti with nations that did not gain their colonial independence until after the Second World War. A study of the Haitian experience in relation to that of other comparable countries could lead both to an earlier identification of the problems involved and to changes in those undesirable factors which can in the long run have an almost paralyzing effect on the economy.

The aim of this essay is to outline the fundamental causes of underdevelopment in Haiti. The discussion will be restricted to agriculture since this sector accounts for about 75-80 per cent of the total population and represents the most important part of the economy.

*Source: *Ekonomisk Debatt*, vol. 8, no. 2, 1980

The Characteristic Features of the Agricultural Sector

Haitian agricultural produce is traditionally divided into two categories: exports and domestic products. The most important export commodity is coffee, which is the major source of cash income for the peasants. Other important export commodities are sugar, sisal and cocoa. Cotton and bananas used to be exported but for different reasons they have now disappeared from the list of products that enter international trade. In recent years, essential oils and beef have instead been added to the list. The major domestic crops which are not subsistence products in the pure sense, since they are sold via a well-developed market system, are corn, sorghum, rice, root crops such as manioc, sweet potatoes and yams, as well as plantains,[1] beans and peas of different types and fruits such as mangoes, avocados, oranges and pineapples.

The majority of Haiti's peasants own their farms. Although the statistics are uncertain on this point, this fact is indisputable. Unlike the majority of Latin American countries, Haiti does not have a 'land problem'. Land is instead relatively evenly distributed between a large number of smallholdings with an average size of 1-1.5 hectares. To the extent that tenant farming does occur, it takes the form of a transaction between peasants from the same social class rather than, as in the case of Spanish and Portuguese America, a transaction between a landless peasant and a rich landowner. This fact is of enormous importance since it precludes the exploitation of the peasants via a monopolistic land market, reductions in rural wages and usurious rates of interest. (This subject will be discussed later.) In addition to the 600,000 smallholdings, there are also a few foreign-owned sugar and sisal plantations. However, they are of marginal importance and account for less than 5 per cent of the cultivated land area.

Haiti has a relatively abundant supply of labor, whereas capital and land may be considered as scarce factors of production. The country is one of the most densely populated in Latin America with 174 persons per square kilometer (1978). Moreover, the majority of the country's population of just under 5 million inhabitants are concentrated in the rural areas: about 80 per cent − the highest figure in Latin America. The rural population are entirely dependent on agriculture for their livelihood. In turn, this has meant that land unsuitable for cultivation has been brought into use. In relative terms, the country is more mountainous than Switzerland. More than half of the land area consists of mountainous slopes of more than 40 degrees. Due to the pressure of population, these steep slopes have also been brought into cultivation.

Haitian peasant agriculture is also short of capital. The average peasant has access to one or two simple hand tools: a hoe and/or a machete. Together with seeds, these implements comprise the entire capital input into agriculture. Irrigation, manure, fertilizers, insecticides or the plow are rarely encountered.

The working population to be employed within agriculture is relatively large. The standard definition of the labor force relates to the age group between 15 and 64 years. However, in the case of Haiti, this definition is quite misleading since children start work long before the age of 15. In addition, there is no retirement age in Haiti. People continue to work for as long as they are able. Furthermore, the ratio of female participation in the labor force is remarkably high, accounting for more than half of the women in the country. Of all the underdeveloped countries for which statistics are available, only Lesotho has a higher female participation ratio than Haiti. The abundant supply of labor in Haiti must be seen in relation to the limited employment opportunities that exist outside agriculture.

Haitian agriculture is well adapted to the country's factor endowment. Agricultural techniques are labor-intensive and maximum use is made of the available land. It is rare that a field is given over to the cultivation of a single crop. As a rule, the same field may contain five, six or more different crops at the same time. Rapid-growing crops are interplanted with slower varieties. Root crops are combined with tree and bush plantation, etc. The soil is rarely left fallow. It may be expected that this would lead to high yields per hectare. However, the shortage of capital combined with the gradual exhaustion of the soil as a result of the intense system of mixed cropping produces yields that are frequently below the average level prevailing in the Third World.

The Problem of Agriculture: Falling Per Capita Incomes

The great problem of Haitian agriculture is its inability to prevent rural per capita incomes from falling. (Haiti is, however, not unique in this respect. Falling or stagnating per capita income is a characteristic of many underdeveloped countries.) Evidence to indicate that rural per capita incomes are falling can be considered under three separate headings. First and foremost, there are the available statistics for agricultural production. Real average GNP per capita (at 1954-5 prices) fell from 419 gourdes in 1954/5-1958/9 to 396 gourdes in 1968/9-1971/2.[2] During the same period agricultural production per capita fell from 207 gourdes to 192 gourdes. Similar conclusions are obtained for individual crops for the period 1950-70.

It cannot be sufficiently emphasized that these figures for agricultural production are likely to be subject to a substantial degree of error. However, they appear to be borne out by the findings of a number of studies dealing with rural nutritional standards. The latter is a relatively well-researched area, due perhaps to the very poverty of the country. The time series data for calorie intake, protein consumption etc., which are, however, also subject to error, would appear to indicate a decline in living standards. Between 1966 and 1975, the daily calorie intake per capita of the rural population would seem to have fallen by approximately 25 per cent.

The third factor that may be interpreted as providing evidence of a gradual decline in living standards for the Haitian peasant is the marked change that has occurred in the traditional co-operative labor team, the *coumbite*, during the past 30 to 40 years. The *coumbite*, which is used especially at the time of sowing and harvesting, i.e. during the busy seasons, consisted traditionally of both work and a marked degree of *consumption* in the form of companionship during work and a feast in the evening following the completion of the day's work.

The work itself was carried out to music and organized hierarchies were frequently developed containing a number of (non-working) dignitaries who took part in the *coumbite*. In extreme cases, the latter could consist of as many as 100 persons. Nowadays, a *coumbite* tends to take the form of a small group of peasants, numbering between 10 and a maximum of 20, who take turns to help each other without any particular external celebrations. In other words, the consumption element has more or less disappeared altogether, which is probably a sign of increasing general poverty. The peasants can no longer afford to organize the more elaborate forms of co-operative work.

Market Imperfections

A frequently presented explanation of the substantial and increasing poverty experienced by the Haitian peasant is that in various ways, he is the subject of exploitation by middlemen and moneylenders. However, in the same way that it was impossible to state that monopoly conditions prevailed in the market for land, this hypothesis is also unsupported by the empirical evidence. We shall return below to a discussion of the credit market. For the moment, let us examine the markets for the products that are bought and sold by the peasants.

First and foremost, it is readily apparent that a considerable propor-tion of agricultural production is sold via a market system. Haiti is far from being a purely subsistence economy. Market relations and trade based on monetary transactions play a considerable role in the life of the Haitian peasant. A distinction has to be drawn between the market for domestic produce and the market for export crops, particularly coffee. In the latter case, a small number of exporters are supplied via a chain of intermediate purchasers, usually known as *spéculateurs*, rather than by means of the extensive, well-developed network of market-places. The marketing of domestic subsistence goods is primarily carried out by itinerant market women — the *Madam Sara* — who have success-fully established efficient trading links between both urban and rural areas as well as between different geographical regions. The *Madam Sara* are also responsible for the sale of goods *to* the peasants.

A high degree of competition exists between the intermediaries in both the marketing systems.[3] Profit margins are often extremely low. Indeed the low level of profits would seem to allow us to speak of a return to labor expended rather than an actual profit. No permanent limitations are usually encountered with regard to freedom of entry. The peasants have considerable freedom in deciding to whom they wish to sell. There are many opportunities to bypass one or several stages in the marketing chain. Price formation is markedly reminiscent of the textbook descriptions of perfect competition. Competition between intermediaries covers not only prices but also, for example, the terms of credit available to the peasants.

Hence the view that the poverty of the Haitian peasant is a result of the behavior of intermediaries is incorrect. The market mechanism operates extremely efficiently, providing a flow of accurate information regarding the prices, quantities and qualities of the traded products. The only notable obstacle to a more efficient marketing and distribu-tion system is the purely physical barrier formed by the inadequate transport system in Haiti, where few roads are negotiable at all times and in all weathers.

Erosion: A Cumulative Process

In order to understand the process whereby incomes are slowly but surely being reduced to subsistence levels, it is essential to start with an examination of population growth and its consequences for the country.

From an international standpoint, the rate of population growth in Haiti is not particularly high. During the first half of the 1970s, the natural growth rate of the population in the country as a whole as well as in the rural areas was around 2 per cent per annum. (The estimated average rate for Latin America was 2.8 per cent.) However, viewed in relation to the rugged Haitian terrain, this rate of population growth has fatal consequences. Population growth is the driving force behind a process of soil destruction that has shown an alarming tendency to accelerate over time.

Erosion is primarily a consequence of the pressure that an expanding population has exerted on the natural forest of the country. Two forces are at work in this process of deforestation. First, trees are felled in order to provide fuel for cooking. Given the relative prices that have prevailed during the past 20 years (and probably even earlier), there are no alternatives to wood and charcoal for the majority of the Haitian population. Trees are also cut down to make way for the cultivation of crops. As the population expands, the plantations extend further and further up the steep hillsides. Given the prevailing technology, the soil becomes rapidly exhausted and is no longer able to be used for agricultural purposes.

When trees are cut down, a given piece of land usually follows a particular sequence. Initially, there is a concentration on the land-intensive crops, mainly coffee, the principal export commodity. From the point of view of erosion, coffee has many advantages since it is a perennial that develops into a bush and tree with a system of roots that helps both to stabilize the soil on the mountain slopes and to provide a vegetation cover against the heavy tropical rains. As the population increases and the agricultural labor force expands, there is a growing tendency, given relative product and factor prices, for relatively labor-intensive crops to expand at the expense of land-intensive crops. Coffee is increasingly replaced by subsistence crops which have a markedly more damaging effect on the soil. Unlike coffee, they are not perennial and yield several crops each year. Consequently, sowing and planting has to take place twice a year – at the start of the two rainy seasons in the spring and fall. As a result, the soil is exposed to the full force of the tropical rains which wash the vital layers of humus down the un-terraced hillsides. After a few years of soil erosion, the land becomes quite worthless for agricultural purposes.

Unfortunately, this process is cumulative at given prices, since a reduction in the supply of cultivable land has the same effect as an increase in population. The relationship between land and labor will be disturbed, with labor-intensive crops once again replacing land-intensive ones. More land is destroyed at an increasingly rapid rate. It might be expected that this stage could be rapidly counteracted by a fall in the output of land-intensive crops while the supply of labor-intensive commodities increased. As a result, the price of the former would increase relative to the price of the latter. The peasants would thereby receive a signal to return to the production of, for instance, coffee. However, during the 1950s and 1960s this was not the case. The price of coffee is mainly determined by factors outside Haiti, factors that are unaffected by the country's own export production. As a result, the price of export crops fell relative to that of subsistence commodities from the early 1950s to the early 1970s which, in turn, led to a further spiral of the process of erosion.

At present, there are unfortunately few incentives for the Haitian peasant to try to stop the growing soil erosion. This process of land destruction contains considerable elements of 'external effects'. There is a marked mutual interdependence between peasants living in the same area. Woodcutting by an individual peasant may have a direct impact on a neighbor's crops, since it may give rise to a flow of water down the hillside. It is therefore not altogether certain that the efforts of an individual peasant to try to prevent erosion will necessarily have a positive effect. These effects may be sabotaged by the failure of neighbors to carry out similar measures. A further complication is that peasants who have extremely low average incomes tend to have a strong preference for present as opposed to future income. The initial costs of erosion control are high, e.g. terracing, whereas the returns accrue mainly in the long run. Consequently, it is unlikely that the peasants will try to solve their own erosion problem.

Is there a total lack of government intervention? The answer to this question depends on what one means by intervention. On paper, Haiti has very strict laws with regard to the felling of trees in mountainous areas. The problem is, however, that these laws are not enforced and that there is no system of control for their implementation. In order to understand the reasons for this neglect, it will be necessary to examine Haitian governments in a historical perspective. From the middle of the nineteenth century onwards, all Haitian governments have shown an almost total lack of interest in the problems of the peasants. This lack of interest has distant historical roots in the land reform of 1809 which broke up the colonial plantation system.

Latin America's First Land Reform

The first rulers of Haiti made a determined effort to keep the large colonial estates intact (particularly the sugar plantations). Attempts were even made to retain slavery – if not in name, at least in practice – by tying the former slaves to the estates as agricultural laborers. In 1809, Alexandre Pétion undertook Latin America's first land reform. Over a period of 30 years, the colonial estates were broken up until not a single plantation was left intact. During the nineteenth century, Haitian agriculture was transformed into peasant smallholdings. Subsequent attempts to reintroduce the plantation system on a large scale have almost all resulted in failure.

There were many reasons for the 1809 land reform. In the first place, Pétion used land redistribution as a political instrument in order to pacify the ex-slave population. However, this was far from the major reason. The colonial estates would sooner or later have collapsed. Above all, they lacked the necessary factors of production. Given the prevailing eighteenth- and nineteenth-century technology, the sugar plantations were in great need of capital. In addition, the intensive use of labor at harvest time was an absolute necessity. Neither capital nor labor were available in the independent Haiti. Much had been lost during the uprising against the French. A domestic capital market was more or less non-existent and free Haitians had no wish to work under conditions which were strongly reminiscent of slavery. Many preferred to flee to inaccessible mountain areas.

The export markets for sugar had been largely cut off during the wars of liberation and the Napoleonic wars. During the first half of the nineteenth century, the price of sugar fell as a result of increased competition in world markets. A further factor was that the governments who ruled Haiti during the nineteenth century failed to ensure an adequate supply of labor on the plantations that were militarily supervised and to prevent peasants squatting on the land at will. No political administration was sufficiently strong to prevent this taking place. Finally, the Haitian inheritance laws which provide for an equal distribution of property among all of the children have been a principal instrument in the subdivision of large properties.

Passive Governments

One of the consequences of the 1809 land reform was that former landowners were forced to find alternative sources of income. The radical change that had taken place in the labor market's pattern of operation prevented large-scale production on the estates. The principal means of accumulating a fortune was to seek personal advance through political involvement. In the absence of any direct control over production, the only means by which the agricultural sector could be deprived of some part of its income was via taxation. Political influence was required in order to gain access to tax revenues. The political arena was transformed into a battlefield where a number of small elite groups fought to further their own interests while at the same time excluding the peasantry from any form of real political influence.

At this time, the peasants had little incentive to react against such an arrangement. They had fought to avoid slavery and to obtain land. By the middle of the nineteenth century they had achieved both objectives and were able to use their rights with little external interference. The peasants largely acquiesced in a situation where 2 per cent of the Haitian population ruled the country.

This combination of clique rule and the confusion of public finance with the private financial interests of politicians had fatal consequences for Haiti's political development. The latter half of the nineteenth century was characterized by increasing political chaos which culminated in the American occupation in 1915. The country was ruled by a series of 'kleptocrats' who managed successfully to ravage the nation's finances and did not hesitate to place the country in debt in order to pocket the loans. Corruption ruled at all levels of the administration. This pattern continued even after the American occupation. The attempts to rid the administration of corruption were a failure. Following the departure of the Americans in 1934, the old order took over the reins of power again. It is hardly an exaggeration to state that Haiti has never had an honest government.

The existence of a weak central authority in Haiti meant that no government has ever shown more than a passive interest in the living and working conditions of the peasantry. On average less than (frequently very much less than) 10 per cent of public expenditure has been allocated to the agricultural sector in spite of the fact that the overwhelming majority of the Haitian population are peasants (approximately 80 per cent at present). It is not until recent decades that a start has been made to some form of indicative planning within agriculture. However, many of the projects that have been started have often failed, not least due to corruption or apathy within the administration.

The Consequences for Public Finance

The pattern of political activity in Haiti that developed as a result of internal feuds within the ruling elite left its mark on the country's finances — both in terms of expenditure and tax revenues. Instead of concentrating on economic development — particularly on agriculture — financial resources have been squandered. Nevertheless, it is the agricultural sector that has borne the heaviest tax burden.

On the expenditure side, three items have been of particular importance. First, there are interest and amortization payments on the national debt. In order to gain recognition as an independent nation, Haiti was forced by France in 1825 to pay an indemnity of 150 million francs. In order to meet the first instalment, a loan of 30 million francs had to be floated in Paris. The French government eventually agreed to reduce the indemnity to 60 million francs to be paid over a period of 30 years. Successive Haitian governments had a relatively good record of punctual debt repayment with the result that the burden of foreign debt was gradually reduced. However, on three subsequent occasions, new foreign debt was incurred mainly (although not officially) in response to the demands of corrupt politicians. Nevertheless, the amortization payments on these loans were met on a regular basis up until the financial chaos immediately prior to the American occupation. During this period, Haiti's foreign debt was consolidated in American hands. Debt repayments were given the highest priority by the occupation authorities. In fact, the country repaid its debt at a faster rate than planned. By 1947, the external debt was no longer a major problem.

The second major item of expenditure relates to the army and the police force. During the whole of the nineteenth century, Haiti was a substantially overmilitarized country. Prior to the treaty with France the country was naturally compelled to maintain a large army. However, even after the 1825 treaty, military expenditure continued to burden the economy. Large sums were absorbed by the military occupation of the Dominican Republic and by two subsequent attempts at invasion. Substantial amounts were also expended on the recruitment of soldiers within or outside the regular army during the political chaos at the turn of the century and on the periodic expansion of the secret police. This pattern of expenditure has been maintained throughout this century. Both the army and the secret police continue to play an important role in political life which is reflected in their share of the national budget.

Finally, a large proportion of government expenditure has been absorbed by the payment of salaries and wages which has limited the resources available for investment. As a result of the extreme use of the spoils system, a change of government leads to a purge of the administration down to the intermediate (and even lower) levels. A new group of people take over as a reward for political services. Simultaneously, the administration has been expanded far beyond the requirements of actual operations.

At the same time as public expenditure has been diverted from agriculture, the burden of taxation has been largely concentrated on the taxation of products which the peasants produce or consume. As is often the case in underdeveloped countries, excise duties on imports and exports comprise the major source of government revenue. These taxes are relatively easy to collect. However, this is not the only reason for the use of this form of taxation. In addition to the lack of an efficient tax administration, the ruling elite also shows a marked unwillingness to tax the upper income groups, i.e. themselves. Consequently, taxation has been concentrated on, for instance, coffee exports and the import or manufacture of commodities that are an essential part of peasant consumption. At the same time, luxury goods are frequently exempted from import duty.

Health and Nutrition

The lack of interest of the Haitian government in the problems of the agricultural sector can be seen directly in at least four specific areas which together combine to depress the productivity of the agricultural population. Standards of nutrition and health are low. The rural population is largely illiterate. Agriculture is unable to obtain credit at reasonable rates of interest. Finally, Haitian peasant agriculture is characterized by technological stagnation. Let us examine each of these factors in turn.

Standards of nutrition are low in rural Haiti. The specific age group that is presumably worst affected is pre-school children. As long as children are solely dependent on breast milk, i.e. during the first six months, the nutritional situation is satisfactory. However, subsequently, children become increasingly liable to protein-calorie malnutrition. In 1970, as many as two-thirds of all Haitian pre-school children suffered from malnutrition. Nutritional standards among adults also show widespread deficiencies. In 1975, it was estimated that the average calorie

deficiency in the rural areas was 35 per cent of the minimum recommended standard.

The standard of public health in Haiti is also far from satisfactory.
Although certain progress was made during the period 1950-75, intestinal parasites, gastro-intestinal disorders related to malnutrition, TB,
tetanus and occasionally malaria are as serious a problem today as they
were 25 years ago. There is a substantial lack of medical facilities in the
rural areas for the prevention and treatment of diseases. In 1973, there
was reported to be only five doctors and seven nurses per 100,000
inhabitants. Local healers of dubious quality were frequently the only
available sources of treatment.

Malnutrition and ill health naturally combine to lower peasant
productivity and thereby have a serious impact on the level of agricultural production. Many peasants are too ill to participate actively in the
labor force. The actual work that is carried out is of poor quality,
spread over relatively few hours and contributes little to production.
The peasants are trapped in a vicious circle. Since they are poor, they
have insufficient to eat and are unable to receive the medical treatment
that they require. They become weak which lowers both the quantity
and quality of their work. In turn this leads to inadequate income
levels. Unfortunately, this problem of malnutrition cannot be solved by
a temporary increase in food consumption. The only viable long-term
solution requires an increase in agricultural production but this cannot
be achieved without an improvement in the standard of nutrition and
health. There is no simple solution to this complex problem.

Educational Discrimination

Within the field of education, the Haitian authorities have also shown a
marked reluctance to give any form of priority to the needs of agriculture. This is evident in several ways. The standard economic approach
to the role of education in economic development is to consider education as an investment in human capital which contributes in different
forms to the productivity of labor. The provision of vocational education or a general school curriculum which could subsequently be extended to include direct instructions on agricultural techniques could
have a number of beneficial effects. Peasants would be better able to
understand the importance of change. Economic and agricultural
decisions would become more comprehensible. In addition, it would
become easier to find out about various products, factors of production

and farming methods.

Assume that the principal function of education is to increase peasant productivity. Viewed in historical perspective, rural education in Haiti has shown little evidence, with the possible exception of the past few years, of any investment in 'human' capital formation. On the contrary, the educational facilities that have been available for the Haitian peasants have been deplorably inadequate in terms of both quantity and quality. In the rural areas, literacy is still as low as 10 per cent, and less than 2 per cent of all rural children of primary school age manage to complete primary school education. The majority are forced to drop out of school after two or three years, often after having repeated classes. Two or three years later, most of the knowledge and skills that were acquired at school have been forgotten, since there has been little opportunity for the children to retain this knowledge intact. Formal agricultural education is rarely encountered within the public school system.

What is the actual function of rural education? Another interpretation of the problem of education put forward by economists is to consider the educational system as a filter for the selection of pupils who show some form of productive potential. Viewed from this completely different perspective, the rural educational system functions as a negative form of screening device that discriminates against the peasants rather than promoting the advancement of certain skills.

In order to understand how this process of discrimination operates, it is necessary to examine how the children are actually taught. In the first place, the language of instruction is French — a language with which most rural children have had little contact before going to school. As a result, the majority of primary school pupils in rural schools have to learn to read and write in a completely foreign language. Naturally, this has a drastic impact on the effectiveness of the teaching. The educational opportunities available to primary school children in rural areas are further limited by the poor quality of teachers, school buildings and materials and by the extensive system of compulsory examinations at the end of each school year. Hence, it is well nigh impossible for peasant children to obtain a school education. The opportunities for social advance via the educational system are minimal, which leads to a further widening of the gulf between the ruling elite and the rural masses.

Problems of Capital Formation

In our discussion of the organization of product markets, no support was found for the argument that peasants were exploited by middlemen. A similar lack of evidence has also been found for a related argument, namely, that peasants are required to pay usurious rates of interest for loans obtained in the informal credit market. It is also alleged that this is a principal cause of their poverty.

The majority of peasants tend to borrow for both investment and consumption purposes. Few peasants are able to save substantial sums of money. These loans are largely obtained outside the organized credit markets. The most commonly utilized sources of credit are the intermediaries with whom the peasant comes into contact in the marketing of agricultural goods. For the most part, these loans are made for consumption purposes — to tide the family over during the difficult period before the coffee harvest brings in cash income.

Interest rates on the informal credit markets are often (but not always) high. During the period prior to the coffee harvest, the peasants have a strong preference for any addition to present income. Consequently, they are prepared to pay extremely high rates of interest. However, this is not to say that these interest rates are the result of usury or monopolistic practices.[4] Loans made at an effective rate of interest of between 50 and 100 per cent are a cheaper method of surviving a temporary fall in income than, for example, the sale of livestock or land which would be repurchased after the coffee harvest. This type of sale-repurchase arrangement is usually subject to considerable transaction costs. On the other hand, the demand for long-term credit to finance capital formation is relatively low. The best long-term investment for the peasants, given the low productivity of traditional technology, is most likely to be in the accumulation of land rather than in agricultural capital formation.

Lenders also tend to show a marked degree of reluctance with regard to long-term credit. From their point of view, high rates of interest are necessary to cover the high degree of risk involved. The longer the duration of the loans, the higher the risk premium required. Potential borrowers are not prepared to pay the rate of interest demanded by potential lenders for long-term credit.

Several half-hearted attempts at providing rural credit have been made by government agricultural agencies. However, they have failed to reach more than 1 per cent of the rural population. One of the principal obstacles has been the tendency to link the provision of credit to the introduction of new technology. For reasons which will be discussed below, the peasants are unwilling to accept technical innovations. The lack of confidence shown by the peasants towards these attempts to extend organized credit has been a further major obstacle. In an economy where contact between government authorities and peasants is limited to taxation, government-organized credit agencies have little chance of success. The latter have also shown a tendency to attract some of the riskier borrowers since, unlike the intermediaries, they have inadequate information on the credit worthiness of their clients. Finally, the costs of borrowing have been in many instances excessively high.

Technological Stagnation

The shortage of credit not only makes it difficult for the Haitian peasant to accumulate agricultural capital but is also a major cause of the almost total degree of technological stagnation within Haitian agriculture.

The agricultural techniques that are currently available to the Haitian peasant are largely the same techniques that were used 100 to 150 years ago. In fact, there is some reason to suspect that Haitian agriculture underwent technological retrogression during the nineteenth century. The resultant low level of technology has remained largely unaltered for more than a century.

The complex underlying causes of this technological stagnation must be sought among a large number of frequently interlocking factors. The rugged terrain of the country has been an important obstacle to technical innovation. For example, it becomes impossible to use a plow when the gradient becomes too steep. Relative factor prices have an even greater bearing on the Haitian peasant's choice of technique. Labor is the relatively cheap factor input while capital (and land) are expensive. Many new technologies tend to require increases in capital input in order to be efficient. This is the case, for example, with high-yield seed varieties that usually require complementary inputs of both irrigation and fertilizers. However, given the high relative price of capital – in terms of labor – it is unlikely that the adoption of new capital-intensive techniques will lead to a decrease in peasant costs.

The problem of factor prices becomes more complex when indivisibilities arise in the use of capital. Draft animals or a tractor are essential complementary inputs in relation to the plow. Indivisibilities also arise in connection with the problem of securing a loan. Given the presence of these indivisibilities and marginal savings, individual peasants may be compelled to borrow a large amount of money in order to finance the introduction of technological change. However, as has been previously discussed, loans are not available at rates of interest below the expected rate of return from the majority of new techniques. The plow can be viewed as a special case of indivisibilities. As it is essentially a labor-saving device, it is the number of hectares plowed that becomes the important consideration. Peasant plots are generally too small to ensure that the saving in wages of labor input is sufficient to outweigh the cost of the plow.

Haitian agriculture is subject to a number of risk factors that can impede the introduction of change. The prices of peasant commodities may fall. Peasants who only produce a small proportion of their subsistence requirements are particularly vulnerable to an increase in the prices of products that are an important part of peasant consumption. Another risk factor is the possibility of increases in the prices of inputs used in peasant production. Harvest failure is another recurrent problem. The peasants have few effective forms of protection against such risks. Poverty prevents them from accumulating sufficient savings to protect themselves against a sudden fall in income. Under these circumstances, it is probable that they will be unwilling to take risks. As a result, innovation will be resisted since its effects are considered to be uncertain.

The profitable introduction of certain new techniques often requires an increase in labor input. The existence of malnutrition may consequently have a detrimental effect on the introduction of these techniques. In these cases, labor performance may well be inadequate. Finally, it is not at all certain that the peasants are adequately informed regarding the various techniques of production that are available. A lack of formal education is likely to restrict the efficiency of their search for new techniques. They are unaware of how and where to search. Unfortunately, they have received little assistance or guidance in their efforts to find new techniques. The general passivity of successive governments in relation to peasant interests is also reflected in this area. Technical guidance exists only on a very limited scale.

Depressing Future

The poverty of the Haitian peasants has not unexpectedly led to a substantial migration from the countryside. Although it began as early as the turn of the century, it accelerated markedly during the 1950s. The migration has taken the form of both an internal migration into the towns and an external migration out of the country. This process may consist of two or more stages. First, there is a move to the nearest town which is then followed by a move to the capital. Naturally, many peasants also migrate directly to Port-au-Prince. The capital is the major point of departure for people leaving Haiti. However, emigration also takes place from other parts of the country.

Until the late 1950s, Haitian emigration was mainly to Cuba and the Dominican Republic. In both cases, Haitians emigrated − temporarily or permanently − to cut sugar cane during the *zafra* (sugar harvest). However, emigration to Cuba came to an abrupt end after Castro came to power. The tourist boom in the Bahamas, in the 1950s, created a new demand for cheap Haitian labor. Migration to the Dominican Republic continued during the 1960s and 1970s. This period has also seen a growing number of Haitians emigrating to the United States, Canada, Guadeloupe, Martinique and other Caribbean islands. A large part of this migration is illegal. It is estimated that 350,000 persons left Haiti between 1960 and 1975. In addition, there is internal migration to the towns and particularly to Port-au-Prince, which grew at an annual rate of more than 6 per cent between 1950 and 1971, one of the highest rates in Latin America.

Migration has lowered the growth rate of the rural population from 2 per cent (the natural rate of increase) to 1.1 per cent. Migration is the principal safety valve through which peasant society can limit the fall in per capita incomes. However, it is an ineffective mechanism. First, it does not actually prevent the fall in incomes. Secondly, there is little employment outside the agricultural sector. The small, export-oriented industrial sector, like other areas of urban economic activity, is unable to absorb the flow of migrant labor. Finally, it ought not to be forgotten that Haiti is situated on an island which makes illegal emigration a highly hazardous enterprise.

The future appears bleak for the Haitian peasant. Soil erosion is destroying Haiti's cultivable land area at an increasing rate. The government's lack of commitment to agricultural development forces the peasants to rely on their own efforts. It is here that the major obstacle to economic development would seem to be. It is evident that Haiti would have enormous problems whatever the government. However, an essential prerequisite for any form of development process is the existence of political will. Condemned to a reliance on their own efforts, the peasants are quite unable to break the vicious downward spiral in which Haitian agriculture is trapped.

Unfortunately, political change does not appear to be forthcoming in the foreseeable future. Haiti's entire history would suggest that the opposite was the case. Consequently, future prospects cannot be anything other than bleak. If peasant incomes continue to fall, the mortality rate may replace migration as the principal mechanism through which population is adjusted to the land area available for cultivation. Malnutrition will continue to increase. Growing numbers of the population (particularly children) will die of starvation. Hence, Haiti will find itself in the painful Malthusian predicament where the population is compelled to reduce its numbers in accordance with the country's diminishing resources.

Notes

1. In contrast to bananas, plantains must be boiled before they can be eaten.
2. From 1919, 5 gourdes = 1 US dollar (by law).
3. This is true only for the marketing of domestic products. Cf. Chapter 10: 'Imperfect Competition in Haitian Coffee Marketing'.
4. This assumes elements of monopoly in the credit market whereas in practice, there is a substantial degree of competition between lenders.

Bibliography

Lundahl, Mats. *Peasants and Poverty: A Study of Haiti*. London, 1979

2 TWO INTERPRETATIONS OF THE HAITIAN REALITY: CRITIQUE OF A CRITIC*

In the Sunday Supplement to *Le Nouveau Monde* of 5 August 1979, my recently published book *Peasants and Poverty: A Study of Haiti*[1] was extensively and critically reviewed by Giovanni Caprio, who presented an interpretation of the problems of the Haitian peasant economy which differs radically from the treatment that is given in my book.[2] This fundamental difference of viewpoints has given rise to some reflections on my part which are hereby offered to the reader. The difference of opinions mainly stems from the fact that Caprio uses a dialectic approach whilst I adopt a more neoclassically oriented one. In order to bring our argument into focus, I will begin with a discussion of Caprio's criticism and thereafter scrutinize the alternative explanation presented by the latter.

Caprio's Interpretation of My Analysis

According to Caprio, my analysis of the peasant sector is cast in terms of a framework which was popular in the 1950s. This framework builds on the notion of vicious circles and leads to the conclusion that the main reason behind the stagnation of Haitian peasant agriculture is lack of capital. The reasoning is furthermore ahistoric, and my discussion is carried out within the framework of an essentially closed economy where insufficient attention is paid to the impact of the world capitalist economy on the peasants, their behavior and standard of living. Hereby, my analysis goes astray from the beginning, since this type of neoclassical analytical framework serves as a theoretical straitjacket which prevents me from reaching the correct conclusions.

The conclusions that Caprio considers correct will be discussed subsequently. Let us, however, begin by looking at his picture of me. Is this an adequate description of my work? To find out, we must briefly recapitulate the theories of vicious circles which were, as Caprio correctly states, in vogue during the 1950s.[3]

* Source: *Conjonction*, no. 152, January 1982

The populations of the underdeveloped countries have low real incomes, so that their overall ability to save is low. Hereby, the underdeveloped economies will be characterized by a general lack of capital which is translated into low labor productivity and hence also into low incomes. A vicious circle thus is at work on the supply side of the economy. Another, similar, circle can be found on the demand side. The low real incomes keep aggregate demand low, so that the incentives for producers to invest in increased productive capacity remain weak. Productivity stays at a low level, and so do real incomes. The two vicious circles are interlocking. As seen, one of the central features in this line of reasoning was the thesis that the roots of underdevelopment were to be found in the lack of capital. If only the economy's rate of capital formation could be increased sufficiently, underdevelopment would soon be a thing of the past.

It is, however, not this type of argument which constitutes the core of my analysis of Haitian agriculture. Instead, I describe the peasant sector in terms of circular and cumulative causation, which happens to be something entirely different. The theories which build on vicious circles are basically static theories which only describe the problems of a particular underdeveloped country at a certain point in time without taking into account how these problems were created and how they have changed over time. To arrive at a causal mechanism, and not only give a snapshot, the analysis must be cast in terms which in addition to the interdependence also bring in a time perspective which is historical. So far, Caprio is right. What has entirely escaped him is that it is the latter approach: the tradition that works in terms of cumulative processes − and *not* the one of the vicious circle − which I have chosen.

My argument runs as follows. Per capita incomes are falling in peasant agriculture. A fundamental reason for this is that population growth in Haiti has detrimental effects on the natural resources of the country. When the rural population grows, in a technologically stagnant agriculture, more land is needed for cultivation purposes and more wood is needed for making charcoal, since no economical substitutes for the latter exist for the vast majority of the population. Hereby, the extent of tree-felling will increase, and a sequence which exhausts and erodes the soil is triggered off. Hitherto tree-clad areas are converted into pastures. Pastures are increasingly used for cultivation, and the output mix of the agricultural sector will be changed in the direction of a higher percentage of labor-intensive crops.

This is fatal. Instead of coffee, the steep mountainsides will carry subsistence crops, and this is in turn highly conducive to erosion. The coffee trees bind the soil in a far better way than the subsistence crops and protect it against the heavy rains. When the coffee trees are up-rooted, erosion takes its toll, and the arable area of the country shrinks. Again, the labor-land ratio increases. Yet more coffee trees are uprooted and more subsistence crops are planted. The erosion process receives an additional impetus. Thus, this process is *cumulative*. Popula-tion growth and erosion combine to depress the incomes of the peas-ants. The cumulative process was further reinforced by the fact that between 1950 and the beginning of the 1970s (the main period under study in my book) the price of coffee (which is basically determined in the world market) fell in relation to the price of subsistence crops.

The sequence described above is not a static vicious circle but a dynamic cumulative process. One may say that this cumulative process constitutes the basic problem with which Haitian peasant agriculture has to cope. The cause is, however, not the lack of capital alone, but as we have seen, if any single factor should be picked out as the most important one, it is the increasing demographic pressure on shrinking natural resources. Increased capital formation can speed up the develop-ment of the peasant sector to the extent that it can help to combat erosion, but increased savings and investment *per se* do not guarantee that the cumulative process would be halted and reversed. To see why, let us go on to look at the second of Caprio's arguments: that my analy-sis is an ahistoric one.

The Need for a Historic Perspective

How should the downward spiral be stopped? It is obvious that the peasants themselves lack the capacity to initiate economic development, however much they desire to do so. Changes must somehow be intro-duced from outside; thus it is the government which carries the main responsibility for initiating and carrying out the necessary reforms. Very few attempts at modernizing the agricultural sector have, how-ever, been made in Haiti, and fewer yet may be qualified as successful. To understand why, a *historical* analysis of government passivity must be carried out — and *this is precisely what I have done*.

Pétion's land reform at the beginning of the nineteenth century eliminated the best way for the dominating classes to create a fortune. These classes could no longer fall back upon landed incomes, but had to look for new ways of making a successful living. Most important among these ways was politics. By dominating the political scene, access to government tax revenues (which could be pocketed) was ensured. The tax proceeds, in turn, came mainly from taxes on the commodities produced or consumed by the peasants. It is no exaggeration to state that most of the Haitian governments have been kleptocracies who have acted with an eye to their own utility rather than being guided by the needs of the masses.

The peasants were completely marginalized from the political process. A tiny elite ran the country and profited from the work of the peasants. This elite did not hesitate to indebt the country internationally during the latter half of the nineteenth century, by procuring loans, the proceeds from which primarily ended up in the pockets of the politicians. This period was characterized by a totally uninhibited race for the spoils and perquisites of office. Haiti became a soft state where corruption was ubiquitous; this state of affairs has continued, albeit in less extreme form, during the twentieth century.

The Haitian politicians severely mortgaged the development possibilities of the country by their foreign borrowing activities. Haiti had to carry the burden of a heavy foreign debt which during the occupation was consolidated in American hands and which continued to affect government finances up to 1947 when the final instalment was paid.

Without going into the historical analysis it is not possible to understand why the Haitian elite were so completely separated from the masses, and without the proper grasp of this separation, the analysis will fail to focus on the main cause of modern Haitian governments' more or less complete lack of comprehension of or interest in the peasants and their problems. This analysis occupies approximately 150 pages in my book, and the historical perspective plays a very important role also in my dissection of education, rural credit, lack of technological change, etc. How this may have escaped Caprio is a puzzle.

Closed or Open Economy?

The fourth main argument in Caprio's criticism contends that I am conducting the analysis in terms of a closed economy, i.e. one which lacks contact with the world market. From the foregoing, it should already be perfectly clear that this is not the case. In the process of taking foreign loans during the past century, the Haitian politicians created a dependence on foreign powers, a dependence which was of course especially pronounced after the American invasion in 1915 but also after the departure of the Marines in 1934, all the way up to 1947. During this period, interest and amortization payments were given priority over all other government expenditures – a priority which was dictated by the American occupation administration. It should, however, be kept in mind that this dependence cannot be understood unless the *domestic* political situation which made indebtedness a reality is brought into the picture. The dependence was not unilaterally imposed from abroad in an act of American imperialist expansion but was in part a consequence of Haitian events.

Thus, the international aspects are brought to the forefront when this is called for. This is also the case with my analysis of the production decisions of the peasants, which serves as foundation for the discussion of erosion. In this discussion I make a distinction between export crops and subsistence crops, and when the development of the relative price of these two crops is discussed, the world market naturally becomes a most important component of the analysis. As a matter of fact, the discussion of the marketing of peasant produce should leave the reader in no doubt as to the high correlation of the world market price for coffee and the price paid to the Haitian producer.

Caprio's Own Interpretation

Why, then, is Caprio so eager to label my analysis 'ahistoric' and to contend that I am neglecting the importance of international factors in Haitian underdevelopment? To answer this question, we must proceed to look at his own view of the problem facing the peasants.

According to Caprio, the roots of the problems of the agricultural sector are to be found in the foreign capitalist penetration of the peasant economy. The 'vicious' circles would disappear if only the dependence on capitalism could be broken and the negative effects of participating in international trade could be overcome.[4] The falling incomes within the peasant sector are a consequence of the operations of capitalism and of the integration of peasant agriculture in a system dominated by the industrialized nations which decide the prices of the agricultural goods exported by Haiti.

This argument suffers from two fundamental weaknesses. It is not possible to contend that the industrial nations fix the price of, for example, coffee, the most important export good produced by the Haitian peasant. In spite of all efforts to regulate the world coffee market, international coffee prices are basically determined by the interplay of demand and supply factors in this market which in the main must be considered competitive. If any single country may be said to hold a decisive influence over international coffee prices, this country is Brazil — a *producer* country — which so far belongs to the group of developing countries and not to the industrialized nations referred to by Caprio.

The second weakness of Caprio's argument is that the peasants are *not forced* to produce export crops. All serious investigations indicate that Haiti's peasants behave rationally in the sense that their production decisions are heavily influenced by the relative prices of different products, some of which happen to be export commodities. As shown by the events of the 1950s and the 1960s, there is little, however, that prevents the peasants from switching into domestic crops and hence reducing their dependence on the world market. During these two decades, products which could either be consumed on the farm or else sold in the domestic market-places were substituted for coffee when the price of the latter fell. This development also indicates that the peasants grow export crops because they want to do so themselves — not because any capitalist penetration imposed from abroad compels them to. Another good example of this is found in sisal production — one of Caprio's main examples of capitalist influence and domination in the agricultural sector. While the large sisal plantations dominated production completely in the 1950s, 20 years later sisal has become a product which primarily is grown as part of the peasant *grappillage*. Around 1970, small, diversified peasant farms accounted for no less than 60 per cent of the total Haitian sisal output. The large-scale capitalist plantations, notably Plantation Dauphin, found themselves in a weak competitive position *vis-à-vis* the peasants.

The conclusion to be drawn from this argument is that the peasants participate in the circuits of international trade of their own free will and that they can withdraw from this trade if they wish, i.e. should the conditions on which they participate become too unfavorable. It is not possible to explain the poverty of the Haitian peasant in terms of any international conspiracy, where he participates in an international trading system where others reap the profits and systematically deprive the peasant of the fruits of his labor.

In this context one should perhaps also stress another point which appears to have escaped Caprio, or which is at least not compatible with his methodology. The analysis of the erosion problem which I sketched above very directly points to the fact that between 1950 and 1970, when peasant real incomes were falling, the output of export commodities *fell* in relation to the production of domestic crops. Had Caprio's thesis been correct, exactly the opposite pattern ought to have been found, with the peasants going ever deeper into dependence on export crops for their incomes. By breaking their dependence on a world market dominated by the industrial powers, the peasants should have been able to improve their standard of living.

At times, Caprio's insistence on the paramount importance of international factors borders on the absurd. Thus, in his discussion on the role of education in rural development, he goes to great pains to demonstrate that today's educational structure does not serve the needs of the country because it imitates the structure prevailing in the developed countries – a structure which is alien to Haiti. I concur. (Although Caprio chooses not to mention it, I reach much the same conclusion in my book.) The point which Caprio fails to perceive, however, is that this is the result of *Haitian* decisions and has nothing to do with imperialist penetration. Already at the beginning of the present century clear-sighted Haitians, notably Dantès Bellegarde,[5] pointed out the problem and actively sought to produce changes. Later, similar positions have been defended e.g. by Jean Price-Mars.[6] Still, their pleas for a different type of education – oriented towards satisfying the needs of the masses – have not been heard, or at least not acted upon, but no external force is responsible. The day the Haitian authorities decide to have a different type of school system, nobody in the world will prevent them from creating one. (Ironically, the only serious attempt to break with the traditional system was made during the American occupation.[7])

The Dialectic Straitjacket

Which type of analysis is desirable when the problems of the Haitian peasant sector are to be discussed? Obviously, Caprio and I hold entirely divergent views when it comes to answering that question. In Caprio's opinion, my analysis has 'an occidentalo-centrist and apologetic character' and does not permit 'the fundamental structures of the Haitian social formation . . . to appear clearly.' Only a method which captures the 'dialectic interaction between exogenous factors . . . and endogenous ones' will permit the right questions to be asked and the right answers to be found. Only the dialectic type of analysis will do.

Here, I fundamentally disagree. A dialectic analysis is likely to go wrong from the very beginning, because it poses the wrong kind of questions. In the case of Haiti, and especially when analyzing the problems of the peasant sector, uncritical use of dialectics will introduce a serious bias into the analysis — as I have tried to exemplify above — and divert attention from the real problems. This is very obvious in Caprio's case. By concentrating on the alleged imperialist/capitalist penetration of the economy, Caprio fails to perceive that the essential problems of the peasant sector are domestic. I do not deny that investments, e.g. by multinational corporations, should be analyzed if a *complete* picture of the Haitian economy and its problems is to be painted. What I very strongly believe, however, is that primary emphasis on international factors is not warranted in a study of the Haitian peasants and their problems. The analyst does much better by concentrating on the domestic factors and letting international aspects come in only to *complement* the study.

One more thing should be made clear. It is never reasonable in development economics, which does not yet possess a dominant paradigm[8] accepted by a majority of researchers, to force the observed reality into a theoretical preconception *a priori* deemed capable of explaining the facts. Yet, this is what Caprio does when he chooses a paradigm which concentrates on international factors. His theory does not stand up when confronted with the facts, but to save the former, a number of observations which are of little or no relevance when it comes to explaining the Haitian reality are brought into the center of the analysis and are twisted and inflated way beyond the permissible. To borrow an expression from Gunnar Myrdal, 'Facts kick.' The selection of theories and methods should be guided by the problem and the observations at hand and not vice versa. Neoclassically inclined economists are often accused by their adversaries of applying their paradigm indiscriminately. (Personally, I tried to avoid this by choosing an interdisciplinary approach to my study.) Caprio, however, errs in the opposite direction. Avoiding the Scylla of neoclassicism he is caught by the Charybdis of historical materialism. There is of course nothing to guarantee that a ready-made mould of international capitalist exploitation of poor peasants yields a better result than naive neoclassicism. Both are essentially *Western* paradigms, originally conceived to explain problems of the industrial nations. In so far as they are to be applied to the case of Haiti, their validity must be demonstrated anew.[9] A doctrinaire view of the world never did the social sciences any good. An open mind, eclecticism if you want, is likely to yield a far better result in terms of research quality than any rough-and-ready formula.

Notes

1. Lundahl (1979).
2. Caprio (1979). Caprio's own interpretation was originally presented in his book *Haiti — wirtschaftliche Entwicklung und periphere Gesellschaftsformation*. Haag + Herchen, Frankfurt am Main, 1979.
3. See particularly Nurkse (1953).
4. Actually, this is not Caprio's own idea. The same argument appears in Pierre-Charles (1967), Chapter 6.
5. See e.g. Bellegarde (1934).
6. See Price-Mars (1959).
7. It is also doubtful to what extent Caprio's attempt to make Rosalvo Bobo an unselfish, fervent anti-imperialist exactly corresponds to the truth. Caprio writes: 'The heroic attempts of . . . Bobo to oppose a politico-economic servitude and to promote the development of the country, the hostility manifested against [him] by the imperialists has for Lundahl not played any role in the development of Haiti's agrarian situation.' This is correct, but Caprio fails to ask why. It cannot be denied that Bobo opposed American concessions in Haiti and the proposed American customs receivership before the occupation, as well as the occupation itself. More interesting than these facts are, however, his possible motives. Unfortunately Gaillard's otherwise excellent *Les blancs débarquent* (1973) doesn't furnish any information in this respect. It must not be forgotten that Bobo was about to become president of Haiti when the Americans intervened. He was at that point the head of the caco troops who had 'precipitated the downfall of Sam and was about to appropriate the rewards of successful revolution by intimidating the Haitian legislature into electing him to the recently vacated presidency' (Schmidt (1971), p. 71). His attitude towards the Americans could obviously also be subject to negotiation when it suited his personal interests. In his well-researched book on the US occupation, Hans Schmidt laconically describes Bobo's vain attempts to become elected as puppet president of Haiti: 'Bobo, seeing his chances for selection deteriorate with each passing day, desperately offered to make any concessions the United States might demand . . .' (ibid., p. 73). An anti-imperialist stand indeed! Finally, even if Bobo had actually played the role assigned to him by Caprio, it is hard to see how this kind of standpoint which (due to the preponderance of the Americans) never had any chance to be converted into actual policy could have affected the development of peasant agriculture.
8. The concept of paradigm in science is discussed in Kuhn (1970).
9. For a discussion of the applicability of Western economics (neoclassical and dialectic) to agrarian societies in less developed countries, see Georgescu-Roegen (1960).

Bibliography

Bellegarde, Dantès. *Un Haïtien parle*. Port-au-Prince, 1934
Caprio, Giovanni. 'Un livre de Mats Lundahl: Le paysans et la pauvreté: une étude sur Haïti', *Le Nouveau Monde*, Supplément du Dimanche, 5 août 1979
Gaillard, Roger. *Les blancs débarquent. Les cent-jours de Rosalvo Bobo*. Port-au-Prince, 1973
Georgescu-Roegen, Nicholas. 'Economic Theory and Agrarian Economics', *Oxford Economic Papers*, vol. 12, 1960
Kuhn, Thomas S *The Structure of Scientific Revolutions*. Second edition. Chicago, 1970

Lundahl, Mats. *Peasants and Poverty: A Study of Haiti*. London, 1979
Nurkse, Ragnar. *Problems of Capital Formation in Underdeveloped Countries*. Oxford, 1953
Pierre-Charles, Gérard. *L'économie haïtienne et sa voie de développement*. Paris, 1967
Price-Mars, Jean. 'Arts, littérature et culture', *De Saint-Domingue à Haïti*. Vire, 1959
Schmidt, Hans. *The United States Occupation of Haiti, 1915-1934*. New Brunswick, 1971

3 HAITIAN UNDERDEVELOPMENT IN A HISTORICAL PERSPECTIVE*

Giovanni Caprio: *Haiti – wirtschaftliche Entwicklung und periphere Gesellschaftsformation* (Frankfurt am Main: Haag + Herchen Verlag, 1979, DM 48). Pp. 338.

Wolf Donner: *Haiti – Naturraumpotential und Entwicklung* (Tübingen: Horst Erdmann Verlag, 1980, DM 48). Pp. 365. Creole translation by Jeannot Hilaire: *Ayiti-potansyèl natirèl é dévelopman* (Fribourg: Komité Ed: Kréyol, 1982) Pp. 353.

Jean Jacques Honorat: *Le manifeste du dernier monde* (Port-au-Prince: Imprimerie Henri Deschamps, 1980, 50 gourdes). Pp. 219.

Benoît Joachim: *Les racines du sous-développement en Haïti* (Port-au-Prince: Imprimerie Henri Deschamps, 1979, 50 gourdes). Pp. 257.

David Nicholls: *From Dessalines to Duvalier. Race, Colour and National Independence in Haiti* (Cambridge: Cambridge University Press, 1979, £17.50). Pp. 357.

The literature on Haiti is growing rapidly. From an economist's perspective, the most interesting works are those that discuss the manifestations of the country's underdevelopment, its evolution in a historical perspective and the possible ways towards a higher standard of living for the majority of the population. These questions are dealt with in different ways in the five books that constitute the basis for the present survey.

Wolf Donner concentrates on the physical manifestations of poverty and underdevelopment and the reasons behind this state from the perspective of physical geography. In Donner's view, Haiti constitutes an example of how a sovereign state in the Tropics has brought its natural base to the verge of physical annihilation without having made any visible progress. Agricultural production is stagnant or, on a per capita basis, falling. When Columbus discovered Hispaniola in 1492, he wrote a highly enthusiastic account of the island's lush vegetation.

*Source: *Journal of Latin American Studies*, vol. 14, no. 2, 1982 (Cambridge University Press, Cambridge)

Today, as a result of human action, the country is virtually denuded. The small forest-clad areas that still remain display severe signs of degeneration and shrink rapidly. Most of the cultivated land is in mountainous terrain which *per se* is not suited for agriculture. With the farming techniques employed in Haiti, erosion has taken a heavy toll during more than two centuries.

Nevertheless, Haitian land is capable of a higher productivity than is currently available. Moreover, according to Donner, this could be achieved by methods that do not destroy the soil. However, that would require a spatial redistribution of the population in order to reduce the pressure on those areas where most damage is being done, a most difficult measure to undertake in a country where the peasant population has a proverbial reputation for clinging to the soil and where interference with peasant ownership of land has always been met with utter suspicion, if not hostility.

Techniques for soil conservation do, however, exist and Donner enumerates them. The problem is rather to persuade the peasants to adopt techniques which they do not perceive to be of any immediate use. Myopia on the part of the farming community, founded in the necessity to produce enough to stay alive in the short run, often precludes the adoption of techniques that in a long-run perspective would prove superior.

The solution attempted hitherto has mainly been one of migration, which each year relieves some of the population pressure in the countryside. This migration goes partly to other countries and partly to urban areas where jobs can be found. However, non-agricultural jobs do not abound. The rapid growth of export-oriented assembly industries during the 1970s did not create more than some 50,000 new jobs, and this proved to be insufficient to absorb the growing labor force. In addition, these industries are heavily dependent on foreign markets, on imported raw materials and on foreign capital. Naturally this makes them vulnerable to a number of circumstances beyond national control. The external population outlet, in turn, is already to an overwhelming extent illegal, and if efficient measures are taken abroad to reduce the immigration of Haitians, as is for example the current trend in the United States, this way out of the population dilemma may easily be closed.

Thus, the Haitian economy is in a straitjacket, and this is especially true of the sector where the majority of the population work: agriculture. The output of this sector today is not large enough to feed the increasing population adequately. Resort has had to be made to food imports. The situation does not show any signs of improvement in the near future; on the contrary, a further deterioration is to be expected.

How did the Haitian economy get into this awkward situation? Two hundred years ago Saint-Domingue produced enough to be the most lucrative colony in the entire world, and after the French had finally been expelled in 1804, the country has been politically sovereign, with the exception of the American occupation between 1915 and 1934. It was the first colony to throw off the yoke of foreign domination. Haiti has had almost 180 years to develop a way to produce a decent standard of living for its population but has failed to do so. Why?

The answer to this question occupies the most important sections of the books by Giovanni Caprio and Benoît Joachim. Both these authors lean heavily on a standard Marxist interpretation of Haitian history. However, their time perspectives differ. Caprio covers the entire period from 1492 to the present while Joachim concentrates on the nineteenth century. The thesis of both books is that Haiti's underdevelopment is intimately connected with the country's historical dependence on colonial and neocolonial economic interests which in different ways have harmed the country. Domestically, this dependence has its counterpart in the domination of the masses by an upper class which shares and serves the foreign interests. This dependence on foreign interests has created a deformed economy which has been characterized by the simultaneous existence of different modes of production (structural heterogeneity), with a form of neofeudalism dominating in the nineteenth century (Joachim) while today, capitalism is paramount (Caprio).

The Caprio-Joachim argument is an interesting and provocative one. Is it the case that Haiti's underdevelopment can be explained mainly with reference to external factors, or could it be that internally generated mechanisms were of equal importance or perhaps carried even greater weight? While Caprio and Joachim stress the former they have a strong tendency to underestimate the importance of the latter.

A good example is given by their treatment of Haiti's foreign debt. In the Caprio-Joachim view, interest and amortization payments on the foreign debt constituted an important method of transferring values from Haiti to the capitalist countries, above all to France and the United States, who are indirectly held responsible for a large portion of Haitian underdevelopment. This, however, is only a half-truth. Debt payments undoubtedly constituted a drain on the Haitian treasury during the nineteenth and twentieth centuries up to 1947. In 1825, the French forced a heavy indemnity on Haiti at gunpoint in order to recognize the country's independence, and a loan had to be taken in

Paris in order to secure payment. New foreign loans were subsequently taken in 1874, 1875 and 1896. In addition, towards the end of the nineteenth and at the beginning of the twentieth century, a number of domestic loans were also taken, where large shares accrued to foreigners residing in the country. Both Caprio and Joachim interpret these loans as a means of neocolonial exploitation.

Such a view is, however, dubious. It is correct that the 1825 loan was forced on the country, but the others were not. Officially they were made to consolidate the foreign debt or to undertake public works. In reality they were mainly the result of domestic politicking. Their purpose was to replenish an empty public treasury in order to allow whoever happened to be in power to obtain a better pecuniary return from holding office.[1] Thus, however much the foreign or domestic debt retarded economic development (with the exception of the 1825 indemnity), this was not so much a result of onerous conditions imposed from abroad as of the low level of domestic politics.

Towards the end of the nineteenth century and at the beginning of the present one, a number of concessions regarding infrastructural investments were given to foreign interests. Joachim and Caprio also interpret these as mechanisms for foreign penetration, and conclude that since little came out of them, their development value to Haiti was more or less negative. These concessions served to keep the country dependent rather than to develop it. Foreign investment also continued during and after the end of the American occupation (1915-34). For Caprio, the establishment of a number of American-owned agricultural companies in Haiti between 1915 and 1934 continued what the infrastructural concessions had started. Haiti would have been in a better position if neither set of investments had been undertaken.

This view also appears to me to be exaggerated. While I certainly do not doubt that little was derived from many of the foreign investments, I hardly think that their absence would have made much difference from a development point of view. Considering in the first place, the quality of the administrations that Haiti possessed around the turn of the century up to 1915 and in the second place, the low quantitative importance of US agricultural investments[2] (only HASCO (sugar) and the Plantation Dauphin (sisal) survived the end of the occupation), the probability that Haiti would have been more developed in the absence of foreign investment during this particular period is low. Again, the role of external factors is stressed while too little attention is paid to the domestic ones.

A third case in point is international trade. In conventional economic theory, trade is held to be at least potentially beneficial for a country. Joachim and Caprio present a different view. The concentration of Haitian exports and imports first on France and thereafter on the United States provides yet another mechanism for foreign domination. This is, however, not clearly demonstrated. The mere fact that international trade took place does not demonstrate anything, nor do vague references to 'unequal exchange'. Furthermore Joachim presents the strange argument that foreign trade revenues did not benefit Haiti, since they had to be used to repay the external debt. This argument confuses the effects of trade *per se* with the effects of foreign debt repayment and, as we know, the debt to a large extent was the result of domestic factors. If Haiti had exported *less*, the country presumably would have been in a *more* precarious situation since interest and amortization payments would then have been even harder to meet.

Dealing with Joachim, there are at least two other arguments that appear somewhat dubious. The first one concerns the development of landholdings and ownership during the nineteenth century. According to Joachim, the agrarian structure even after the land reforms that took place, beginning in 1809, continued to be characterized by the existence of a class of large landowners who exploited a peasant class that rented land on a share tenancy basis. This contention, however, violates the known facts. It is not true that nineteenth-century rural Haiti worked in this way. Recent investigations have demonstrated both how and why the breakdown of the colonial plantation system took place and why the sharecropping system did not work in the manner envisaged by Joachim.[3] Hence the neofeudal argument runs counter to the observed facts. The mechanisms necessary to conserve a large-scale ownership structure were simply not present.

The second point deals with the color issue. Joachim states that attempts to interpret Haiti's history in terms of color conflicts only serve to hide the real nature of the underdevelopment problem, namely the existence of a hybrid economic structure which was basically feudal but which was simultaneously disturbed by the domination of international capitalism. In this context, it is interesting to compare Joachim's view with that of David Nicholls, since Nicholls's book deals precisely with the importance of ideas based on color and race as a determinant of the course of politics and historical events in Haiti.

In a sense, Nicholls presents the reader with an idealistic view of history: 'the ideas and beliefs of Haitians, which must be seen largely as the products of their history, have influenced their actions . . . the story of the country cannot therefore be told without a knowledge of these ideas.'[4] His point of departure is the difference between the two concepts of race and color. *Race*, in Nicholls's book, refers to 'a set of persons who regard themselves and are generally regarded as being connected in some significant way by extrafamilial common descent', whereas *color* refers to 'pheno-typical or somatic characteristics, specifically to skin color, type of hair, nose and lips'.[5]

Race and color have played very different roles in the history of Haiti. The idea of race has served to unify the nation, at least up to the 1960s. All Haitians basically think of themselves as having a common African ancestry. This feeling has been an important factor in the struggle for and defense of political independence. Color, on the other hand, has frequently served to divide the nation since the color issue has given rise to different ideologies which are in turn largely based on the color of the proponents of these ideologies themselves. The ideological disputes naturally were confined to elite circles but in the process of bidding for power both mulattoes and Negroes have invoked the color question when it has been to their advantage to do so. For any government it has been of importance to ensure that large parts of the population tacitly and passively have accepted its presence, even though the political struggle has by and large been limited to the elite minority.

It is in this light, according to Nicholls, that the color issue has to be seen. Thus, mulatto politicians in their contact with the black masses have stressed the unity and harmony between the two color groups, whereas Negro politicians have put emphasis on color as a line of division between the masses and the mulatto elite members. Such was the pattern that persisted between 1804 and 1915. During the occupation, however, the first seeds of what was later to become the *Négritude* movement were sown and with that emerged a new tendency among young Negro intellectuals to put more emphasis on race.[6] It was contended that there were wide psychological differences between the white and Nego races. Consequently, it was argued, the Haitians should cease looking for intellectual guidance and standards in Europe and should instead build on the African cultural heritage. The idea was not shared by a majority of the mulattoes who kept and nurtured the old association with France. Thus, after the occupation, race became more of a dividing issue — a tendency which was to be reinforced under Estimé, when the Négritude theoreticians were able for the first time to cash in politically on their ideas, and even more under Duvalier.

Nicholls asserts that between 1804 and 1915 political struggle in Haiti was mainly a struggle for power along color lines. The problem of adhering to such a view is of course a tendency to view Haitian history through what Nicholls himself calls *lunettes bicouleures*, i.e. to attempt to trace all divisions of opinions and all internal strife back to the color question. Nicholls has not quite succeeded in avoiding falling into this trap as is most noticeably evident in the chapter on Papa Doc, where he attempts an interesting reinterpretaion of the phenomenon of papadocracy. Instead of subscribing to the view that Duvalier was a maximizer of private wealth and power or the view that he was a maniac who had studied too much voodoo and sociology, Nicholls contends that Duvalier assumed power endowed with certain ideas — the Négritude theories — which he wanted to translate into practical political action. He projected himself as a spokesman for the masses, sometimes with religious overtones, when comparing himself with Jesus Christ. These ideas, according to Nicholls, go a long way towards explaining the harsh treatment of his political opponents — real or imagined.

At this point, I think that Nicholls stretches his thesis too far. The Duvalier phenomenon is much too complex to be reduced to one or two dimensions.[7] The complete picture certainly does include elements of the other two views as well. A president moved mainly by ideological reasons would hardly be suspected of transferring more than US$7 million per year out of the country for personal purposes.[8] To understand this, one has to view Duvalier in a quite different perspective, as a link in the virtually uninterrupted chain of selfish Haitian politicians, seeking office to share the spoils, that goes way back into the nineteenth century.[9] Nor does it sound very plausible that someone comparing himself with Christ does not display a trait or two that may be of a certain psychiatric interest.[10]

His view of Duvalier leads Nicholls to at least one very strange conclusion:

> Perhaps the most significant result of Duvalier's 'revolution' will turn out to be the sense which was given to the mass of the peasants that they were really citizens and what they did was important . . . and a growing belief that something can be done to affect the course of events. This is partly due to the countrywide organisation of the VSN [*tonton macoutes*] and to the populist rhetoric of the regime . . . If people are told often enough that they are important, they may begin to believe it.[11]

I doubt that this conclusion is correct. The history of the relations of the Haitian masses, particularly the peasants, with the governments is not one of taking the words of politicians for granted. The peasants have proved remarkably passive when it comes to 'affecting the course' of, at least, economic events by introducing or accepting novel behavior. One explanation of this 'conservative' behavior is the risks that changes may entail.[12] There is no reason to believe that risk aversion should not be an important consideration in the field of political action as well, especially since the political arena is one which is completely alien to the peasants.

Nicholls's book is of special interest to economists in that it casts a sidelight on the hotly debated issue that we have already touched upon, namely, that of whether Haitian underdevelopment should be considered the outcome of a domestic process or as a result of the intervention of international economic and political factors. What Nicholls shows is that in their fight for political power, neither Negroes nor mulattoes have hesitated to offer to mortgage the country politically and economically to foreign interests in return for an upper hand in domestic political life. Thus, to a certain extent *domestic* factors were also responsible for the possible negative effects of *foreign* investment, e.g. during the decade preceding the American occupation, and perhaps even for provoking the occupation itself, if it can be assumed that the main cause of the latter was an American desire to secure continued and widened economic influence in Haiti.[13]

What can be done to solve Haiti's development problems? An imaginative prescription is given by Jean Jacques Honorat. His point of departure is that Western large-scale technology with its emphasis on a capitalist mode of production and large markets will not lead to development. Rather, it may serve to reinforce dependence and aggravate underdevelopment. Nor will an intermediate technology as advocated, e.g. by Schumacher[14] (smallness, simplicity, capital cheapness) do the trick. In Honorat's view, this will never create a sufficient level of productivity to allow the Haitian producers to compete with imports from the capitalist countries. Moreover, the country is too small to allow for complete self-reliance. Instead, a domestic innovation capacity must be created which can create an appropriate technology which is productive enough to be competitive.

For Honorat, the only possible way to development is one which rests on the principle of self-reliance. Contacts with the Western world via trade and capital movements must be excluded. Such contacts only operate to the benefit of the developed countries. Honorat professes to share the critical attitude of the indigenist movement against the dominant European culture. However, Haiti is too small to be able to stay out of international trade altogether. But trade with developed nations would not be beneficial. The solution envisaged is the integration with other Third World countries in common markets, e.g. in the Caribbean.

Instead of growing export crops, the concentration should be on food crops with a view towards achieving self-sufficiency in food production. Industries should also be located in rural areas and not concentrated in the neighborhood of Port-au-Prince. These industries should have a high labor intensity, and use local inputs and local cheap energy. The overriding long-term goal should be national self-sufficiency. Development should concentrate on the peasants because Haiti is a peasant country and should build on established peasant structures like the extended family and the collective work team to reverse the flow of migrants to urban areas. Land should be owned and used collectively instead of, as now, individually.

Honorat's technological solution presents a curious mixture of the rational and the mystic. On the one hand, he points to a number of instances of simple innovations which would benefit the peasants in their daily life, and others that would not, as when he stresses that it does not make sense to train doctors in methods which are heavily dependent on access to a highly sophisticated Western medical technology if they have to work in an environment which lacks all these facilities. On the other hand, he stresses the eager co-operation of the Haitian peasant in all enterprises to improve his standard of living and the transformation of his country. This, as I have already stressed, is clearly not the case. The peasant is not unconditionally willing to undertake technological improvements, and this is fairly well documented. It all depends on under which circumstances technological change is suggested. Collectivization of land in particular is likely to meet diehard resistance.

Strangely enough, at the same time he puts emphasis on the tendency of the average Haitian to seek non-rational explanations for natural and social phenomena and the magico-religious fatalism. He then contrasts Western positivism and Haitian mysticism and calls into question the view that holds the former to be superior to the latter from a development point of view. This is interpreted as an apologetic exercise in favor of Western ideals. According to Honorat, the reason why the Haitian peasant does not interpret his world in Western abstract terms is that Western domination has reduced his existence to one of submission, subsistence and escapism. For Honorat the reasons for the unequal development are to be sought in the difference in *Weltanschauung* and perception of the world. However, there is a historical difference as well. The white Europeans were better prepared for the type of violence required to conquer others.[15]

There is, however, no fundamental contradiction between disciplined work and the existentialist foundation of Haitian culture. Honorat suggests that mysticism and positivism may be complementary ('deux volets du dyptique de la science'). He argues that Third World man must strip the Western world of experimental analysis to 'reestablish the fertile unity of knowledge and the indispensable union of man with the universal being'.[16] He claims furthermore that recent developments in Western science appear to be leading to a total revision of thinking. The examples he quotes are frightening: the alleged psychokinetic faculties to move objects by mental exercise only, or to provoke chemical reactions by means of cerebral waves, psycho-galvanic measurements of the spiritual life of vegetables à la scientologist Ron Hubbard and parapsychology in general. Honorat goes on to allege that this type of thinking, which is supposedly related to Third World mysticism, would be of relevance when it comes to solving the problems that beset Haiti. Poor Haiti! The argument cannot be saved by reference to any egalitarian pluralism or to the alleged ethnocentrism of Western technology. It is simply rubbish, unless it is a bad joke.

Notes

1. Cf. Lundahl (1979), Chapters 7 and 8.
2. Ibid., pp. 266-7.
3. See, in particular, Lacerte (1974-5); Murray (1977), Chapter 3; and Lundahl (1979), Chapter 6.
4. Nicholls, *From Dessalines to Duvalier*, p. 15.
5. Ibid., pp. 1, 2.
6. The American occupation of Haiti served as a rallying point for a Haitian literature of protest and national consciousness. A *littérature de combat* emerged which was not to be without a certain influence on political life during a later period of Haiti's history. (A fascinating account of this is given in Dash (1981).) Young writers proceeded to re-evaluate Haitian society. The values of the traditional elite were challenged. Nationalism and cultural authenticity with emphasis on the African past, as expressed by the indigenist movement, put Haiti and the specifically Haitian into focus and repudiated the influence of American civilization.

Much of this vigorous literary movement was translated 'into politically absolutist solutions' (Dash (1981), p. 98) where the *Négritude* movement in due time was exploited by Duvalier in his mythical insistence on nationalism, coupled with muddled racial theories which were perfectly suited to back up a dictatorship building not on the interests of the traditional elites but on the emerging black bourgeoisie instead.

7. Cf. e.g. García-Zamor (1970).
8. Quoted by Donner, *Haiti*, note, p. 338.

9. For a discussion of this tradition, see Lundahl (1979), Chapter 7.

10. Cf. the discussion in Rotberg with Clague (1971), pp. 348 ff.

11. Nicholls, *From Dessalines to Duvalier*, pp. 237, 246.

12. Resistance to change in Haitian agriculture is discussed in detail in Chapter 14 of this book and in Lundahl (forthcoming).

13. The causes of the American occupation of Haiti are discussed in Schmidt (1971) and in Castor (1971).

14. Cf. Schumacher (1974).

15. This has much in common with the argument advanced in Cipolla (1965).

16. Honorat, *Le manifeste du dernier monde*, p. 119.

Bibliography

Castor, Suzy. *La occupación norteamericana de Haití y sus consecuencias*. (Siglo Veintiuno, México, 1971)

Cipolla, Carlo M. *Guns and Sails in the Early Phase of European Expansion, 1400-1700*. (Collins, London, 1965)

Dash, J. Michael. *Literature and Ideology in Haiti, 1915-1961*. (MacMillan, London and Basingstoke, 1981)

García-Zamor, Jean-Claude. 'Papadocracy', *Caribbean Review*, Spring 1970

Lacerte, Robert K. 'The First Land Reform in Latin America: The Reforms of Alexander Pétion, 1809-1814', *Inter-American Economic Affairs*, vol. 28, 1974-5

Lundahl, Mats. *Peasants and Poverty: A Study of Haiti*. (Croom Helm, London, 1979)

Lundahl, Mats. 'Peasants, Government and Technological Change in Haitian Agriculture' in Hans F. Illy (ed.). *Public Administration and Rural Development in the Caribbean*, (Munich, Weltforum, forthcoming)

Murray, Gerald F. 'The Evolution of Haitian Peasant Land Tenure: A Case Study in Agrarian Adaptation to Population Growth', PhD thesis, (Columbia University, New York, 1977)

Rotberg, Robert I. with Clague, Christopher K. *Haiti: The Politics of Squalor*. (Houghton Mifflin, Boston, 1971)

Schmidt, Hans. *The United States Occupation of Haiti, 1915-1934*. (Rutgers, New Brunswick, 1971)

Schumacher, E.F. *Small is Beautiful*. (Sphere Books, London, 1974)

4 WRITTEN IN BLOOD. THE STORY OF THE HAITIAN PEOPLE, 1492-1971*

Written in Blood (Boston: Houghton Mifflin, 1978, pp. 785) is the joint effort of Colonel Robert Debs Heinl, Jr and his wife. Colonel Heinl is the 'spit-and-polish Marine'[1] (also a Yale graduate and the author of a number of books on military history) who was in command of the US Marine Corps training mission to Haiti from 1959 to 1963 (when he was expelled by Papa Doc after considerable tension caused by Heinl's stern refusal to sanction training of Duvalier's paramilitary corps, the dreaded *tonton macoutes*).

The Heinls have undertaken a very ambitious task, that of writing a comprehensive history of Haiti from the European discovery by Columbus in 1492 to the death of Papa Doc in 1971. Unfortunately, they do not quite succeed in their endeavor. The claim on the dust cover, that 'unless new materials are discovered, the substance and interpretation are as definitive and authoritative as any publication is likely to be', is exaggerated. The reason is that the Heinl book represents history written in a somewhat old-fashioned manner. Events, actions and people are brought to the foreground while the more profound analysis of causes and trends is understated and is sometimes lacking altogether.

Not surprisingly, the book is strong on military history, but wars, uprisings, coups, etc. tell only a limited part of the Haitian story. It is not possible to understand contemporary Haiti and its problems without analyzing how present-day conditions evolved in a historical perspective, involving dictatorship, corruption and underdevelopment in general and stagnation of the most important sector of the economy — peasant agriculture — in particular.

The book is generally weak on economic matters. A glance at the bibliography shows that the authors are not familiar with the important books by for example Paul Moral and Gérard Pierre-Charles,[2] not to mention works dealing with particular aspects of economic life. This neglect shows up in several instances. The authors fail to mention the importance of sugar for the colonial economy of Saint-Domingue. Less than a page is devoted to discussing the most important event of the

*Source: *Ibero-Americana*, vol. 12, no. 1, 1983

entire nineteenth century, the 1809 land reform and the ensuing subdivision of the large colonial estates into what finally became small
peasant holdings of the type that still dominate rural Haiti. It is this
subdivision of landholdings which constitutes Alexandre Pétion's ultimate monument in Haiti's history, not 'his place among the liberators
of the Americas'.[3] The Heinls likewise fail to stress and analyze the
development of a soft state in nineteenth-century Haiti. When President Boyer was ousted in 1843, Haiti's 'social structure was solidified,
and its economic life formed'.[4] This is correct, but the interesting
point is *why* rather than *how* this development took place. One would
expect such a statement to be backed by a thorough analysis of the
reasons behind this fundamental change, but it is not. Visible events are
accounted for, but only in a way which leaves the reader with considerable doubts as to the mechanisms leading up to the formation of the
peasant nation.

Superficiality does damage in two more ways. The book is a very
difficult one to read, even for those who are well acquainted with the
main features of Haiti's history. This, in turn is mainly a result of the
overwhelming amount of detail. The book abounds with names, both
of people and places. This is to be regretted, since in the end it leaves
the impression that a particular variety of Gresham's law operates,
whereby cute but irrelevant details drive the analytical sections out of
the book. Sometimes it degenerates into a mere gossip chronicle.

Secondly, the authors take the title of their book too literally. The
atrocities committed in the course of Haiti's history are accounted for
in juicy detail.[5] An unsystematic count shows that the book contains at
least 30 such passages.

The two most interesting parts of the Heinl work are those dealing
with the American occupation and with the Duvalier regime. Although
it is difficult to escape the impression that the Heinls have a tendency
to defend the occupation, a couple of interesting points are made.
Particularly interesting is the authors' conclusion that the old claim that
a majority of the Marines in Haiti were Southerners who 'knew how to
handle the niggers', is unfounded. The claim was never raised during
the occupation itself but is a product of posterity which does not
correspond to actual events. After searching the existing archives the
authors conclude that 'In short, a Southerners-only policy for Marines
would not only have foundered on the rocks of administrative practi-
cality, but would have left recorded tracks, which do not exist.'[6]

The economic analysis of the occupation and its consequences could,
however, have been more thorough. The authors fail to note the priority

given to American interests in the repayment of the Haitian foreign debt (which had been consolidated into American hands in 1922). In fact, the interests of the bondholders were always allowed to take precedence over the attempts to foster economic development, and for some time after the occupation had ended. Haiti was forced to maintain a unique record in Latin America by not defaulting on debt payments even during the depression years of the thirties, but this conservative wisdom did not pay. Even though the Haitians met their foreign obligations, assistance from abroad to lay the foundations for development failed to materialize for a long time.

The section on the Duvalier regime, finally, is a good one, perhaps the best in the book. The Heinls have made excellent use of their first-hand knowledge of the darkest years and the turbulent events of that period. It is, however, a bit surprising to find that relatively little is added to previous knowledge.

To sum up, the Heinl book is a difficult one to read. It is marred by the inclusion of too many irrelevant details and lacks a systematic analysis of the driving forces in Haitian history. The strength is in the description of events rather than in the interpretation. The lack of economic analysis is especially unfortunate, since economics and history are intimately connected in the Haitian case. It is not possible to understand the economy unless a historical perspective is taken and any analysis of the history that is not founded in a solid knowledge of economic factors has a tendency to become somewhat superficial. In a way, the Heinl book could be read more as a novel – to get a feeling for the *ambiance* – than as a non-fiction historical work. In that perspective, its qualities are more easily appreciated.

Notes

1. Diederich and Burt (1972), p. 133.
2. Moral (1959, 1961); Pierre-Charles (1965).
3. Heinl and Heinl, *Written in Blood*, p. 159.
4. Ibid., p. 179.
5. Here, the dust cover is more to the point: 'as gory as an abattoir'.
6. Heinl and Heinl, *Written in Blood*, p. 490.

Bibliography

Diederich, Bernard and Burt, Al. *Papa Doc. Haiti and its Dictator*. Harmondsworth, 1972
Moral, Paul. *L'économie haïtienne*. Port-au-Prince, 1959
Moral, Paul. *Le paysan haïtien*. Paris, 1961
Pierre-Charles, Gérard. *La economía y su vía de desarrollo*. México, 1965

II. MAN AND LAND

5 POPULATION PRESSURE AND AGRARIAN PROPERTY RIGHTS IN HAITI*

This chapter demonstrates that population pressure on the land has been an important determinant of agrarian property rights in Haiti, including property rights in human beings. Major changes in the density of the population are identified and linked to redefinitions of property rights. The chapter ends with a discussion of possible future monopolization of landholdings in Haiti.

Introduction

Furubotn and Pejovich define *property rights* as 'the sanctioned behavioral relations among men that arise from the existence of things and pertain to their use', and argue that the 'prevailing system of property rights in the community can be described, then, as the set of economic and social relations defining the position of each individual with respect to the utilization of scarce resources.'[1] For a long time, property rights constituted a neglected field in economic theory – presumably, mainly as a result of the increasing mathematization of the discipline after the Second World War. During the past decade, however, the concept has played an increasingly important role in economic research, especially in attempts to link theory with empirical evidence. According to Furubotn and Pejovich, the aim of the property rights approach to economics is to establish operationally meaningful, i.e. empirically testable, propositions about the economy, given postulates on maximizing behavior and the sovereignty of individuals' preferences or values in guiding economic choice. For such an approach to yield fruitful insights, the institutional environment within which economic activity takes place must be specified with great care.[2]

The development of property rights and institutions can itself be subjected to economic analysis. This chapter attempts to link the concept of property rights with the degree of population pressure on the land in the setting of an underdeveloped agrarian economy: that of Haiti. It will be shown how changes in population pressure, and, hence,

*Source: *Statsvetenskaplig Tidskrift*, vol. 83, no. 5, 1980

in relative factor supplies, have constituted an important determinant of the system of property rights in Haitian agriculture from the French colonial period up to the present time. In this context, the 'things' referred to by Furubotn and Pejovich are not only land but also men — those men who work the land. The major changes in population density have been linked to important changes not only in relations between the laboring and non-laboring classes, which pertain to the use of agricultural land, but also in the relations connected with the use of labor. Property rights in both land and human beings have been re-defined and the degree of population pressure has had an important role to play in this process. This has not been a role which could be unequivocally predicted from a known man/land ratio or from a change in this ratio, but one which has differed as a number of circum-stances exogenous to population growth have differed.

The Rise of the Plantation System

Present-day Haiti was a French colony from 1697 to 1791. With res-pect to property rights, the main characteristic of Saint-Domingue, as the colony was known, was the combination of large-scale plantations with slave labor. By the time of the French Revolution, some 450,000 Negro slaves[3] were sustaining an economy which produced a number of export crops, notably sugar and coffee, on fairly large-sized plantations. The largest were the sugar plantations which ranged from 150 to 300 hectares, while coffee and indigo plantations were usually less than 100 hectares.[4] Sugar was the most important crop. It was basically the technical requirements of sugar production in combination with an extreme demographic situation which produced the system of property rights that prevailed in Saint-Domingue and then, in a slightly modified form, in independent Haiti for more than a decade after liberation from the French.

Sugarcane came to Hispaniola at the beginning of the sixteenth century. The West Indian climate presented extremely favorable con-ditions for its cultivation and Hispaniola and the rest of the Caribbean islands possessed a strong comparative advantage in sugar production. The structure of this advantage was not such, however, that it could be acted upon directly. The technology available to the sugar planters required comparatively heavy concentrations of capital, land and labor for profitable operations.[5] Each plantation had to have a crushing mill, the optimum economic size of which was fairly large. This optimum, in turn, determined the optimum size of the plantation and the size of the required labor force.

Establishing plantations of the requisite size was easy, but the recruitment of the necessary labor force presented a formidable problem for the planters. The reason is to be found in demographic changes. When Columbus discovered Hispaniola in 1492 the island sustained a large Indian population, estimates of which range from 200,000 to 1,200,000.[6] A century later hardly a soul of this population was left. Spanish practices of forced (*encomienda*) labor in combination with imported European diseases and outright slaughter in battle had taken a heavy toll. This meant that there was plenty of land to turn into plantations, but also that Negro slaves had to be imported from Africa to man them. This practice was already underway in 1502, but it was not until the French period that the slave traffic reached its peak, with average annual imports possibly exceeding 20,000 people.[7]

The dwindling population was less of a problem during the Spanish period, when extraction of alluvial gold was the Spaniards' principal economic interest. When this activity ceased, cattle grazing and livestock trade became the dominant activities occupying this position as early as the 1530s and 1540s. Cattle ranching is a highly land-intensive activity requiring very little labor with the cattle being allowed to stray across vast open ranges. The basic economic units in this system were the *hatos*, 'immense possessions . . . where horses and cattle [were] raised with little care'.[8] By 1650, *hatos* may have covered as much as one-third of the area of Hispaniola.[9] Cattle ranching was quite in harmony with the factor proportions prevailing in the island, but after the formal cession of Saint-Domingue to France by the Treaty of Ryswick in 1697, this equilibrium was upset. The French colonists, who had penetrated western Hispaniola at least 75 years earlier, had been hesitant to undertake the large investments required to make sugarcane a profitable crop as long as the territorial status of Saint-Domingue remained uncertain. With the Spanish threat removed, sugar cultivation was expanded rapidly across the French colony. Large plantations emerged and property rights were created not only in land, but also in men as an artificial means of overcoming the obstacle posed by an extreme demographic situation where plantation labor on a voluntary or forced basis was unavailable locally.

It must also be mentioned that, although the slavery-based plantation system was the 'final' solution of the labor force problem, it was not the only one attempted. At an earlier stage, indentured laborers (*engagés*) had been brought in from France on contracts specifying the number of years (usually three) they had to work before gaining complete freedom.[10] This, however, was no solution to the problem of mobilizing labor for the sugar estates. The coercive measures at the disposal of the planters *vis-à-vis* the *engagés* were too weak. An indentured laborer could be held only for a limited number of years, could not be driven as relentlessly as a slave and when the labor contract expired he was a free man. With plenty of unsettled land available, backbreaking labor on a sugar estate would never have attracted a single ex-*engagé*. The necessary effort could only be extracted from slave labor. For sugar to be a profitable crop, extremely strong property rights had to be established not primarily in land, which was plentiful, but in human beings.[11]

A Nation of Free Peasants

After the French were expelled from Haiti, slavery was abolished in 1793 and 50 years later Haiti was a nation where free peasants were making an independent living on land which belonged mainly to them. During the intervening years, Haiti's entire economic system had been profoundly reshaped. The set of property rights had undergone a fundamental change and once again one of the main determinants of change was to be found in the relative availability of production factors.

Based as they were on slavery, the large plantations — *la grande culture* — gradually disappeared after 1793. The institution of slavery could be upheld only as long as there was a supply of slaves and slaves were available only as long as effective sanctions excluded the Negro masses from other ways of making a living. After independence, the range of opportunities increased as a result of the drastically increased availability of land together with weak public administrations.

The transition from slavery-based plantations to free peasant smallholdings did not take place immediately after the end of French rule. On the contrary, the first rulers of independent Haiti felt that the plantation system should be preserved and made strenuous efforts to retain it.[12] Much of the system had been physically destroyed during more than ten years of intermittent warfare, but enough was left for a restoration of *la grande culture* to be a feasible option. Thus, up to the historically significant year 1809, the year of the first land reform in Latin America, an agrarian system which differed from slavery in name only existed in Haiti. Ex-slaves who during the turmoil produced by the wars of liberation had been acting mainly as independent agricultural small-scale producers were, as far as possible, brought back to the estates. The plantations were rented to members of the emerging Haitian elite and strict military supervision of the agricultural workers was resorted to in order to secure the necessary labor input.

The restoration was only a temporary episode, however. In 1809, Alexandre Pétion, president in the southern half of the country, decided to set his serfs free and to redistribute the large landholdings. Ten years later, Henry Christophe followed suit in his northern kingdom. By 1840 Haiti had become a nation of free peasants and this situation was to be reinforced during the rest of the nineteenth century. In 30 years, the system of agrarian property rights had been completely transformed. No one now held any rights in his fellow men, and, one way or another, the peasant population had access to land which they could till for their own benefit: as outright owners, as squatters or as sharecroppers. This constituted one of the most decisive events in Haiti's economic history. The creation of an economy comprised of free peasants set Haiti on a course which diverged widely from the pattern typical of most of Latin America.[13]

The transition from plantations to peasant holdings can be traced to a large extent to the changing effective supply of labor and land.[14] To understand how this worked we may take a brief look at the phenomenon of *marronage*. During the colonial period this term referred to the escape, organized or unorganized, of slaves from the French plantations. These runaway slaves fled to remote regions outside the effective control of the colonial administration where they attempted to make a living as subsistence farmers.[15] *Marronage* never developed into a mass movement. Its success was ultimately conditioned by the amount of land available for illegal squatting without interference by the authorities and during the colonial period this area was limited in practice. The planters and their administrative machinery were sufficiently strong to ensure that *marronage* was a solution for a minority of dissatisfied slaves only. Policing expeditions were regularly sent out when it was felt that the strength of the maroon communities exceeded the tolerable level.

During and after the wars of liberation the extent of *marronage* increased.[16] When the French administrative apparatus had been destroyed and the balance of power no longer weighed so heavily against the Negro masses and when, in addition, many colonial plantations had been abandoned and lay without effective ownership, the area available to those ex-slaves who preferred independent subsistence farming to militarily supervised serfdom increased. Now, the masses were provided with an attractive alternative to remaining as landless workers on plantation estates with a rigid discipline.

The increased availability of land had important repercussions in the labor market. During the wars most ex-slaves, when given a choice, preferred to work on their own small plots instead of going back to the plantation system. In Saint-Domingue part of the slaves' subsistence was secured by providing them with small garden plots, the produce of which the slaves could dispose of themselves, in markets or by direct consumption. To a certain extent, these 'provision' plots provided the colonists with foodstuffs.[17] During the wars of liberation when imports of food or their distribution within Saint-Domingue were disrupted, the food supply gradually came to depend on the 'slave gardens', and it appears that a very widespread reaction among the ex-slaves was simply to remain as cultivators on their 'old' plots.[18] Presumably, it was the very knowledge of this which made the first Haitian rulers take the decision to reinstitute the plantation system on a *forced* labor basis. Any attempted solution based on a free choice would have failed. On the macro-economic level, the situation was turned further against the plantation system by the population decline which eventually resulted from the wars. From 1790 to 1805 the Haitian population declined by an estimated 150,000.[19] Of these, 40,000 were whites[20] but the majority of the remainder were Negro ex-slaves.

Thus, the relative supply of land had increased, while that of labor had decreased. Only artificial administrative devices could for a time guarantee the survival of the 'colonial' pattern of property rights and when the administrative apparatus had been sufficiently weakened the pattern broke down. Toussaint and Dessalines could muster enough strength to keep the old military system working for some time. Since no agreement had been reached with France regarding the territorial status of the country, the threat of renewed war activities had not been removed when Dessalines was murdered in 1806. When Haiti was divided into two states intermittently waging a civil war upon each other following his death, successively less money and energy could be spent on preventing the system of property rights from falling apart. At the same time the costs of supervision and enforcement had increased. The masses had tasted freedom during the revolutionary wars and were less prepared than ever to go back to the plantations. The beginning of the end came in 1809 in the southern part and ten years later in the north. Although there were occasional attempts,[21] no subsequent Haitian administration was able to reverse this order of things. The new system had come to stay. When rights were seriously threatened, rural protest movements arose which sometimes turned into outright peasant revolts.[22] Subsequent changes in the agrarian property rights system have been modifications within the peasant mode of production rather than profound transformations involving the relative freedom of men.

Securing Peasant Ownership

By 1842 probably none of the colonial plantations remained in their original form. Around one-third of the population were peasant-owners, another third were squatters and most of the remainder were sharecroppers.[23] All of them were smallholders. This distribution of land did not remain unchanged, however, during the nineteenth century. Before 1900 the majority of the Haitian peasants could probably safely be termed 'owners'. The reason for this development was the comparatively strong bargaining position conferred on the peasants by the low man/land ratio. In 1978 the population density amounted to 174 persons per square kilometer.[24] In the 1820s, the maximum figure was 25,[25] a figure which was to increase only slowly during the course of the nineteenth century. To see how peasant 'owners' came to dominate the scene we will outline more details of the change from large plantations to smallholdings.

When the attempt to preserve the colonial plantations was made at the beginning of the nineteenth century most of the land was declared government property and, thereafter, was rented to high army officers and other members of the new upper class. As the colonial property rights structure finally began to crumble under Pétion and his successors this government property was transferred to private hands. At the same time the landed elite found that plantation labor was no longer available in the quantities and on the conditions necessary for profitable operation and took steps to adapt to the changing circumstances. Since cultivating the soil themselves was out of the question, the first option was to lease the land to the peasants against collection of some type of rent, usually a share-rent: one-half of the crop. This strategy was obviously feasible only for a limited period, however, because the interests of landlord and peasant often clashed when it came to the exact determination of contractual obligations.

The area of conflict was in the physical harvesting of the crops planted under sharecropping arrangements.[26] In contemporary Haiti the sharing arrangement means that a division of the rented plot is made *before* the plot is harvested and the landlord *himself* must harvest his half and see that the produce is marketed. Presumably, the same type of arrangement became the rule in nineteenth-century Haiti.[27] This posed a very obvious problem for the landlord class:

> Except for the owners of coffee plantations . . .[28] the nineteenth century Haitian landlord was in the almost ludicrous position of having fields cultivated in crops which did not really interest him, and of having furthermore to harvest those peasant crops himself. As a last straw he was also obliged, if he was to make any money of the arrangement, to himself arrange for the marketing of that produce within the arena of a popular market system dominated by energetic female peasants. If the image of a self-respecting member of the gentry digging up his own sweet potatoes is humorous, the image of his genteel, French-speaking wife lugging them to a local market to sell them in noisy competition with skillful peasant *machând* is absurd.[29]

Thus, except for the case of coffee, this type of sharecropping contract was more or less doomed from the beginning. Only during the first few years after the initial redistribution of land would we expect to meet it and then presumably with the sharecropper harvesting the portion of the landlord as well. Unfortunately, no statistics have so far been uncovered to support the hypothesis, but it seems reasonable to expect that a majority of the sharecropping contracts in 1842, referred to above, dealt with coffee plantations.

Due to the comparatively easy availability of land for cultivation the Haitian peasants were in a much better position to oppose landlord claims than their counterparts in most parts of the world. Sharecropping was not a viable solution from the point of view of the landlords and, therefore, it gradually disappeared. Instead, the predominant pattern became one where the peasants actually *owned* their fields — generally without deeds. This situation arose in two different ways, by laissez-faire squatting and by alienation of parcels by the landlords through actual sales.

The bulk of the literature on Haiti puts the emphasis on the importance of squatting.[30] When the landlords found that going back to the plantation system was impossible and that sharecropping was not viable, they simply gave up, withdrawing to an urban life and allowing their tenants or other peasants free reign. Recently, however, Gerald Murray has strongly challenged this traditional view and pointed to the possibility that most peasants actually acquired their land via regular purchases based, on the one hand, on the need of the landowning group to capitalize on land which its members did not want to cultivate themselves and for which no hired fieldhands could be found, and, on the other, on cash accumulated by the peasants from transactions in the domestic marketing circuit.[31]

Murray's interpretation is interesting since it simultaneously provides an explanation of why in spite of a general absence of written titles, peasant holdings appear to have been fairly secure and highly marketable in Haiti.[32] A sales transaction should constitute a firmer basis for both tenure and further transactions than simple squatting. Two more considerations could, however, be added here. In the first place, the sales to which Murray refers took place during a period when land was plentiful in relation to the population. There was enough land for everyone who wanted a plot at least up to the last quarter of the nineteenth century.[33] In this situation, few people (and especially not outside interests) were likely to question even unwritten land rights, since the labor necessary to produce an income from the land was lacking.

The second point is one which has relevance also to the contemporary situation. Rural Haiti is a relatively classless society[34] and a vast majority of all land transactions take place within the context of the rural world, i.e. between people of basically the same social standing — people sharing the same values. Such people are not likely to question the rules of a game which has evolved within more or less the same setting during a century and a half. The situation would be different if rural Haiti had been socially highly stratified and land transactions had been carried out mainly on an *inter*class rather than an *intra*class basis.

By the end of the nineteenth century the transition from slavery-based plantations to a society where the vast majority of cultivators were peasants who owned the land themselves had been completed. The history of the development of property rights during the twentieth century is not well known. No cadastral survey has even been undertaken in Haiti which can shed light on the contemporary situation. An attempt was made during the American occupation of the country (1915-34) to straighten out the land tenure situation, presumably to prepare the way for American-owned plantations. Aerial photography was carried out but before the photographs had been interpreted the building where the negatives were stored burned down 'in an unexplained fire'.[35] To evaluate today's situation, we are left with the rather unreliable figures of the 1950 census and a number of local surveys.

Presumably, however, no major changes have taken place. The available information is difficult to interpret but, in the main, it indicates that a majority of all Haitian peasants own their land. The 1950 census indicated that up to 85 per cent of the peasants were 'owners'. This impression is confirmed by at least two later major surveys, one nation-wide in 1970 and another of more than 7,000 farmers in the *arrondissement* of Cap-Haïtien in 1974, in which it was found that 60 per cent of all parcels and 75 per cent of all the land, respectively, were cultivated by the owners themselves.[36] According to all three sources, the incidence of tenant farming and sharecropping was low: some 8 per cent in 1950 (peasants owning *no* land − not part-time tenants), 28 per cent of all parcels in 1970, and 14 per cent of the area in the 1974 Cap survey. The generally accepted picture of today's landholding system in Haiti is that a majority of the peasants still own their land with or without deeds and that most of the land *area* is held in this way.

Future Monopolization of Land?

Let us end with a brief look at the future. From the mid-nineteenth century up to the present time Haiti has stood out as an exception to the land tenure pattern prevailing in most Latin American states. Land has not been concentrated in the hands of a minority while the mass of the rural population have been landless laborers, tenants or minifundistas working on artificially overcrowded marginal soils. Haiti has not had any 'land problem' in that sense. Rather, the main difficulty has been to maintain fertility on fairly equitably distributed plots in the face of population growth. In this struggle, the Haitian peasant has generally not been successful,[37] but at least, one can claim, he has been spared exploitation by a landlord class. Can we expect the same pattern to continue into the future or will the growth of the Haitian rural population lead to dramatic shifts in the structure of agrarian property rights towards increasing concentration of land and, hence, also to exploitation of the landless?

Most of the literature which deals with the possibility or existence of land concentration in Haiti is concerned with attacks on peasant freedom by a class of absentee landlords. A number of authors have, in fact, attempted to prove that such a concentration of land already exists in Haiti.[38] However, such an interpretation violates the observable facts.[39] Haiti *de facto* is a country where most of the rural population has access to land on terms which cannot be qualified as monopolistic.

What then is the likelihood of the emergence of such a class? It is well known that very few Haitian peasants can present any written titles to their land.[40] Furthermore, Haitian history points to a number of instances where, when the value of the land has increased, peasants have been subject to eviction by outsiders.[41] However, such cases must be considered rare. Murray found that in a community he studied in depth this had *never* occurred.[42] The main reason appeared to be that although very few peasants could present individual titles to the plots they owned, the *grâ-pyês* generally still existed. This 'big' deed to the undivided land of a family estate some generations ago was kept by some relative and could be used to trace subsequent land transactions.[43] The existence of such documents undoubtedly makes alienation of peasant land difficult for outsiders.

A problem may arise even among those possessing legal deeds. Unwritten property rights, as we have already pointed out, are generally regarded as valid by the peasant class from which potential 'insiders' would come. This convention is reinforced by a second factor based on sorcery. In Murray's community the most important threat to peasant security was not seen as coming from outsiders but rather from distant kin who actually *did* have legal rights to land but who, by emigrating or otherwise, had in practice forfeited their rights. In such cases it is, of course, possible that generations later heirs could come up with a legal title. This type of intruder was, however, regarded as being particularly vulnerable to sorcery exercised by those actually *using* the land.[44] Thus, the likelihood that people with legal rights to land which they had chosen to leave would come back to claim that land seems low.[45]

Population growth may possibly disrupt this relative security. One such pattern has been suggested by Murray. His point of departure is that an individual who can today buy land in Haiti will never lack the labor to make the land productive and, hence, to make the transaction worthwhile.[46] This, according to Murray, is ensured by the existence of potential sharecroppers. He then goes on to argue that

it is precisely such a situation which is conducive to the emergence of patterns of land concentration. Such a danger would exist no matter what the pre-existing tenure mode were. But in a society such as Haiti, where even at a 'grass roots' level land has traditionally been alienable, the danger is especially great. For where there is land purchase, there must also be land sale and — ipso facto — the emergence of at least temporary resource differentials. And where land is further transmitted via inheritance, as is true of Haiti, these differentials will easily be intergenerationally perpetuated. Furthermore, since the children of the better-off start life in a somewhat stronger economic position than the children of the less well off, they are more likely to purchase more land, the differentials will thus increase, and land concentration will have set in.[47]

This has not occurred so far, however, because there is another mechanism which serves as a periodic regulator of the distribution of land, namely, voodoo. For reasons connected with the need to finance voodoo ceremonies at various times over the life cycle, land has to be put on the market for sale. Murray found that a majority of all land sales in the community were motivated by these needs. The result of these transactions, as Murray sees it, has been to reduce class differentials based on land tenure:

> The mechanism has not eliminated differentials, but it has kept them within the basic confines of a life-cycle modality of resource management, and has prevented the emergence of intergenerationally perpetuated local strata.[48]

Such a view of the land market is highly dubious. This double role as a generator and moderator of class differences is definitely not inherent in the market mechanism. *A priori* there is no reason to expect that those with more land are better farmers who will improve their economic positions and, therefore, also buy more land.[49] Neither should we expect that those with less land are necessarily the main sellers. Finally, there is nothing in the market mechanism which guarantees that the land coming from voodoo-induced transactions is land which is alienated by those holding relatively much land. All these propositions have to be proved before Murray's case can be established.

Perhaps the most realistic type of mechanism based on population growth which may eventually undermine the prevailing set of agrarian property rights in Haiti is to be found in increasing poverty itself.[50] There is a tendency for rural incomes to fall over time. So far, one of the main regulators here has been migration to the capital city and abroad. In the future there are, however, no guarantees that emigration to other countries will continue to provide a safety valve. It may very well be that other countries feel that too many Haitians are coming in and they may, therefore, take steps to curtail immigration.[51] In such a situation greater stress will be placed on the domestic economy to provide the population with non-agricultural employment. Hitherto, the economy has failed to do so. If the rural population continues to grow, marginal peasants may find themselves in a situation where they have to increase their indebtedness with land as collateral and this may lead to an eventual transfer of land into the hands of moneylenders. Alternatively, land may have to be sold to cover immediate needs. This is a familiar pattern in other agrarian communities.[52]

Concentration of land tends to lead to monopsonization of the labor market. When large segments of the population lack land of their own they become increasingly dependent on landowners for employment. In this situation exploitation may be a reality.[53] Whether such a situation will develop in Haiti remains to be seen. So far, nothing indicates that it is imminent, but it may be prudent to concentrate some attention on uncovering possible hidden or unknown trends in the development of agrarian property rights. One cannot simply trust the market mechanism since there is, of course, nothing inherent in that mechanism which guarantees that the development of property rights takes the most 'desirable' course. In this sense the market is neutral. It all depends on the circumstances under which the market mechanism is allowed to work.

Notes

University of Lund. Thanks are due to Carl-Johan Dahlman, Lennart Jörberg, Bo Larsson and Jim Love for their constructive criticisms of an earlier version of this essay.

1. Furubotn and Pejovich (1972), p. 1139.
2. Ibid., p. 1157.
3. Moreau de Saint-Méry (1958), p. 28.
4. Lepkowski (1968), pp. 48-9.
5. For details regarding the sugar economy see Lundahl (1979), pp. 256-9.
6. The estimates of the indigenous population vary widely from source to source. For a sample see e.g. Palmer (1976), p. 38; Cauvin (1977), p. 39; Lundahl (1979), p. 189; Caprio (1979), p. 28 and the sources indicated in these works. Cook and Borah (1971) discuss the aboriginal population of Hispaniola at length.
7. Lundahl (1979), p. 189.
8. Moreau de Saint-Méry (1796), p. 65.
9. Palmer (1976), p. 51.
10. The *engagé* system is discussed in Debien (1952).
11. In this respect, the colonial economy is consistent with the Domar hypothesis regarding the causes of slavery or serfdom which states that out of free land, free peasants and non-working landowners, any pair of elements, but not all three, can exist simultaneously (Domar, 1970). For an efficient exploitation of the possibilities offered by sugarcane when land was plentiful and when landowners would not work themselves on the land, laborers had to be enslaved to

prevent them from taking advantage of the easy availability of land. Also, owner-ship of land was monopolized by the free citizens of the colony.

12. See Lundahl (1979), pp. 259-63.

13. This course is analyzed at length in ibid.

14. See ibid, Chapter 6 for a discussion of all the factors involved.

15. Extensive discussions of *marronage* can be found in Debbasch (1961, 1962); Debien (1966); and Fouchard (1972).

16. Lepkowski (1968), note, p. 80.

17. Murray (1977), p. 49.

18. Ibid., pp. 57-64.

19. Lundahl (1979), p. 272.

20. Ibid., p. 320.

21. See ibid, pp. 264-8.

22. See Nicholls (1979), esp. pp. 30-1.

23. Leyburn (1966), p. 76.

24. Lundahl (1979), p. 55.

25. Franklin (1828), p. 404.

26. A second area of conflict, suggested by Murray (1977), pp. 94-6, that of the choice of crop to be planted, is harder to accept. Murray argues that 'the entire orientation of landowners of the period was the production of crops for export, above all the production of sugar cane which had underwritten so many colonial fortunes' (ibid., p. 94) while the peasants preferred to grow crops which could be sold via the internal marketing system with which the peasants were familiar since the colonial period. Exceptions here were coffee and cotton — 'simply because the trees were already there . . .' (ibid., p. 95). The sales of export crops were conducted via licensed government traders with whom peasant contacts were 'disadvantageous and perhaps perilous' (ibid.), while the marketing of domestic crops took place via a network of market women basically coming from the peasant class itself.

There are at least two difficulties with such an argument. In the first place, sugar quickly ceased to be an export crop in the post-independence period. With the technology of the period, as we have already discussed, sugar processing required high concentrations of capital, labor and land, and such concentrations were simply beyond the means of the small peasant producers who rented the land. It is therefore not likely that the landlords would have insisted on sugar cane being grown, especially not since increased competition from Cuba and other Caribbean islands as well as from European beetsugar made the price of sugar-decline during the first half of the nineteenth century (Lundahl, 1979, p. 274). The second difficulty lies in the fact that an argument which holds that sales of export products are difficult due to the risks entailed in dealing with government licensed intermediaries and which simultaneously maintains that there was no conflict over the choice of crop in the case of coffee is self-contradictory, since coffee is the prime example of a crop marketed in this way. Rather, the absence of conflict in the case of coffee should have been due to the extremely low labor requirements connected with this crop.

The standard procedure was to leave virtually everything except harvesting to nature. (Cf. Lundahl, 1979, pp. 236-7, 564-5.) Hence, the attraction of coffee for the peasants was that it could be cultivated without much labor effort and still yield an income to be added to that resulting from the cultivation of foodstuffs. (Murray employs the latter argument as well but attempts to reconcile it with that of the choice of marketing channels.)

27. Murray (1977), pp. 96-7.

28. Cf. note 26.

29. Murray (1977), p. 97.

30. Especially the highly influential works by Leyburn (1966), pp. 76-9, and Moral (1961), pp. 27-8. Cf. also Lepkowski (1968), pp. 120-1.

31. Murray (1977), pp. 107-8.

32. Cf. ibid., pp. 349-54.

33. Ibid., p. 410.

34. For discussions of the Haitian class system, see the numerous references quoted in Lundahl (1979), note 83, p. 361.

35. Schmidt (1971), p. 179.

36. Lundahl (1979), p. 48.

37. This is the main theme in Lundahl (1979). Cf., however, also Palmer (1976), pp. 167-71, for an exception to this pattern.

38. E.g. Casimir (1964); Brisson (1968); Pierre-Charles (1969); Jean (1974).

39. Cf. Lundahl (1979), pp. 51-2; Zuvekas (1978), pp. 92-8.

40. According to Murray (1977), p. 351, probably fewer than 1 per cent.

41. Lundahl (1979), pp. 603-4.

42. Murray (1977), p. 352.

43. Ibid., pp. 310-11, 352-3.

44. Ibid., pp. 320-2.

45. Palmer (1976), p. 149, however, reports the opposite pattern, where those remaining in the countryside do not dare touch fallow land owned by people who have left the community.

46. Murray (1977), pp. 463-5.

47. Ibid., pp. 463-4.

48. Ibid., p. 465.

49. In economies of the Haitian type, there is frequently a low correlation between the initial wealth of a person and his entrepreneurial abilities. Cf. McKinnon (1973), p. 11.

50. Cf. Lundahl (1979), pp. 645-6.

51. Emigration from Haiti is dealt with in ibid., pp. 623-8 and Zuvekas (1978), pp. 73-6.

52. Cf. Myrdal (1968), pp. 1039-47.

53. Cf. Griffin (1976).

Bibliography

Brisson, Gérald. *Les relations agraires dans l'Haïti contemporaine.* Mimeo. México, D.F. (?), 1968

Caprio, Giovanni. *Haiti — wirtschaftliche Entwicklung und periphere Gesellschafts-formation.* Frankfurt-/Main. 1979

Casimir, Jean. 'Aperçu sur la structure économique d'Haïti', *América Latina,* vol. 7, 1964

Cauvin, Henri. 'The Haitian Economy: A Case Study of Underdevelopment', PhD thesis, New School for Social Research, New York, 1977

Cook, Sherborne F. and Borah, Woodrow. 'The Aboriginal Population of Hispaniola' in *Essays in Population History,* Berkeley, 1971

Debbasch, Yvan. 'Le marronage: Essai sur la désertion de l'esclave antillais', *L'Année Sociologique,* vol. 3, 1961, 1962

Debien, Gabriel. *Les engagés pour les Antilles (1634-1715).* Paris, 1952

Debien, Gabriel. 'Le marronage aux Antilles Françaises au XVIIIe siècle', *Caribbean Studies,* vol. 6, 1966

Domar, Evsey D. 'The Causes of Slavery or Serfdom: A Hypothesis', *Journal of Economic History,* vol. 30, 1970

Fouchard, Jean. *Les marrons de la liberté*. Paris 1972
Franklin, James. *The Present State of Hayti (Saint Domingo) with Remarks on its Agriculture, Commerce, Laws, Religion, Finances and Population, etc. etc.* London, 1828
Furubotn, Eirik G. and Pejovich, Svetozar. 'Property Rights and Economic Theory: A Survey of Recent Literature', *Journal of Economic Literature*, vol. 10, 1972
Griffin, Keith. *Land Concentration and Rural Poverty*. London and Basingstoke, 1976
Jean, Rodrigue. *Classes sociales et sous-développement en Haïti*. Ville St-Laurent, 1974
Lepkowski, Tadeusz. *Haïti. Tomo I*. Habana, 1968
Leyburn, James G. *The Haitian People*. Revised edition, New Haven, 1966
Lundahl, Mats. *Peasants and Poverty: A Study of Haiti*. London and New York, 1979
McKinnon, Ronald I. *Money and Capital in Economic Development*. Washington, DC, 1973
Moral, Paul. *Le paysan haïtien (Etude sur la vie rurale en Haïti)*. Paris, 1961
Moreau de Saint-Méry, Médéric-Louis-Elie. *A Topographical and Political Description of the Spanish Part of Saint Domingue*. 2 volumes, Philadelphia, 1796
Moreau de Saint-Méry, Médéric-Louis-Elie. *Description topographique, physique, civile, politique et historique de la partie Française de L'isle Saint-Domingue*. New edition, 3 volumes. Paris, 1958
Murray, Gerald F. 'The Evolution of Haitian Peasant Land Tenure: A Case Study in Agrarian Adaptation to Population Growth', PhD thesis, Columbia University, New York, 1977
Myrdal, Gunnar. *Asian Drama. An Inquiry into the Poverty of Nations*. New York, 1968
Nicholls, David. 'Rural Protest and Peasant Revolt in Haiti (1804-1869)', in Malcolm Cross and Arnaud Marks (eds.). *Peasants, Plantations and Rural Communities in the Caribbean*. Guildford and Leiden, 1979
Palmer, Ernest Charles. 'Land Use and Landscape Change along the Dominican-Haitian Border', PhD thesis, University of Florida, Gainesville, 1976
Pierre-Charles, Gérard. *Haití: Radiografia de una dictadura — Haití bajo el régimen del doctor Duvalier*. México, D.F., 1969
Schmidt, Hans. *The United States Occupation of Haiti, 1915-1934*. New Brunswick, 1971
Zuvekas, Clarence, Jr. *Agricultural Development in Haiti. An Assessment of Sector Problems, Policies, and Prospects Under Conditions of Severe Soil Erosion*. Mimeo. US/AID, Washington, DC, 1978

6 INTERGENERATIONAL SHARECROPPING IN HAITI: A RE-INTERPRETATION OF THE MURRAY THESIS*

This chapter questions a recent interpretation of increased intergenerational sharecropping in Haiti as a labor-mobilizing device and offers a re-interpretation based on the increasing relative price of land.

I

The generally accepted picture of the agrarian structure of Haiti is that of a peasant nation where the majority of the farming population own the land they till with or, more usually, without written deeds. Thus, the 1950 census indicated that up to 85 per cent of the peasants could be classified as 'owners', while only 8 per cent were reported to be tenants or sharecroppers.[1] These figures are, however, known to be fairly unreliable since they do not refer to the *area* held under each type of arrangement. In addition, the percentage of tenants and sharecroppers refers only to those owning *no* land whatsoever, i.e. it gives no idea of what the importance of, for example, part-time sharecropping may be. Still, the picture given by the 1950 census figures appears by and large to be consistent with that emerging from two more recent and better organized surveys,[2] the first undertaken on a nationwide basis in 1970 and the second covering 7,355 farms in the *arrondissement* of Cap-Haïtien in 1974. The former indicated that 60 per cent of all plots were cultivated by owner-cultivators, while 14 per cent were cultivated by tenants who were not sharecroppers, the latter category accounting for another 14 per cent. The Cap survey showed that 75 per cent of the agricultural area in the Cap district was peasant-owned and that only 8 and 6 per cent were leased out under fixed rents and sharecropping arrangements, respectively.[3]

In contrast, periodic local surveys have given the impression that the extent of tenant farming and sharecropping may be higher than indicated by the conventional, accepted estimates. The strongest claims have been made by Gerald F. Murray who studied a community in the

*Source: Journal of Economic Studies, vol. 9, no. 1, 1982

Cul-de-Sac plain, east of the capital. Murray found that no less than 54 per cent of all *plots* in the community were being *sharecropped*, while only 35 per cent were actually *owned*[4] and concludes that share-cropping is 'the major access-route to cropping land'.[5] It is extremely difficult to know to what extent Murray's findings can be generalized to other parts of Haiti. Obviously, this is a matter which needs more research. It is, however, not possible to dismiss Murray's empirical findings, based on almost two years of intensive fieldwork, before the results can be compared with the results of other surveys where definitions are clear enough to permit valid comparisons.

The type of sharecropping encountered by Murray is unusual in that it is simultaneously *intraclass* and *intergenerational*. Both landlords and tenants are peasants and sharecropping is mainly a life-cycle phenomenon. Young peasants often gain access to land via sharecropping, then later they purchase land and eventually they begin to share out land to younger people.[6]

The incidence of intergenerational sharecropping appears to have increased during the present century, at least in the community studied by Murray, and in his view this increase represents a major change in the structure of agrarian property rights − the development of a new type of response to population pressure on the land. On the other hand, as we will argue presently, it may very well be that the question of whether sharecropping or some other type of tenancy is the predominant form is an irrelevant one and that overdue concentration of the analysis on the type of tenancy only serves to hide or at least obscure the true nature of the response to population growth. The development of sharecropping may by nothing but a *surface* phenomenon − at least viewed in the context of demographic change.[7] To see why this may be so, let us look at Murray's argument.

II

As early as the end of the nineteenth century most arable land in Haiti was either cultivated or at least being claimed by some 'owner'. This meant that young peasants who were about to start an independent life could no longer find any land upon which they could freely squat or which they could afford to purchase. Instead, they came to rely upon a type of pre-inheritance grant of land from their parents. In exchange for labor on their parents' land, young men in their teens or early twenties received a piece of land (traditionally one-fourth of a *carreau*)[8] the proceeds from which they could pocket themselves.[9] Today, the pattern is a different one, at least in the community studied by Murray. In the first place, the age at which the pre-inheritance grant is received is higher, but more importantly, according to Murray, a totally new pattern has emerged where intraclass sharecropping on parental as well as on non-parental land appears to be an increasingly important vehicle for gaining access to land among the young.

What is then the reason for this changing pattern, according to Murray? Central to his view is the concept of access to land as a mechanism of recruiting filial labor. By granting their sons a plot of pre-inheritance land the fathers managed to procure the necessary labor for cultivation of their own land. The sons were in a sense 'tied' to their parents. 'Now in possession of his "own" provisionally granted plot, the young man was in no position to scoot off and moonlight on the plots of labor-needy neighbors . . . And it is in this light − its use as a vehicle of control − that the pre-inheritance grant of land is most penetratingly analyzed.'[10] When the population grew this system came under stress, according to Murray, in two ways. Average holdings grew smaller over time and, as this occurred, granting the traditional one-fourth of a *carreau* became too expensive. Whereas formerly, when land was less scarce, the grant could be taken out of land which was marginal when it came to sustaining the family, a comparable grant today entails parting with land that *must* be cropped to provide a living. Thus, pre-inheritance grants are diminished or delayed.

There is, however, also a tendency for these grants to disappear and for young men to procure their first land under a sharecropping contract, either from outsiders or from their fathers. According to Murray, the reason for this is that population growth undermines the labor supply from the point of view of the fathers:

> The increased man/land ratio which demographic increment has locally produced would logically be predicted to generate a *surplus* of labor. And a potential surplus may well exist. But human labor must be motivated and mobilized. By causing sons to go elsewhere for land, local demographic increment has in effect undermined the traditional labor-mobilization sequence and made paradoxically common a situational labor shortage for semi-abandoned fathers whose sons are off sharecropping land for someone else.[11]

In this situation, the fathers are forced to resort to sharecropping as well:

It would be convenient for the landowners if they could continue to receive the labor of their sons *without* granting the traditional pre-inheritance land. But they can not. They choose then a slightly lesser evil and make part of their land available for other community members to sharecrop. The landowner does not enjoy *all* the fruits of that plot: but then again he does not have to forfeit as much land in the form of 'no strings attached' pre-inheritance land to his sons. By turning to the alternative of sharing out part of his landholdings, he is making himself somewhat less dependent on his sons as a source of labor.[12]

Often the share tenant is a son. Hence, at least in the community studied by Murray, a pattern has emerged where fathers are frequently their sons' landlords.

In Murray's analysis the increasing incidence of filial or non-filial sharecropping appears as an *essential* device for ensuring that the necessary labor to cultivate the land is forthcoming. Without sharecropping the system could break down in the face of population growth.

Because land became too scarce, parents could no longer as easily 'capture' their sons' labor via generous land grants. The shift to *sharecropping* has permitted the mobilization of critical labor to continue to be made via land presentations, as under the old system. What has changed is the context: the intrafamilial linkages of inheritance land and filial labor have ceded to the largely extradomestic manoeuvres of landlord/tenant bonds. But the basic systemic linkage between land-giving and labor-giving, a critical feature of the old system, has been maintained.[13]

This interpretation of the sequence is questionable, however, because it concentrates attention on what may be nothing but a superficial phenomenon behind which other more important changes are to be found. These other changes are related to the increasing relative price of land.[14] If the analysis begins from the increase of the relative price of land rather than from the alleged need for labor mobilization, a somewhat different sequence emerges – one which makes it possible to explain why sharecropping has not become the dominant form of land tenure in contemporary Haiti.[15]

III

Let us start with the growth of population. This growth has two important consequences. First, farms today are generally smaller than they were a few generations ago.[16] This means, in turn, that each individual peasant/father now needs less labor on his land than was the case earlier, e.g. around the turn of the century. Secondly, the growth of the population has led to increasing scarcity of land, i.e. to a higher price of land in relation to labor, especially since increased population pressure is prone to cause erosion.[17]

Thus, the father who under the traditional system would normally grant a son one-fourth of a *carreau* has two good reasons for not doing so. He needs less labor, and the price of labor has decreased in terms of land. In time, such a situation should lead to a renegotiation of the terms on which the sons can get land in exchange for their labor and this is precisely what has taken place. The size of the pre-inheritance grants has declined and the time of the grant has been delayed.

Where the son does not find the terms of the new labor contract acceptable, he will go elsewhere in search of land and become a share-cropper for someone else. According to Murray, this will also force his father to lease land under share contracts. This, however, is not necessarily true. In the first place, the amount of labor provided by those sons who *do* accept the new terms may be enough on the smaller farm and secondly, the son leaving is not likely to find a share contract which gives him a better deal than he could get from his father on, for example, a smaller pre-inheritance plot. If the market works, as it apparently does in Haiti, the market mechanism will establish an equilibrium where the effective wage in land or in cash under the traditional system equals what the son would get under a share contract. Unless other considerations enter the picture,[18] there is no need for a peasant/father to give a better deal in terms of share contracts than in terms of pre-inheritance grants.

This proposition is easily demonstrated. In Figure 6.1, the share contract which corresponds to a given wage can be found. On the vertical axis we measure the value of the marginal product of labor on a given plot as well as the wage. On the horizontal axis we have the amount of labor employed.

Assume that under competitive conditions OA units of labor are employed under the traditional system at an implicit wage of OE (paid in land from which the tenant receives the rent). If instead a share contract is chosen, we find the share rent which is the equivalent of this wage by rotating the VMP curve inwards until the areas of the two triangles BCD and DEF are equal, i.e. at the mid-point of EC. Then, given that the sharecropper also provides an amount of labor which is equal to OA on the plot, total production remains unaltered. If the share tenant provides less labor than OA, he can always be evicted and another tenant found. Under competitive conditions, no tenant will obtain a contract unless he provides at least this amount of labor. The sharecropper receives an income of OFBA, equal to the income from a pre-inheritance plot of OECA, while the landlord retains FGCB, which equals EGC, the landlord's share under the traditional type of contract. The share rent to be specified in the contract is FG/OG.[19]

Figure 6.1

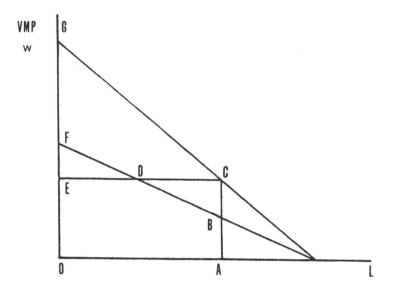

Thus, there is no fundamental difference between the traditional system of allocating pre-inheritance plots and sharecropping as far as labor mobilization is concerned. Either system will do. The conclusion is obvious. It is not the employment of sharecropping *per se* which constitutes the main change in property rights. Regardless of whether sharecropping or the traditional system is chosen, the most important impact of population growth is rather that it changes the relative bargaining positions of those who own land and those who do not. To buy or rent a plot of a given size today a person must supply more money or labor than a couple of generations ago.[20] Whether this change in contractual arrangement appears within what Murray calls the traditional system or whether it takes the form of a share rent is irrelevant.

This alternative interpretation is consistent with Murray's empirical data. One advantage of the sharecropping system which Murray stresses is that a transition to that system entailed no novelties in the sense that the system had existed alongside the traditional one for a long time. What he chooses to underplay is that the two systems *continue* to exist side by side. Even in the youngest age group of peasants investigated, those born after 1938, Murray found that no less than 60 per cent cropped their *first* garden on their parents' land while at the same time 66 per cent had *at some time* sharecropped for their parents. It may then be argued, as Murray does, that the relative incidence has changed. Among those born before 1923, the comparable figures were 83 and 43 per cent respectively.[21] The pattern is, however, also quite compatible with an interpretation in terms of harder contractual obligations. Since pre-inheritance land as a rule is today granted later, the *first* plot is more likely to come from sharecropping outside or inside the family on harder terms than a few decades ago and to be supplemented later either by pre-inheritance land, by more land held under share contracts, or by both.

The conclusion to be drawn from the foregoing is that it is not possible to explain the increased incidence of sharecropping, in so far as a real trend does exist, as a response to an increasing difficulty to mobilize filial labor because sons prefer outside share contracts. The choice of contract is of no importance from that point of view.

It is of course possible to think of other explanations which may save that part of Murray's argument which states that the incidence of sharecropping is increasing while pre-inheritance grants are on their way out. Thus, one may attempt to retain Murray's hypothesis that sharecropping represents a superior way for a father to mobilize the labor of his sons but without assuming that the sons can obtain better deals outside the family. In rural Haiti, a declining standard of living has been observed for some decades.[22] It is then quite possible that fathers may feel that they cannot count on filial labor under the traditional system as the degree of economic hardship increases. There is, of course, always a temptation for sons to devote most of their time and efforts to their 'own' pre-inheritance plots to increase their own incomes, and less to their parents' fields. With enough land available to provide both fathers and sons with sufficient incomes, the fathers would presumably not complain too much, but when the standard of living falls towards the subsistence level, an intergenerational conflict may arise as to the desired allocation of the sons' efforts. In this situation a shift may take place from informal understandings on how much labor the sons have to provide to the fathers towards more formal sharecropping arrangements where the efforts expended benefit fathers and sons equally. Then the intergenerational allocation conflict disappears.

It should, however, be noted that this type of argument involves a difficulty which can also be found in Murray's argument, namely, that it is always possible to find pre-inheritance contracts which, from the point of view of labor mobilization, are equivalent to a given share contract as long as the father/landlord has influence over the labor effort expended by his sons/tenants. The empirical evidence presented by Murray is difficult to interpret on this point, since Murray never deals directly with the present hypothesis. He emphasizes that 'it is well known that a father who can provide his sons with abundant land could control the energies and labor of his sons'.[23]

At the same time he shows that those sons who still receive pre-inheritance grants tend to spend more labor on their fathers' gardens than those who do not.[24] On the other hand, he demonstrates that 'young men *are* in fact now putting in, on the aggregate, less time on parents' gardens than was true in the days of old'.[25] What his data do not show, however, is whether those who today receive, say, a quarter of a *carreau* as a pre-inheritance grant provide more or less labor for their parents than was the case a generation or two ago. This — whether sons receiving pre-inheritance grants can get away with less work on parental land — is the crux of the matter.

We may also formulate a second hypothesis which builds on the declining rural standard of living but which is not directly connected with labor mobilization. This argument runs in terms of the relative permanency of pre-inheritance grants and share leases. If the former are regarded as more permanent transfers of land than the latter, i.e. if the property rights granted to the sons under the first type of arrangement are stronger and less alienable than those that can be obtained under a share contract, fathers today, being closer to the subsistence level than fathers one or two generations back, may be reluctant to give their land away in pre-inheritance grants and may prefer sharecropping arrangements instead.

The problem with this argument is that of establishing how strong the property rights vested in a pre-inheritance grant actually are. It is known that such grants do not necessarily entail any permanent transfer of land from fathers to sons. 'What father gave, father could take away. The maintenance of his newly acquired land was contingent on the young man's fidelity to local domestic norms, particularly that rule which bound him to *regular unremunerated labor in his father's gardens.*'[26] Against this, however, we have to set the notorious uncertainty of sharecropping arrangements which can always be terminated when the period of lease expires.[27] Pre-inheritance grants do not have to be permanent to be regarded as more secure for the sons than share contracts. Local norms may prescribe that a father should not take back a pre-inheritance grant as long as the son provides the required amount of labor on the parental fields. Norms may, however, change. It may very well be the case that the relative security of the two types of contract is equivalent in the same way as their relative ability to mobilize labor and that the evolution of security over time does not differ between the two. Unfortunately, Murray's work does not shed any light on these problems.

Sharccropping is a phenomenon which is not so easy to understand, especially since its incidence may differ from region to region.[28] Much more research is needed to explain its existence in Haiti. Unfortunately, the theoretical literature does not offer a coherent view.[29] Still, I think that critical employment of existing theory on the subject may be a strategy not to be discarded without discussion when interpreting field data.[30]

Notes

A preliminary version of this essay was presented at the fourth Arne Ryde Symposium (on the Theory of Economic Institutions) at Frostavallen, 4 September 1979. Thanks are due to Carl-Johan Dahlman and Lennart Jörberg for their comments on that version. I have also benefitted from comments by Christopher K. Clague and from communication with Gerald F. Murray. Needless to say, the opinion stated here is only my own.

1. Lundahl (1979), pp. 48-9.
2. Unfortunately, the results of the 1971 census are not yet available.
3. Lundahl (1979), pp. 48, 50.
4. Murray (1977), p. 377. It should be kept in mind, however, that Murray does not give any figures with respect to the relative *areas* owned and sharecropped.
5. Ibid., p. 376.
6. At the same time, they remain sharecroppers on the land of others. The main reason for this pattern, according to Murray, is probably that hereby the peasants manage to diversify their land with respect to crops, soil types and hydraulic conditions, thereby decreasing the risk of, e.g., crop failures (Murray, 1977, pp. 490-1).

7. Murray's work has been met with acclaim: 'This excellent study of how land tenure patterns have changed in response to population growth should be required reading for all students of rural Haiti.' Zuvekas (1978), note, p. 84. This makes a discussion of his interpretation doubly important.

8. One *carreau* = 1.29 hectares.

9. A short account of the system, as it appeared in the Marbial valley in the late forties, can be found in Bastien (1951), pp. 37-40.

10. Murray (1977), pp. 412, 414.

11. Ibid., p. 424.

12. Ibid., p. 427.

13. Ibid., p. 495.

14. What Murray assumes with respect to the relative price of land and labor is not quite clear. On the one hand, he agrees that land is scarce in today's Haiti, while it was abundant during the nineteenth century (ibid., pp. 409ff). On the other hand, he attempts to establish a case for increasing scarcity of labor as the population grows (ibid., pp. 419ff). Obviously, land and labor cannot be scarce at the same time. The alternative interpretation offered here begins from increasing scarcity of land (increasing abundance of labor), but in the face of increasing abundance of labor it is difficult to understand why special strategies need to be designed to mobilize it. This contradictory feature of Murray's analysis makes it hard to accept.

15. It must be stressed that Murray's findings with respect to the incidence of sharecropping run counter to all other evidence published so far.

16. Cf. Lundahl (1979), Chapter 6.

17. This process is analyzed in ibid., Chapter 5.

18. Transaction costs, however, appear to be higher for share contracts than, e.g., for fixed-rent or wage contracts (Cheung, 1969:1, pp. 25-6). It can also be shown that share contracts offer no advantages from the point of view of risk sharing. It is *at best* equivalent to a combination of fixed-rent and fixed-wage contracts. (See e.g., Newbery, 1975, pp. 110-16.)

19. See Johnson (1950) and Griffin (1976), pp. 192-4.

20. This type of contractual renegotiation as a response to shifts in relative bargaining power when relative factor prices change is common. See, for example, North and Thomas (1973) *passim* and Davis (1973), Chapter 6, for evidence from Medieval Europe and from the sixteenth and seventeenth centuries. In Haiti, the same type of change has been observed by Palmer in the Belladère region during the present century: 'In Belladère . . . renting is increasingly common as more and more farmers inherit impracticably small plots. At the same time, however, as land becomes scarcer and more valuable, large landowners are more hesitant to put their properties up for rent.' (Palmer, 1976, p. 147.)

21. Murray's argument is correct only if these changes also represent a change in the relative land area held under each type of arrangement. In order to find out the relative importance of sharecropping and pre-inheritance land for a particular age group, the *total amount of land* held under each arrangement should be compared. Murray, however, does not give any figures with respect to areas.

22. See Lundahl (1979), Chapter 3.

23. Murray (1977), p. 444.

24. Ibid., pp. 446-7.

25. Ibid., p. 444.

26. Ibid., p. 412. Italics in the original.

27. Lundahl (1979), p. 603.

28. See, for example, the findings of Palmer who, in a study of the Belladère area in the early 1970s, found *no* sharecropping whatsoever (Palmer, 1976, p. 209).

According to the peasants in the area this was 'because the low yields make it impractical' (ibid., p. 148).

29. The reader may consult, e.g., Johnson (1950); Cheung (1968, 1969:1, 2); Griffin (1974), pp. 22-6; Bardham and Srinivasan (1971); Rao (1971); Newbery (1973, 1975); and Bell and Zusman (1976). A comparison of theories is made by Bell (1977).

30. Strangely enough, not a single reference to the theoretical literature on sharecropping appears in Murray's bibliography.

Bibliography

Bardhan, P.K. and Srinivasan, T.N. 'Crop-sharing Tenancy in Agriculture: A Theoretical and Empirical Analysis', *American Economic Review*, vol. 61, 1971

Bastien, R. *La familia rural haitiana, Valle de Marbial*. México, 1951

Bell, C. 'Alternative Theories of Sharecropping: Some Tests, using Evidence from Northeast India', *Journal of Development Studies*, vol. 13, 1977

Bell, C. and Zusman, P. 'A Bargaining Theoretic Approach to Crop-sharing Contracts', *American Economic Review*, vol. 66, 1976

Cheung, S.N.S. 'Private Property Rights and Sharecropping', *Journal of Political Economy*, vol. 76, 1968

Cheung, S.N.S. 'Transaction Costs, Risk Aversion and the Choice of Contractual Arrangements', *Journal of Law and Economics*, vol. 12, 1969:1

Cheung, S.N.S. *The Theory of Share Tenancy*, Chicago, 1969:2

Davis, R. *The Rise of the Atlantic Economies*. Ithaca, 1973

Griffin, K. *The Political Economy of Agrarian Change: An Essay on the Green Revolution*. Cambridge, Mass., 1974

Griffin, K. *Land Concentration and Rural Poverty*. London, 1976

Johnson, D.G. 'Resource Allocation under Share Contracts', *Journal of Political Economy*, vol. 58, 1950

Lundahl, M. *Peasants and Poverty: A Study of Haiti*. London, 1979

Murray, G.F. 'The Evolution of Haitian Land Tenure: A Case Study in Agrarian Adaptation to Population Growth', PhD thesis, Columbia University, New York, 1977

Newbery, D.M.G. *Crop-sharing Tenancy in an Equilibrium Model*. Paper delivered to the European Meeting of the Econometric Society, Oslo, 28-31 August 1973

Newbery, D.M.G. 'The Choice of Rental Contract in Peasant Agriculture' in L.G. Reynolds (ed.). *Agriculture in Development Theory*. New Haven, 1975

North, D.C. and Thomas, R.P. *The Rise of the Western World: A New Economic History*. Cambridge, 1973

Palmer, E.C. 'Land Use and Landscape Change along the Dominican-Haitian Border', PhD thesis, University of Florida, Gainesville, 1976

Rao, C.H. Hanumantha. 'Uncertainty, Entrepreneurship and Sharecropping in India', *Journal of Political Economy*, vol. 79, 1971

Zuvekas, C. Jr. *Agricultural Development in Haiti: An Assessment of Sector Problems, Politics and Prospects under Conditions of Severe Soil Erosion*. Mimeo, US/AID, Washington, DC, 1978

7 A NOTE ON HAITIAN MIGRATION TO CUBA, 1890-1934*

Summary

Important migratory movements took place between Haiti and Cuba between the First World War and 1930. These migrations which were both permanent and temporary were due almost exclusively to economic factors. The influx of Haitians represented an important addition to the labor force for the Cuban sugar harvest during a period of rapid expansion in the sugar industry, while at the same time this migration helped considerably to reduce the population pressure which had mounted in Haiti during the course of the nineteenth century and which after the turn of the century was visible in the form of increasing scarcity of arable land.

The migration of Haitian cane-cutters to Cuba is a theme which has been subject to little systematic research. The present note represents an attempt to present the most important characteristics of Haitian-Cuban migration and at the same time offers an analysis of the causes of migration.

'Fifteen years I spent in Cuba, fifteen years, every day cutting sugar cane, *oui*, every day, from sunrise to dusk-dark. At first, the bones in your back get all twisted up like a corkscrew. But there's something makes you stand it. What? Tell me, do you know what it is?' He clenched his fists as he talked. 'It's being mad — that's what! Being mad makes you grit your teeth and tighten your belt when you're hungry . . .'

Jacques Roumain, *Masters of the Dew*

The Forerunners

The first migration from Haiti to Cuba took place in the wake of the Haitian revolution against the French colonial power in 1791, when large numbers of ex-*colons* took refuge in Cuba to escape certain death

*Source: *Cuban Studies*, vol. 12, no. 2, 1982

at the hands of the rebelling slaves, 'as it seems, under the auspices of a curious society which made propaganda in France'.[1] Between 1795 and 1805 more than 30,000 refugees from Haiti arrived in Santiago de Cuba, one-third of whom were whites.[2] This arrival of the French had a very definite impact on the Cuban economy in that French coffee growers were instrumental in creating a flourishing coffee industry in central and eastern Cuba. A high price on the European market, in combination with the relative ease and low costs connected with creating a coffee farm, made coffee an attractive crop whose cultivation was rapidly expanded in Cuba from 1790 to 1810.[3] The coffee of Saint-Domingue was reputedly one of the finest in the world. It was of a quality sometimes equal to that of mocha,[4] and with the aid of the French experience in high-quality coffee production that had been accumulated over 65 years,[5] Cuban coffee exports rose from only 80 tons in 1790-2 to more than 20,000 tons in 1844.[6]

However, the success of Cuban coffee hardly lasted beyond the first generation of French immigrants. Coffee was quickly overtaken by sugar for the simple reason that the former yielded a smaller profit than the latter. In addition, in 1834 the United States imposed a high tariff on coffee imports as well as tonnage duties on Spanish boats entering US ports. Furthermore, Cuba was hit by a series of devastating hurricanes that ruined the crops of 1845 and 1847. Finally, Brazilian production of coffee expanded enormously after 1840. As a result, Cuban coffee exports had fallen below 12,000 tons by 1844.[7] A generation later, the remaining coffee farms had declined to a point where they supplied only a third-rate crop.[8]

The first wave of migration from Haiti to Cuba was intimately connected with Cuba's development of an important export crop. This was even more true of the second, and principal, wave of migration, but in a very different fashion. The migration of unskilled cane-cutters that took place after the turn of the century differed in that the know-how was Cuban (or rather American) and the Haitians supplied only their sheer physical effort and resistance; whereas in the case of the French planters, the immigrants had supplied the technical know-how. The Haitians were common laborers and not entrepreneurs.

The most important wave of migration did not begin until more than a century after the arrival of the French planters. Around 1900, imports of contract labor had, however, reached proportions which were large enough to lead to vehement protests from white Cubans who wanted to increase the ratio of whites to blacks in the Cuban population. Allegedly, more than 1,000 black immigrants from Haiti, Jamaica and Turks Islands arrived in seven months in the year 1900.[9]

The Causes of Migration

Protests were of little avail. Migration was determined not by racist political pressure groups in Cuba but by economic factors which were strong enough to sweep aside any ideologically-based restrictions on immigration. Here, both demand and supply factors were at work. Let us begin by examining the former.

Demand

In the 1890s, Cuban sugar production began a process of expansion. Output grew from a figure of 632,000 tons in 1890 to reach the magic figure of one million tons for the first time in history in 1894-5. This was due, among other things, to technological advances, the abolition in the United States of tariffs on primary imports such as sugar, and the substitution of cheaper contract labor for slaves, whose maintenance cost exceeded that of hiring free labor in the market.[10] This achievement proved to be only temporary. In 1894 a 40 per cent duty on imported sugar was again levied in the US, and in 1894-5 the world market price of sugar fell drastically. Production could be maintained during 1895 only by an increase in exports to Spain. However, as a result of the outbreak of civil warfare in the same year, production fell rapidly to almost one-fifth of its 1894-5 level and remained at just over 300,000 tons until after the turn of the century.[11] As peaceful conditions returned, sugar production managed to surpass the one-million-ton level, especially after the signing of the US-Cuban reciprocity treaty in 1903, which gave Cuban sugar a 20 per cent tariff preference in the United States market and which triggered sizeable American investments in Cuban sugar.[12] By 1912 the effects of the treaty were clearly visible. Cuban sugar was sovereign in the United States, where it had driven all European, West Indian, or other non-favored sugar off the market. In 1913 the two-million-ton level was reached. The outbreak of the First World War caused the price of sugar almost to double in two months; and as the war subsequently converted the European beet fields into battlegrounds, a further strong stimulus was given to sugar production. The Allies increasingly came to depend on Cuba for sugar purchases, and it was at this point that the forests of Oriente province succumbed to the sugar *centrales*.[13]

The tenfold increase in sugar production which took place between

1898 and 1917 meant that increased inputs of labor were required to cut the sugarcane. At the same time, however, as a consequence of the wars beginning in 1895, Cuba had lost some 200,000-300,000 people by 1899.[14] The census taken in the latter year also noted that 'No country for which data are available has such a small proportion of children below the age of five years as the island of Cuba'.[15] In the countryside, the situation was further aggravated by the fact that during the wars large numbers of the rural population had been forced to take refuge in the major cities.[16] An effort was made to increase the supply of labor by encouraging the settlement of Spanish farmers in Cuba, but generally they could not be persuaded to settle in the countryside, preferring the higher wages and other attractions of the cities, notably Havana. At this point, the *centrales* turned their attention towards the neighboring islands of the West Indies, including Haiti.[17]

Officially, there was a ban on black immigration to Cuba. The *Orden Militar* 155 from 1902 prohibited the entry of contract labor for employment in agriculture, which meant that the import of Haitian, Jamaican and Chinese labor was officially forbidden.[18] However, as a result of the expansion of their industry, the sugar interests were not slow in demanding that immigration be permitted.[19]

Supply

On the supply side, the most important reason for migration from Haiti to Cuba is to be found in the growth of the Haitian population. After the expulsion of the French at the beginning of the nineteenth century, the Haitian population fell, perhaps by as much as 150,000, between 1789 and 1805.[20] For a while this left ample room for the ex-slaves to expand across the Haitian part of the island of Hispaniola without incurring a decline in their per capita incomes. The history of rural Haiti during the first half of the nineteenth century is one of a newly-created nation of peasant squatters who grabbed land wherever it could be found. Gradually, however, demographic growth caught up with the area of arable land, so that during the last quarter of the nineteenth century it was no longer possible to respond to population growth by simply continuing to combine land and labor in fixed proportions. Diminishing returns to labor began to set in. A situation had been reached where all the arable land in Haiti was either worked or claimed by some owner.[21] Land was a scarce resource in the Haitian economy, and pressure was exerted on the redundant population to emigrate. Thus it appears as if most of the emigrants to Cuba were landless peasants with few alternative economic opportunities in their native country.[22] In his study of the life of the Haitian peasant, Paul Moral has claimed that a majority of all the Haitians who left for Cuba up to 1923 were 'destitute'.[23]

This push out of Haiti may have been artificially reinforced by some events which took place during the American occupation of Haiti after 1915. The occupation authorities undoubtedly encouraged emigration for several reasons. In the first place, leading officials considered the country to be overpopulated. In his 1925 report, the American High Commissioner pointed to the problems created by the population pressure[24] and four years later, in an analysis of the occupation, Financial Adviser-General Receiver Arthur Millspaugh concluded that the country was overpopulated[25] in relation to the poor natural resource endowment. In the light of this growing awareness of the demographic problem, the active encouragement of emigration can be seen as a logical escape route.

Secondly, as Hans Schmidt has emphasized in his study of the American occupation of Haiti, the interests of the United States always came first when a decision was made by the occupation authorities.[26] Emigration could serve these interests in at least two different ways. In the first place, it brought needed labor to the American-owned sugar plantations in Cuba, and secondly, it created a source of revenue in the form of an emigration tax which for years constituted the most important item of Haitian internal revenue.[27] These revenues, in turn, were primarily spent on interest and amortization payments on the Haitian external debt, which had been consolidated in American hands between 1922 and 1925.[28]

In addition to the reasons just advanced, Marxist writers, notably Suzy Castor, have pointed to the alienation of agricultural land from the peasants by American interests after the beginning of the American occupation.[29] *L'Union Nationaliste*, a patriot organization that was founded after the arrival of the Marines in Haiti, was very strongly concerned about the land concessions given by the occupation authorities, including the puppet government, to American interests.[30] In 1930 the Union denounced the alienation of agricultural land from 'thousands of peasants' who, as a consequence of the land concession policy, were allegedly faced with the choice of whether to remain in the countryside as landless laborers or to migrate.[31] A number of leading Haitian intellectuals voiced their protests. Percival Thoby warned against the 'tentacles of dollar imperialism' and pointed out that small peasants and squatters could not be sacrificed in a policy which erroneously attempted to attract American capital to develop the agricultural resources of Haiti;[32] Georges Séjourné and François Dalencour unanimously sounded an alarm against the creation of a rural, landless proletariat which would subsequently be at the mercy of the foreign corporations' demand for cheap labor.[33]

It cannot be denied that American policy, at least during the first half of the occupation, was based on the perceived need for the introduction of large-scale agriculture. The occupation authorities did all they possibly could to attract plantation agriculture to Haiti. Between 1915 and 1930, at least 33 different legislative measures were applied to this end.[34] The main problem in this respect was to secure legal title to the land deemed suitable for concessions. In order to achieve this purpose, the American-drafted 1918 constitution allowed foreign ownership of land for the first time in the history of independent Haiti. Moreover, it was necessary to prepare a cadastral survey to establish who owned what, since clear titles were generally absent. An aerial survey was carried out in 1925-6, and an attempt was made to let an American lawyer draft a land legislation bill. Both efforts failed. The building where the photos were stored burned down, possibly as a consequence of arson, and the Haitian puppet government opposed both the bill and the cadastral survey.[35]

The occupation managed to establish a total of perhaps 28,000 hectares of American-owned plantations in Haiti between 1915 and 1927.[36] It is not known with any degree of accuracy to what extent eviction of peasants was resorted to in the process, but in at least one instance, that of creating the Plantation Dauphin — at one time the largest sisal plantation in the world — the dispossession of smallholders is known to have been massive.[37] According to Suzy Castor, altogether some 50,000 peasants were evicted in northern Haiti.[38]

Nevertheless, the exact influence of the American eviction of peasants is difficult to establish. However, the increasing demand for cane-cutters in Cuba (the largest employers were the United Fruit and the General Sugar Companies, with the former employing 8,000 Haitians in 1926 and 12,000 in 1927),[39] combined with the mounting Haitian population pressure, gave rise to a wage differential which was great enough to induce a large-scale movement of Haitians to the neighboring island. According to Arthur Millspaugh, the average daily wage in Haiti in 1923 was about 30 US cents, while in Cuba the wages of unskilled workers were four to five times as high;[40] Haitian laborers in the Cuban cane fields received from US $1 to $1.50 per day.

Migration and Living Conditions

Given the potential supply of Haitians and the market for unskilled labor in sugar production, it was, of course, only a matter of time before the issue was clarified in Cuba. The decisive, triggering event was the black revolt in 1912,[41] following which the United Fruit Company applied for permission to import West Indians to work on the plantations of Oriente province. The permission was readily granted by President Gómez in early 1913. A few months later President Menocal again allowed the company to bring in *braceros.*[42]

The Haitians quickly gained a reputation for being faster and less demanding than, for example, Jamaicans.[43] As a result, a steady stream of Haitians poured into Cuba for fifteen years. These workers were typified by Manuel, the protagonist of the most famous of all Haitian novels, Jacques Roumain's *Gouverneurs de la rosée,*[44] who was a *viejo*, a Haitian who had been in Cuba and who had subsequently returned home, having only departed for the *zafra* but in the end staying for fifteen years. Manuel was not alone. Beginning in 1915, numerous boats departed from Cayes, Port-au-Prince or Port-de-Paix with Haitian peasants recruited by representatives of the Cuban sugar companies who established themselves in the ports of emigration.[45]

Table 7.1 provides three estimates of the legal migration from Haiti to Cuba between 1913 and 1931,[46] two based on Cuban sources and one giving Haitian data. According to the Cuban figures, some 150,000-190,000 Haitians legally migrated from Haiti to Cuba during this period; but as a comparison with the Haitian figures for 1922-9 shows, actual migration may well have been higher. Most of the early migration was illegal.[47] Moreover, the methods that were subsequently employed to recruit Haitians were by no means always confined to legally accepted devices. Graft and trickery in the issues of visas and passports were common enough, and legal measures undertaken in Haiti to put an end to this traffic after 1923 — increases in passport fees, regulation of the activities of the recruiting companies, increased control of individual emigration — were fruitless.[48]

It is difficult to determine what the real number of immigrants may have been. Suzy Castor estimates that from one-third to one-half of the total migration was illegal, with altogether some 30,000-40,000 people migrating from Haiti to Cuba every year between 1915 and 1929,[49] which corresponds to a total of 450,000-600,000 migrants. Juan Pérez de la Riva arrives at a figure in the same range — around 500,000 — for the years 1903-31 — by adding the figures for immigration of

Haitians (corresponding to the first estimate in Table 7.1) and those for 'entry of passengers'. This estimate is based on the assumption that there is no overlap between the two series and that the former series consists only of cane-cutters who had been contracted in Haiti, whereas the latter gives a reasonable approximation of the number of cutters who possessed enough money to pay the fare themselves and went to Cuba on their own. A further addition was also made to take account of 106,000 'passengers' who were officially classified as United States citizens, although they were supposedly Haitians smuggled into Cuba outside the legal quotas.[50]

Table 7.1: Legal Haitian Migration to Cuba, 1913-31 (Number of Migrants)

Year	Cuban figures[a]	Cuban figures[b]	Haitian figures
1913	1,200	1,512	
1914	98	117	
1915	2,453	2,490	
1916	4,922	4,878	
1917	10,136	10,241	
1918	10,460	11,268	
1919	10,044	7,329	
1920	35,971	30,722	
1921	12,483	12,567	
1922	639	1,437	10,152
1923	11,088	10,553	20,117
1924	21,013	20,430	21,517
1925	18,750	12,198	22,970
1926	12,346	10,423	21,619
1927	14,312	5,949	14,098
1928	14,353	707	} 5,500
1929	4,339	274	
1930	5,126	2,769	
1931	22	336	
Total 1922-9:	96,840	61,971	115,973
Grand total:	189,755	146,200	

Sources: Cuban figures (1); 1913-19: Juan Pérez de la Riva, 'Cuba y la migración antillana 1900-1931', *Anuario de Estudios Cubanos*, no. 2 (1979), pp. 38-9 (taken from Cuba, Secretaría de Hacienda, *Inmigración y movimiento de pasajeros* (La Habana, one yearly bulletin); 1920-1: *Memorias inéditas del censo de 1931* (La Habana: Editorial de Ciencias Sociales, 1978), p. 290; 'Número total de inmigrantes por nacionalidades'. Since the series presented by Pérez de la Riva coincides exactly with that given in the *Memorias* for 1920-9 (with the exception of 1922, for which no figure is available in Pérez de la Riva), the two series have been linked here.
Cuban figures (b); 1913-19: Emily Greene Balch, 'Notes on the Land Situation in Haiti', in Emily Greene Balch (ed.), *Occupied Haiti* (New York: The Writers Publishing Company, 1927), p. 77 (taken from *Inmigración y movimiento de pasajeros*; 1920-31: *Memorias inéditas*, p. 296: 'Entrada de pasajeros por pases de procedencia'. Since the latter series contains the same figures as those given by Balch for the two overlapping years 1920 and 1921, the two series have been linked here.
Haitian figures: Suzy Castor, *La ocupación norteamericana de Haití y sus consecuencias* (México, D.F.: Siglo Veintiuno, 1971), p. 83 (taken from the Annual Reports of the Financial Adviser-General Receiver, Washington, DC, 1925-6, p. 97; 1928-9, p. 67).

Both Castor's and Pérez de la Riva's figures may, however, be over-estimates. Quite probably the latter contains a measure of double counting, since they build on the assumption that there is no overlap whatsoever between the two series of 'immigrants' and 'passengers'. The practice of counting all 'passengers' as cane-cutters may be a dubious one even if no overlap exists, since a number of other temporary visitors, who had nothing whatsoever to do with the sugar sector, would then have spuriously inflated the migration figures.

Castor's contention that from one-third to one-half of the total migration was illegal should probably also be revised downwards. Although the illegal portion of the migration was probably quite high during the first few years after 1912, it may not have been necessary to bring in other than legally contracted labor during the 1920s. Table 7.2 shows that the United Fruit Company consistently utilized less than its official quota between 1923 and 1928. This quota could always be (and always was) increased when the company so desired.[51] At any rate, completely illegal migration, where immigrant boats landed at deserted spots, does not appear to have been very common in comparison with the entry of legally contracted cutters.[52] To the extent that other companies behaved in the same manner as United Fruit, the alleged importance of illegal immigration is thus reduced. Perhaps it is more correct to assume that one-third constitutes a maximum estimate, corresponding to a total migration of 450,000 people between 1913 and 1931.

Table 7.2: Imports of Haitian Braceros by the United Fruit Company, 1923-30

Year	Officially authorized quota	Real number of immigrants
1923	4,000	3,904
1924	5,000	4,783
1925	{ 5,000 + 1,200	5,976
1926	{ 8,000 + 1,500	8,621
1927	10,500	9,619
1928	10,500	9,606
1929	9,600	n.a.
1930	2,000	n.a.

n.a. = not available
Source: *United Fruit Company: Un caso del dominio imperialista en Cuba* (La Habana: Editorial de Ciencias Sociales, 1976), p. 217.

This type of measurement, however, is subject to double counting in another sense since the policy of the Cuban sugar companies was to repatriate the Haitians after the *zafra* rather than to keep them in the country. The cost of repatriation and subsequent recontracting and transport was obviously lower than that of keeping the Haitians on the company premises during the dead season.[53] This is borne out by the figures of Table 7.3, which shows that in 1927 only a quarter of the Haitians recruited by United Fruit went to Cuba for the first time.[54]

Table 7.3: Number of Previous Trips to Cuba by Haitian Braceros Contracted by the United Fruit Company in 1927

Number of previous trips	Number of workers
None	2,777
1	3,633
2	2,744
3	1,237
4	367
5	140
6	48
7	34
8	12
9	5
10	3
Total	11,000

Source: *United Fruit Company*, p. 220.

With time, regular cane-cutter routes developed between Haiti and Cuba. Thus, the United Fruit Company made Port-de-Paix the center of Haitian emigration. The transit stop at Port-de-Paix gave the company a profitable return freight on the Honduras route.[55] The fact that much of the migration was temporary makes it hard to determine the number of Haitians who lived in Cuba during any particular year. In 1920, the total number of Haitian residents presumably amounted to 70,000;[56] ten years later, according to the Haitian consul of Camagüey, the number of Haitians in that province alone was as high as 30,000.[57] In 1931, according to the census taken that year, Cuba had 77,535 resident Haitians, 88 per cent of whom were male, constituting a total of 18 per cent of all foreigners.[58] Pérez de la Riva estimates the maximum to have been 165,000 in 1929, before the introduction of the Smoot-Hawley tariff in the United States (cf. below)[59] and claims that the 1931 census figure must be viewed as a substantial underestimate since the American-owned sugar companies chose to hide the Haitians when unemployment figures began to rise in Cuba. To some extent this is true,[60] but probably not to the extent claimed by Pérez de la Riva. The 1931 sugar output amounted to only 60 per cent of the 1929 figure,[61] and the number of unemployed Cubans had increased sufficiently to cut the need for Haitians substantially.[62]

How did the Haitians fare in Cuba? When Roumain's Manuel returned home, he was 'the man who had crossed the sea, who had lived in the strange country of Cuba. He was crowned with a halo of mysteries and legends.'[63] The *viejo* became an important part of daily life in Haiti:

> the *viejos* constituted already a sort of aristocracy, distinct from the mass of *engagés* who had not succeeded. At each new crossing, the freelance *viejo* brought in relatives and friends. When he returned home, he created a sensation with his loud jewelry, his eccentric clothes, his broad-rimmed felt hat, his sunglasses, and his Spanish jargon. At Port-de-Paix, Cayes, or Petit Goave, the return of the 'Cubans' in July was the big event of the year: business picked up; the greenbacks, genuine or counterfeit, circulated; provincial life woke up.[64]

Still, most of the emigrants never managed to make any fortunes. Manuel brought home little money from Cuba.[65] Earning the daily wage in Cuba was not simple. The conditions facing the Haitians were deplorable. 'They live and die like dogs. *Matar a un haitiano o a un perro*: to kill a Haitian or a dog is one and the same thing, say the rural police. They're just like wild beasts,' asserts Manuel in *Gouverneurs de la rosée.*[66] His assertion closely resembles the conclusion drawn by Paul Moral:

> They are subjected to exhausting work, subdued by the draconic conditions of the employer, exposed to the exactions of the rural police without finding any protection extended to them by the Haitian consular representatives. They suffer the mean intrigues of the plantation agents and live miserably in the filthy barracks of the large 'fincas', losing their meager savings on gambling and drinking, often deserting the plantation to maroon for a while before they end up in the shantytowns of Santiago. 'Haitiano' in Cuba has become synonymous with 'poor devil'[67]

Suzy Castor arrives at similar conclusions when pointing out that the successful *viejos* never constituted more than a minority:

A small fraction of these emigrants managed to command a better life. These are the so-called 'viejos' who have constituted a colorful theme in the Haitian literature. They came back with a few hundred dollars' savings, good clothing, shoes, gold teeth, and sunglasses. But the majority returned as poor as before, after suffering innumerable humiliations and being physically exhausted after working 10 to 15 hard hours a day in the cane fields. The work contract turns the immigrant into a serf, almost a slave.[68]

Conditions like these naturally made many Haitians return home. In addition, the work on the plantations was highly seasonal. Thus, a majority of the cane-cutters are believed to have returned to their country of origin sooner or later. Emily Greene Balch and Arthur Millspaugh both place the figure at some two-thirds.[69]

Around 1930 migration began to taper off. In 1928, after a diplomatic controversy with Cuba, the Haitian government attempted to curb the outflow. In July President Borno prohibited emigration, which explains the low numbers of legal emigrants in 1928-9. According to Haitian figures, only 5,500 officially emigrated to Cuba, while 5,530 returned.[70] The ban was, however, lifted again in December, and things would presumably have gone back to normal had not certain events within the sugar industry intervened.[71]

In 1925, Cuban sugar output had managed to pass five million tons for the first time, but the sugar price was on its way down. The consumption of sugar in the United States — the major market — failed to keep pace with the growth of the population, so that in spite of continued high output levels for a few years, export incomes declined. A number of measures were taken to restrict the Cuban output in order to keep prices high. With the market continuously threatened by overproduction, an attempt was made to secure the co-operation of European beet sugar producers. Despite these efforts, the year 1929 saw a new five-million-ton crop put on the market. In the meantime, the United States raised its tariffs on sugar (the Smoot-Hawley tariff). The sugar price kept falling, and large portions of the 1929 crop remained unsold.

New attempts were made to restrict output, and in 1931 the so-called Chadbourne plan, under which sugar production was to be cut back heavily, was signed by a majority of the world's sugar producers. The Cuban share on the USA market dropped from almost 50 per cent in 1930 to slightly over 25 in 1933. Since the Chadbourne agreement failed to include protected areas, domestic producers and producers in

Hawaii, Puerto Rico and the Philippines took over. The plan also failed to prevent sugar prices from dropping. With the onset of the depression and the general fall of prices of primary products, Cuban incomes from sugar exports in 1932 hit their lowest level since 1901. Thus the Cuban sugar industry gradually went into a slump. 'The unemployed in the sugar industry grew to great regiments; most of those who had work in 1932 had a total of a bare eighty days . . . mills closing, work and capital unobtainable, the international market at its lowest point, everywhere decay and misery.'[72]

In this situation the Cuban government decided to repatriate large numbers of Haitian plantation workers. Resentment loomed large among Cuban workers who had witnessed an uninterrupted flow of Haitians into the country for years, underbidding them in the labor market when the economy was in a state of depression. At this point, the demographic balance to some extent was also beginning to be re-established. At any rate, enough Cubans were available to meet the demand of the *centrales*.[73] In November 1933 a law was promulgated which stipulated that at least 50 per cent of the labor force in industry, commerce and agriculture had to be Cuban, and in December another law decreed that all those immigrants who resided illegally in the country were subject to deportation.[74] The *Guardia Rural* immediately took action. Haitians were beaten or otherwise harassed and even murdered. Immigrant ships were not allowed to land.[75] In July 1934 an estimated 8,000 Haitians had been repatriated.[76]

Epilogue

The 1934 repatriation constituted the end of Haitian large-scale emigration to Cuba. The one-third of the Haitian migrants who did not eventually return to their home country were absorbed into the Cuban population. In the course of a single generation (up to 1953), the official number of Haitians residing in Cuba had fallen to 27,543.[77] With Fidel Castro's subsequent victory and rise to power in 1959, Cuba was more or less totally cut off as an escape valve for the rising Haitian population. The abysmal difference in political outlook between the two countries made migration a most difficult affair. Robert Rotberg gives the total number of Haitians in Cuba as 50,000 at the end of the 1960s,[78] but this figure is almost certain to be an overstatement. According to the 1970 Cuban census, the number of residents born in Haiti was 22,579, of whom no less than 55 per cent were concentrated in Oriente province and 43 per cent in Camagüey.[79] Those departing for Cuba since the beginning of the Castro era had mainly been people with radical political ideas who would have been exiled.[80] Aaron Segal has estimated their number between 1960 and 1974 to be in the order of 1,000 people, while the total number of Haitians living in Cuba was approximately 15,000 in the mid-seventies.[81] Today, emigration from Haiti to Cuba must be considered an event of the past. The 1970 census is eloquent on this point. More than 88 per cent of the Haitians resident in Cuba were 60 years old or more, and 91 per cent of these in turn were men.[82] They had come in their youth and early manhood to cut sugarcane.

Notes

The research has been funded by the Swedish Council for Research in the Humanities and Social Sciences and SAREC. Thanks are due to Claes Brundenius and two anonymous referees for constructive criticism of an earlier version.

   1. Le Riverend (1971), p. 155.
   2. Pérez de la Riva (1979), p. 17.
   3. Le Riverend (1971), p. 168.
   4. Lundahl (1979), pp. 593ff. A detailed account of coffee-growing techniques in Saint-Domingue is given in Moral (1955).
   5. Lundahl (1979), p. 40.
   6. Thomas (1971), p. 129. The history of Cuban coffee is presented in Pérez de la Riva (1944).
   7. Ibid., p. 131. In addition, the coffee industry failed to bring about the necessary technological change (Le Riverend, 1971, p. 167).
   8. Thomas (1971), p. 241.
   9. Ibid., p. 431.
   10. See Thomas, ibid., Chapter 23, for details. (Sugar output figures are found on pp. 1562-4.) The changing labor market is discussed in, e.g., Le Riverend (1971), Chapter 28.
   11. Cf. Thomas (1971), Chapters 24 et seq.
   12. Ibid., pp. 469-70. Large investments had, however, also been made between 1899 and 1902 (Le Riverend, 1971, p. 480).
   13. See Thomas (1971), Chapter 45, for a description of events. See also, e.g., Guerra (1976), Chapter 9, for a discussion of the factors behind the expansion of sugar production at this time. The case of United Fruit is studied in detail in *United Fruit Company: Un caso del dominio imperialista en Cuba* (La Habana: 1976).
   14. Le Riverend (1971), p. 563 (200,000); Thomas (1971), p. 423 (300,000).
   15. Quoted by Le Riverend, ibid., p. 563.
   16. Ibid., p. 564. The figure was 8.3 per cent.
   17. Thomas (1971), p. 540.
   18. Le Riverend (1971), p. 565.
   19. Wingfield (1966), p. 93. *United Fruit Company*, pp. 206-12, gives details regarding the problems of this particular company.
   20. Lundahl (1979), p. 272.

21. Murray (1977), p. 410.
22. Cf. Wingfield (1971), p. 94.
23. Moral (1961), p. 70.
24. United States, Department of State (1925), p. 7.
25. Millspaugh (1929).
26. Schmidt (1971), p. 234.
27. Moral (1961), p. 69. In 1925-6 the proceeds from the emigration tax amounted to more than one million gourdes (US$ 200,000). Castor (1971), p. 86.
28. For details, see Lundahl (1979), pp. 366-75.
29. Castor (1971), pp. 82-3.
30. See L'Union Nationaliste (1930).
31. Ibid.
32. Ibid.
33. See ibid. and Dalencour (1923).
34. Castor (1975), p. 55.
35. Lundahl (1979), p. 286.
36. Ibid., p. 267.
37. Ibid., pp. 286-7.
38. Castor (1975), note, p. 56.
39. Schmidt (1971), p. 171. Figures from Castor (1971), p. 85.
40. Millspaugh (1931), p. 143.
41. Thomas (1971), p. 522.
42. Ibid., pp. 524-5; Pérez de la Riva (1979), p. 28; *United Fruit Company*, p. 212.
43. Wingfield (1966), p. 94. Linguistic and cultural isolation from the rest of the population, in combination with lack of support from the Haitian diplomatic representation, made it easier for the sugar companies to obtain favorable deals with Haitian workers than with the Jamaicans, who spoke English, making negotiation easier, and who were supported by the British representation in Cuba. Pérez de la Riva (1979), p. 27.
44. Roumain (1944). English translation as *Masters of the Dew* (New York, 1947).
45. Moral (1961), p. 69.
46. Le Riverend (1971), p. 565, estimates that 175,000 Haitians came to Cuba between 1913 and 1933.
47. Wingfield (1966), p. 94; *United Fruit Company* (1976), p. 213.
48. Moral (1961), p. 70.
49. Castor (1971), p. 84.
50. Pérez de la Riva (1979), pp. 34-5, 38-9. The figures for 'pasajeros' presented in Table VIII:1 do not coincide with those given in *Memorias* (1978), p. 296, used in the present Table 7.1.
51. *United Fruit Company*, p. 218.
52. Pérez de la Riva (1979), p. 51.
53. Ibid., p. 51; *United Fruit Company* (1976), pp. 218-19.
54. See also Pérez de la Riva (1979), p. 27.
55. Moral (1961), p. 70.
56. Ibid.
57. Castor (1971), p. 84.
58. *Memorias* (1978), pp. 74, 77. Between 1920 and 1931, 25 per cent of all immigrants to Cuba were Haitians. According to these figures, only Spain (47.5 per cent) accounted for larger numbers.
59. Pérez de la Riva (1979), p. 53.
60. Cf. *United Fruit Company* (1976), p. 223.

61. Thomas (1971), p. 1563.
62. *United Fruit Company* (1976), p. 223.
63. Roumain (1947), p. 62.
64. Moral (1961), pp. 70-1.
65. Roumain (1947), p. 54.
66. Ibid., p. 29.
67. Moral (1961), p. 70.
68. Castor (1971), pp. 84-5. See also Pérez de la Riva (1979), pp. 50ff.
69. Balch (1927), p. 77; Millspaugh (1931), note, p. 43. The claim by Georges Séjourné that out of more than 300,000 who left Haiti for Cuba nobody returned home appears exaggerated, to say the least. Quoted by Castor (1971), p. 83.
70. Millspaugh (1931), p. 144.
71. For details regarding the following, see Thomas (1971), Chapter 47.
72. Ibid., p. 563.
73. Le Riverend (1971), p. 566.
74. Pérez de la Riva (1979), p. 70.
75. Ibid., p. 72; Leyburn (1966), p. 271.
76. Pérez de la Riva (1979), p. 72.
77. Brand (1965), p. 20. This figure is likely to be an understatement, however. Cf. Segal (1975), p. 198.
78. Rotberg with Clague (1971), p. 249.
79. República de Cuba (1975), Tabla 7.
80. Segal (1979), p.199.
81. Ibid., p. 200.
82. República de Cuba (1975), Tabla 7.

Bibliography

Balch, Emily Greene (ed.). 'Notes on the Land Situation in Haiti' in *Occupied Haiti*. New York, 1927
Brand, William. *Impressions of Haiti*. The Hague, 1965
Castor, Suzy. *La ocupación norteamericana de Haiti y sus consecuencias*. Mexico, 1971
Castor, Suzy. *La ocupación norteamericana de Haití sus consecuencias*. México, 1971
Castor, Suzy. 'El impacto de la ocupación norteamericana en Haití (1915-1934) y en la República Dominicana (1915-1934)' in Gérard Pierre-Charles (ed.). *Política y Sociología en Haití y la República Dominicana*. México, 1975
Dalencour, François. *Le sauvetage national par le retour à la terre*. Port-au-Prince, 1923
Guerra, Ramiro. *Azúcar y población en las Antillas*. La Habana, 1976
Le Riverend, Julio. *Historia ecónomica de Cuba*. La Habana, 1971
Leyburn, James. *The Haitian People*. Second edition. New Haven, 1966
Lundahl, Mats. *Peasants and Poverty: A Study of Haiti*. London, 1979
Millspaugh, Arthur C. 'Our Haitian Problem', *Foreign Affairs*, vol. 7, 1929
Millspaugh, Arthur C. *Haiti under American Control 1915-1930*. Boston 1931
Moral, Paul. 'La culture de café en Haïti; des plantations coloniales aux "jardins" actuels', *Cahiers d'Outre-Mer*, vol. 15, 1955
Moral, Paul. *Le paysan haïtien (Etude sur la vie rurale en Haïti)*. Paris, 1961
Murray, Gerald F. 'The Evolution of Haïtien Peasant Land Tenure: A Case Study in Agrarian Adaptation to Population Growth', PhD thesis, Columbia University, New York, 1977
Pérez de la Riva, Francisco. *El café. Historia de su cultivo y explotación en Cuba*. La Habana, 1944

Pérez de la Riva, Juan. 'Cuba y la migración antillana 1900-1931', *Anuario de Estudios Cubanos*, no. 2, 1979

República de Cuba, Junta Central de Planificación. *Censo de población y vivienda 1970*. La Habana, 1975

Rotberg, Robert I. with Clague, Christopher K. *Haiti: The Politics of Squalor*. Boston, 1971

Roumain, Jacques. *Gouverneurs de la rosée*. Port-au-Prince, 1944. English trans. *Masters of the Day*. New York, 1947

Schmidt, Hans. *The United States Occupation of Haiti, 1915-1934*. New Brunswick, 1971

Segal, Aaron Lee. 'Haiti' in Aaron Segal (ed.). *Population Policies in the Caribbean*. Lexington, Mass., 1975

Thomas, Hugh. *Cuba. The Pursuit of Freedom*. New York, 1971

L'Union Nationaliste. *Dépossessions*. Port-au-Prince, 1930

United States, Department of State. *Report of the American High Commissioner at Port-au-Prince, Haiti: 1925*. Washington, DC, 1925

Wingfield, Roland. 'Haiti. A Case Study of an Underdeveloped Area', PhD thesis, Louisiana State University, Baton Rouge, 1966

8 HAITIAN MIGRATION TO THE DOMINICAN REPUBLIC*

Haiti and the Dominican Republic share the physical territory of the island of Hispaniola. They do not share it equally, however, the Dominicans possessing some two-thirds, with only half as much left to a Haitian population which is only slightly lower than the Dominican one. Both countries are poor, but neither is poverty shared alike. Haiti is the poorest country in Latin America with a gross national product per capita which was estimated by the World Bank to equal some US$260 in 1978 whereas the corresponding figure for the Dominican Republic was 3.5 times as high, or US$910, according to the same source.[1] This income gap has led to a steady stream of temporary and permanent migrants from Haiti to the Dominican Republic for a full century.

This migration, although a well-known phenomenon to all students of the two countries, is not well researched. Relatively little is known especially with regard to the magnitude of the migration but also with respect to its determinants, and quantitative data which can be used for analytical purposes are scanty. The purpose of the present essay therefore is a modest one. In the sections that follow, we will sketch some of the most important features of Haitian-Dominican migration and advance a few hypotheses regarding the mechanisms determining the migration process in order to set the stage for meaningful future discussions and empirical data-gathering in the field.

The Early Migrations: The Maroons

The first Negro slaves were brought to Hispaniola in 1502. The aboriginal Indians of the island were quickly exterminated after the European discovery, and to make up for this loss of labor, the Spaniards decided to replace the Indians with Africans. Around the same time, sugarcane was introduced from the Canary Islands. This was an event which was to have a tremendous impact on the future economy of the western part of the island. The Spaniards never showed more than a fickle

*This chapter was written with Rosemary Vargas

interest for the fate of that part which in turn left western Hispaniola open for French penetration. With time, a colonial economy based on sugar exports developed there, while cattle ranching became the dominant activity in the eastern, Spanish, part.

Cattle ranching was labor-extensive with cattle being allowed to roam freely across unfenced open ranges, while sugar production for technical reasons required heavy concentrations of labor.[2] During the heyday of the slave traffic according to contemporary sources some 33,000 Negroes were imported annually.[3]

Around 1750, some nine-tenths of the total investment of a sugar plantation (excluding the land) was commonly in slaves.[4] At the outbreak of the wars of liberation, in 1791, the slave population of Saint-Domingue amounted to some 450,000 people.[5]

This economic system, based entirely on the coercion of unfree labor, naturally created strong incentives for the slaves to attempt to escape their fate by running away and establishing themselves as subsistence squatters in remote areas which could not be efficiently controlled by the colonial administration. *Marronage* became an alternative to slavery for a courageous minority of blacks. Frequently, the escape route took the runaway slaves to the Spanish part of the island. From there, they were not repatriated. In 1677, twelve Negro slaves were reported to have fled to the Spanish side, where they were received by the governor who allowed them to stay and live freely. Given the political tension at the time between Spain and France, the governor had good reasons for what he was doing. Escapes of slaves inflicted serious economic losses on the French *colons*. As the rumor of the successful crossing to Spanish territory spread, the number of runaway emigrants quickly increased to 50, who in 1678 were settled on an unoccupied land east of the Ozama River, where a new community, San Lorenzo de los Minas, had been founded the year before. A patrol system was devised whereby refugee slaves from the French side were tracked down and brought to this community.[6]

By the Treaty of Ryswick in 1697, Spain officially acknowledged French possession of the western third of Hispaniola. This did not, however, mean that the Spanish policy towards French maroon slaves changed. The Spanish side kept its attraction for the latter. The risk of repatriation, although existing in theory, was virtually nil. The border between the two colonies was not well defined but subject to a long dispute. Consequently, the governor in Santo Domingo and the Spanish Crown had no interest in keeping the refugees out. In 1720, there were some 2,000 escaped Saint-Domingue slaves on the Spanish side. In 1751, the figure had risen to 3,000.[7]

The treatment given the refugees varied. All of them were not given their freedom. Some had to purchase it. Others were not freed at all but only found themselves with Spanish masters instead of French. The treatment differed somewhat according to the time and the circumstances and especially with the character of the administration in Santo Domingo. Before 1701, the standard procedure appears to have been a more or less mock interrogation where the slave was made to state that he had escaped because he wanted to live a more Christian life. Subsequently, after serving a five-year labor sentence, he was freed.[8] After that year, however, the normal fate of a refugee was to remain a slave. Conditions in the Spanish colony were still much better than on the French side. The economy of the latter was to a large extent built on sugar. At the time of the harvest, sugar production required an almost round-the-clock labor effort where maximum use was made of the exhausted slaves to bring the cane to the mills and crush it before fermentation set in.[9] The Spanish economy, on the other hand, was land- not labor-intensive. The escaped slaves were made cattle herders instead and could live largely independent lives following the cattle across the *hatos*. (For the Spanish, the refugees constituted a welcome addition to the labor force.) Besides, manumission was, comparatively speaking, much more liberally practiced on the Spanish side than in Saint-Domingue, especially after 1713 when an attempt was made to limit the number of *affranchis* in the French West Indies.[10] All those who had escaped to the Spanish colony had a reasonable chance of being manumitted sooner or later.[11]

Small wonder, then, that many slaves on the French side nourished the hope of escaping across the border 'to live there independently or share the Spanish indolence there', as Moreau de Saint-Méry expressed it.[12] In 1776 the French colonial administration noted that 'the escapes most frequently are made to the Spanish [part]'.[13] At that time the towns on the Spanish side of the border were inhabited mainly by maroons from the French side. Moreau found that in San Rafael and San Miguel de la Atalaya 'the Spanish racial features which originally occupied those lands have disappeared without leaving a trace in the region'.[14]

Another factor which facilitated escape across the border was that the latter was not well defined and that it was comparatively easier for the Spanish colonists than for the French to gain a foothold in the border regions. The Treaty of Ryswick had stated that the boundary between the French and Spanish provinces was to follow the *de facto* division in 1697.[15] To establish that division was, however, far from easy. The French and Spanish interpretations differed widely. It was not until 1731 that the governors of both parties agreed to use the Massacre River as a demarcation line in the north. The rest of the border remained undefined until 1777, when the legal dispute was finally settled.[16] During the 80 years between 1697 and 1777, the Spaniards managed to occupy most of the disputed borderlands. In this, they were greatly aided by their economic system which was built on cattle ranching and not on sugar cultivation. All the Spanish had to do was to send their cattle to graze in the region, tended by a handful of people who lived in the open, whereas sugar cultivation required both a large number of slaves and a heavy concentration of capital, mainly in the crushing mill which was attached to each plantation.[17] 'In the same space where a Spaniard settles in two days a hundred French with five thousand Negroes can do so only in several years', noted a contemporary observer in 1773.[18] In turn, Spanish dominance of the borderlands made escaping across the border easier, since with no French population, except escaped maroons, living close to the frontier, the French administration had only a weak incentive to control the border area.

Without effective Spanish co-operation it was impossible to prevent the maroons from crossing the border. Not only the passive official Spanish interest in controlling border passage but also the more active help by the Spanish subjects living in the border area facilitated the traffic. In this region, contraband commerce with the maroon communities on the French side had developed,[19] and the Spaniards had a positive interest in not allowing relations with the communities, and hence with the fugitives themselves, to deteriorate. The creation of *maréchaussées*, special forces whose only task was to hunt maroons, beginning in Léogâne in 1705, and extended to the entire colony in 1733, could do nothing to change this situation.[20]

At any rate, French authority ceased at the border. Once the fugitives had reached the Spanish side, extradition required official sanction from the authorities in Santo Domingo. Theoretically, the sanction existed. The first convention regarding mutual aid between the two crowns in matters pertaining to extradition of escaped slaves was signed shortly after the Treaty of Ryswick, and another agreement was included in the Aranjuez Treaty of 1777.[21] In practice, however, the documents were dead as soon as they had been signed. The Spanish produced only words but no deeds. During the early eighteenth century, at least four different missions were sent to Santo Domingo by the French *colons* to persuade the Spanish authorities effectively to put an end to the migration of maroons. Nothing whatsoever came out of these attempts. Neither did resident Spanish lobbyists paid by the French manage to break the passive attitude of most Spanish governors.[22] In 1730 the governor of Saint-Domingue complained that 'They publish, they write everything that should be executed, they do not restore anything of what is due, and they do not execute anything of what has been promised'.[23] Ingenious pretexts were invented not to repatriate slave refugees.[24] Towards the end of the eighteenth century, Moreau summed up the Spanish policy in a single, laconic sentence: 'To think that the religious exactitude that has been promised reigns in this part of the government would be to hide the truth cowardly.'[25]

The Nineteenth Century: Haitian Expansion

The history of Haitian-Dominican relations during the nineteenth century, after Haiti had gained its independence from France in 1804, was characterized above all by Haitian incursions and invasions of Spanish, and later Dominican, territory. As early as 1801, Toussaint had invaded the eastern part of the island, and in 1805, Dessalines did the same. Much more important, however, were the occupation of the Spanish part by Boyer for 22 years (1822-44) and the subsequent invasions by Soulouque in 1849, 1851 and 1855, who hoped to regain what the Haitians had lost after the fall of Boyer.

During the period when Haiti was still a French colony, extensive cattle ranching took place in the border region between the French and Spanish colonies. At the same time a substantial overland trade had developed between the border areas of the two colonies. Both were destroyed during the first half of the nineteenth century.[26] The invading Haitian armies lived off the border regions when making their inroads into Dominican territory, requesting that towns and villages provide food for men and animals. The border towns were repeatedly drained of cattle that were slaughtered by the Haitian armies. As a result, the cattle ranchers on the Dominican side withdrew from the border, either to Santo Domingo or emigrating abroad. The *hatos* were abandoned and the remaining cattle were allowed to stray freely. At the same time, trade was cut off.

This state of affairs left ample scope for Haitian migration to the eastern part of the island. In 'push' terms no such migration was warranted. The population of the Haitian part of Hispaniola had fallen by an estimated 150,000 as a result of the wars of liberation.[27] This left plenty of room for those who remained. It took at least the first 50 years of the century,[28] and quite probably another 25 years as well,[29] to settle the western part. The Dominican evacuation of the border region, however, provided a strong enough pull to speed up migration. The population of Santo Domingo had also declined from some 125,000 in 1789 to 63,000 in 1819, according to the census taken during the latter year.[30] A virtual mass emigration arose from the first Haitian invasions in 1801 and 1805. Venezuela, Colombia, Puerto Rico and, particularly, Cuba, all received large numbers of immigrants. A contemporary observer noted that 'All of the Spanish population decided to emigrate to other lands, and the only ones who did not leave were those who absolutely could not do so'.[31]

The result was that in the 30 years up to 1819, the Dominican population was reduced by almost 50 per cent. The Haitian occupation added another reason for Dominican emigration. Large landowners were forced to leave the country so that the Haitian government could confiscate their holdings.[32] Resentment loomed large among the Dominican landowners:

> The houses and the landed property of everybody were abandoned to the Haitians or were sold to them at such extremely low prices that, on due consideration, the sales contracts were laughable parodies rather than adjustments and agreements founded in reason, in the price or in the nature of things. Houses worth four, six, eight, ten and twelve thousand pesos were sold for two or three hundred pesos in local currency. In this way, the Haitians were able to become masters, protected by the shadow of legitimate titles, of houses, possessions and property belonging to the Church or of these unfortunate Dominicans who were wandering about looking for a shelter that could protect them from abuses by the Haitians.[33]

The population vacuum was filled by Haitians. By 1841, the population had increased to 130,000 as a result of Haitian immigration,[34] which was coupled during this period with the confiscation of landed property from Dominican emigrants and the outright annexation of a part of the Dominican territory as well.[35] After the liberation from the French, the Haitians pushed steadily eastwards into the much less densely settled, partly evacuated, Dominican territory. This continued for many years, and when the Haitians had to leave Santo Domingo in 1844, they retained large portions of the Central Plain with the towns of Hincha, Las Cahobas, San Miguel de la Atalaya and San Rafael. Immigration and *de facto* occupation went hand in hand. The border areas were too thinly populated to offer much resistance, and the political turmoil ensuing after the Haitian occupation prevented the Dominicans from taking determined action to expel the Haitian settlers.

Thus, the Central Plain remained under Haitian control — and more Dominican land was in danger. The Haitian settlements were gradually extended into the San Juan Valley. In 1884, Pedro Bonó expressed a profound fear and preoccupation with the fact that the frontier was 'exposed to a perpetual and progressive invasion of foreigners (Haitians) which is daily reducing the influence of the Dominicans who, unarmed and exhausted, will disappear completely from that region'.[36]

The Rise of Sugar

As the Haitian occupation came to an end in 1844, the Dominican Republic emerged for the first time as an independent country. The principal economic activity continued to be cattle ranching which, as we know, was an activity that required large land tracts but comparatively little labor.[37] In spite of the Haitian immigration during the occupation, the country continued to be underpopulated at the beginning of the 1870s. In 1871, the total population of the country was estimated to be some 150,000.[38] Thus, land-intensive goods were produced and not labor-intensive.

In the coastal region southwest of Santo Domingo, there were some sugar plantations which continued to cultivate sugarcane and produce sugar by means of the traditional wooden sugar mills.[39] These plantations, however, faced a problem when it came to obtaining labor,[40] since cultivation and the manufacture of sugar were activities that required concentrated efforts.

Sugar soon became the most important product of the Dominican Republic — a fact that was to have an enormous importance for migration from Haiti, up to the present time. The expansion of Dominican sugar production began when large numbers of Cubans came into the country as a result of the aborted Cuban attempt to rid that island of Spanish sovereignty between 1868 and 1878.[41] 'Thousands of Cubans were busy working in the city [of Puerto Plata] or in the neighboring countryside at the same time as they were conspiring against Spain', wrote Eugenio María de Hostos.[42] During the course of a few years, some 5,000 Cuban exiles arrived in the Dominican Republic.[43] Some of these were planters who had brought some money that was invested in cane land and in modern machinery for sugar manufacturing using steam engines and railroads to transport the cane. The traditional animal-powered *trapiches* were replaced by modern *ingenios*. The first of these was founded in 1875 and during the next seven years another 30 sugar plantations were founded, representing an investment of 21 million Dominican pesos or US$6 million.[44]

The Cubans were soon followed by other foreigners, notably Americans. The *ingenios* quickly proved their superiority to the *trapiches*. The lower cost entailed in sugar production in the former quickly put the latter out of business. Overall sugar output, destined mainly for the United States market, increased rapidly, from some 8 million pounds in 1880 to 35 million pounds in 1886 and 100 million pounds in 1905.[45]

The new large-scale sugar technology required large amounts of labor. During the harvest season, the demand for labor was so strong that it was possible to 'gain in a few days the wage that before was gained only in weeks . . . and even in months'.[46] In this way, many Dominican peasants were made to leave their homesteads and move to the new sugar area, east of Santo Domingo, temporarily or permanently.[47]

The domestic supply of labor was, however, not large enough to satisfy the demand from sugar plantations and *ingenios*: immigrants were attracted as well. In the first place, the Dominican Republic was sparsely populated when sugar production began to expand. The subsequent rise in population figures to a large extent was due to immigration.[48] Secondly, work in the cane fields and in the sugar mills was highly temporary. Outside the harvest season there was nothing to do.

To some extent, this presented a conflict for those Dominicans who in addition to the work offered by the sugar companies also had some land to work.[49] Finally, owing to the higher population pressure elsewhere — and especially on the Haitian side of the border[50] — immigrant workers were prepared to work for lower wages than Dominicans. Some immigrants, known as *cocolos*,[51] came from the British West Indian islands, but a majority came from Haiti. In 1884, Hostos calculated that 35 *ingenios* used 5,500 domestic and 500 foreign day laborers.[52] As early as 1885 the number of Haitians in the sugar industry was large enough to call forth vehement protests from Dominicans who suggested that immigration of Haitians be stopped on racial grounds.[53]

Although hard data are scarce, since the immigration of Haitians was more or less uncontrolled, there is no doubt that immigration figures rose substantially as the sugar industry expanded during the next few decades. In Table 8.1, official Dominican immigration figures (flows) are presented. Between 1916 and 1925 the Ministry of Agriculture and Immigration published information regarding Haitian immigration in its *Memorias.*[54]

Table 8.1: Official Immigration of Haitian Workers in the Dominican Republic, 1916-25

1916-18	400
1918-19	300
1919-20	1,489
1923	4,100
1924	555
1925	2,500

Source: Hernández (1973), p. 55.

The 1919-20 *Memoria* indicated that 10,124 Haitians were legally in the country, and the 1920 Dominican census recorded a total of 28,258 Haitian residents.[55] It is clear that the flow figures in the table are far from reality, since they do not take any of the uncontrolled, clandestine migration into account. Between 1916 and 1925 some 145,000-155,000 Haitians *legally* migrated to Cuba, i.e. some 15,000 per year.[56] The illegal migrants included some one-third to one-half of the total which puts the annual migration from Haiti to Cuba somewhere between 22,500 and 30,000.[57] According to some contemporary sources at least, the migration to the Dominican Republic should have been even higher,[58] a 'veritable border "osmosis", anarchic and uncontrolled'.[59] The census figure also appears to be too low. The criteria employed for classifying a person as 'Haitian' were probably not efficient enough. The figure appears too low in the light of the heavy density of Haitians in the western part of the Dominican Republic.[60]

During the American occupation of the Dominican Republic, from 1916 to 1924, active encouragement was given to the expansion of the sugar industry and hence to the demand for labor. During the First World War, the European beet sugar producers in for example Germany, France, Russia and Romania were put out of competition. An excess demand for sugar ensued in the international market with prices in the Dominican Republic rising from US$5.50 per *quintal* (100 kilos) in

1914 to \$12.50 in 1918 and \$22.50 in 1920.[61] During this *Dance of the Millions*, economic and social life in the Dominican Republic received a tremendous impetus from sugar production:

> During this short period, some towns like Santiago, La Vega, San Pedro de Macorís and Puerto Plata ascended to an urban category which they had not known before. Sugar made of Macorís a city with large houses of armed concrete and streetcars in the streets to transport passengers. Puerto Plata and Santiago with tobacco and La Vega and Sánchez with cocoa, favored by the railroads, were also converted into noisy commercial centers where day after day new buildings and stores were erected and the families who had commercial interests became rich over a night.[62]

> Some cities installed electric lights and, for the first time, paved their streets and constructed sewerage systems, while also the social clubs proliferated, literary societies were founded and theaters and parks were constructed.[63]

The expansion of sugar production was also facilitated by a number of political measures. Some of these dated from the period before the occupation. In 1911, the Dominican government had conferred important advantages on American investors, by granting tax exemption on their products for eight years, and by lowering machinery and port duties for foreign investors to half of what local investors paid.[64] Most important of all, whenever roads, railroads or ports were deemed to be important for foreign enterprise, the Dominican government undertook to expropriate the necessary land. By this law, the communally owned *hatos* were also subdivided so that the expanding sugar corporations could acquire the necessary land tracts for their operations. In 1920, during the American occupation, land legislation was completed by a law providing for the registration of land titles. A land court was set up for this purpose and a land tax was imposed to ensure the use of uncultivated land.[65] In 1919, a list was devised of 245 goods that could be imported free of duty and of 700 goods where only low duties had to be paid.[66] This favored sugar production in two ways. In the first place machinery for the sugar *centrales* could now be imported without the payment of duty and secondly, since tobacco, cocoa and coffee could also be imported freely, relative prices were shifted in favor of sugar.

The sugar plantations did not fail to expand. When coffee and cocoa growers were ruined as a result of exposure to low-cost foreign competition and an export tax on these two products,[67] their land had to be sold, usually to sugar interests. The land legislation also facilitated this expansion. The American-owned Central Romana company, for example, was able to obtain title to what had hitherto been two whole villages. Some 150 Dominican families were evicted and the villages were burned to leave room for sugar production.[68] This type of transaction became so unpopular that in 1920 a peasant rebellion was triggered off. It subsequently was put down by the occupation forces.

The occupation forces also proceeded to regulate the labor supply directly. During the United States occupation of Haiti, the American administration actively encouraged emigration from the latter country. Haiti was considered to be overpopulated. In itself this was sufficient reason for the Americans to try to stimulate emigration. However, there was also a purely financial reason. Those who left the country legally had to pay an emigration tax, the proceeds of which were mainly used to liquidate the Haitian foreign debt which had been consolidated during the occupation into American hands.[69]

On the Dominican side, complementary measures were taken. In 1919, the American Military Governor issued a series of executive orders which all aimed at ensuring the supply of workers for the sugar industry (and for public works). Thus, it became prohibited to induce Dominican workers to leave the country or to transport them if the purpose was to employ them abroad. Haitian immigrants were not allowed to leave the Dominican Republic before the *zafra* for which they had come had finished. After that, however, the employers were to ensure that the Haitians departed no later than within a month.[70]

In spite of these regulations, the individual sugar *centrales* could not always be certain that enough labor would be forthcoming for the harvest. Thus, a letter from the Santa Fé sugar *ingenio* voiced the following complaints to the Department of Agriculture and Immigration:

> we have met the insuperable difficulty . . . that the majority of the workers imported during this period that have not been repatriated have not remained with this sugar mill. Some have spread to the neighboring mills, others have returned by themselves to their respective countries without giving notice, others are dedicated in other places to tasks which differ from the agricultural ones, working in docks, factories, work-shops and warehouses situated in different localities.[71]

Other observers, however, held a different opinion:

> A Haitian day-laborer at home is paid 30 American cents by the Public Works Department, and 20 to 30 outside. The writer is positive, after surveys in both countries, that the Haitian profits by his seasonal move but that his presence has a bad effect on wage levels in Santo Domingo ... At any rate the Dominicans would be glad to dispense with their 100,000 or so of annual Haitian visitors. This alien and undesired element is about a tenth of the population of the country ...
>
> Cheap imported seasonal labor digs a pit of subsistence wages at the feet of the Dominican worker in the interest of the sugar business.[72]

The most interesting information conveyed by the quotation is the one regarding the wage level. If the figures given are reasonably correct, the movement of Haitians across the border would tend to have led to a wage rate equalization between the Dominican Republic and Haiti. In the latter country, according to Arthur Millspaugh, who was Financial Adviser-General Receiver of the United States occupation forces in Haiti between 1927 and 1929, the average wage for unskilled labor in Haiti was about 20 US cents in 1923.[73]

The Post-occupation Period

When the American occupation of the Dominican Republic ended, in 1924, the Dominican economy was highly dependent on sugar production.[74] Sugar has continued to be the most important economic activity up to the present day. By the same token, Haitian immigration has maintained its importance. Both sugar production and migration have been subject to fluctuations, due on the one hand to the price level prevailing in the international sugar market and on the other to the state of relative political ease or tension between Haiti and the Dominican Republic. However, clandestine migration has hardly ever ceased even though at times the legal migratory flow has been interrupted.

The cane-cutters were not the only Haitians to migrate to the Dominican Republic during the 1920s and 1930s. The border between the two countries had been disputed for a long time. Arbitration had been attempted by the Pope in 1895 and 1901 and by the World Court in 1911. In 1912 a temporary settlement was reached with the aid of the United States. However, this did not end the dispute. In 1929 another border treaty was signed, but it was not until 1935 that the Haitian-Dominican border was finally demarcated.[75]

In the meantime Haitian squatters continued to settle on Dominican territory:

> Haitian influence spread unchecked into the San Juan Valley until the late 1930s. Haitian Creole became the lingua franca within the valley; indeed, in the town of Elías Piña there were relatively few native Spanish speakers. Older residents affirm that Elías Piña had become, in effect, a Haitian village.[76]

Parts of the western Dominican Republic became 'haitianized'. Haitian money circulated freely and was accepted as legal tender even in Santiago de Caballeros. In the south Haitian money penetrated all the way to Azua.[77] The 1935 census provides some interesting information regarding the character of Haitian immigration. It reveals a figure of 52,657 Haitian immigrants, of whom more than 50,000 were illiterate, more than 32,000 were males and 41,000 were qualified as *jornaleros*. Almost 50,000 lived in rural areas.[78] Hence virtually all those who did not count as family dependants were either sugar workers or squatter farmers. Some were also active in retail commerce.

The haitianization of the border area did not fail to provoke anti-Haitian feelings in the Dominican Republic and measures were gradually taken to bring this process to a halt. As early as 1900 Hostos had suggested that the Dominican government should be instrumental in bringing colonists to the frontier to strengthen the Dominican influence and seven years later a law was passed which allocated government funds to such colonization. In 1925 a government commission was appointed to select suitable areas for agricultural colonies in order to stop the Haitian penetration.[79]

These measures failed to have any effect. In the mid-1930s the price of sugar in the world market was rising slowly after having reached its lowest level so far during the twentieth century in 1933.[80] Haitians kept slipping into the Dominican Republic, legally or illegally, to work in the sugar industry.[81] In 1937, however, Haitian immigration came to an immediate stop. During that year, for reasons that are not quite clear, Trujillo unleashed a massacre on the Haitian immigrants:

> It has been variously speculated that he was angry with Vincent [the Haitian president] for incautiously having liquidated several

Dominican agents in Haiti; or that he was piqued at a sullen reception by ex-Haitians in the border village of Restauración ceded to the Dominican Republic; or that he acted out historic racial fears and hatreds going back to 1822; or that, as Vincent told Sheperd, the British minister, the massacre was a pre-election ploy by Trujillo to goad Haiti into invasion and disaster or otherwise provide a pretext for Dominican intervention; or that — deeply ambitious (as his own Foreign Minister later confided to the American minister) to unify and rule all Hispaniola — Trujillo chose this moment to teach Haiti a lesson. No answer is wholly satisfactory. The act . . . must speak for itself.[82]

The act consisted in indiscriminate butchering of from 15,000 to 25,000 Haitians — men, women and children — with machetes, clubs, knives, bayonets and (more seldom) firearms[83] at the beginning of October 1937, mainly along the border River Massacre, but also further eastward into Dominican territory, as far away as San Pedro de Macorís, Samaná Bay and Barahona.[84] This terrible deed which was carried out at the direct orders of *el Benefactor* sent many thousands of Haitians back to their country.

During the same month, the border between Haiti and the Dominican Republic was closed. The movement of Haitians across the border was stopped — but only temporarily. Although great care was taken by Trujillo to hide the facts of the massacre,[85] the news soon leaked to the world. The matter had to be settled via a symbolic payment of US$750,000. The first instalment, of $250,000, was used for the creation of five agricultural colonies on the Haitian side of the border. A total of 4,400 hectares were distributed to 1,425 families, a project which soon failed for lack of continuity.[86]

For some years Trujillo continued his efforts to repatriate Haitians. Between 1937 and 1944 a deportation program was in operation. This program officially required that an indemnity be paid to the Haitians who had improved the lands they were working before repatriation could take place, but in practice many Haitians were deported without payment up to the 1944-5 *zafra*.[87] To complement the deportation program, a 1938 law put a $500 head tax on all non-white immigrants to the Dominican Republic.[88] Four years later, a Haitian law also attempted to regulate the flow of migration.[89]

During the same year, Trujillo began a dominicanization program. By constructing a number of villages along the border, backed by a series of military posts, Dominican families were given land in agricultural colonies and the town of Elías Piña was completely modernized and furnished with a host of public facilities and infrastructural arrangements. Roads were constructed and irrigation canals were dug. As a result, the border area was settled by Dominicans and the zone was incorporated with the rest of the country.[90]

Neither of these measures was efficient in preventing migration. The year after the massacre, 1938, Haitians again crossed the border in secrecy to work in the Dominican sugar industry,[91] and during the 1944-5 harvest season, the Haitian and Dominican governments again agreed that Haitian workers could hold jobs on the Dominican side of the frontier.[92] It is impossible to say how quickly the pre-1937 level of migration was reattained. The estimates of the number of Haitians working in Dominican agriculture in 1938 vary between 20,000 and 60,000. The latter figure includes the families of the workers.[93] In 1943 the number of Haitian cane-cutters was estimated to be some 30,000.[94] However, the reliability of these figures and their possible significance cannot be easily appreciated since the methods of estimation are likely to differ considerably.

The attitude of Trujillo towards Haitian immigration may have changed during the 1950s. As the Second World War was coming to an end, he perceived that the profit level of the sugar industry was sufficiently high to warrant an inroad. In 1949 he had the Ingenio Catarey, near Villa Altagracia, constructed as his private property. This was followed a year later by the Central Río Haina which was to be the largest sugar mill in the country. In addition to these construction activities, foreign-owned sugar estates and *ingenios* were also purchased until he controlled a majority of the sugar-producing companies in the country. Only the Casa Vicini and the South Puerto Rico Sugar Company (which owned the Central Romana) remained outside Trujillo's sugar empire,[95] which controlled 63 per cent of the industry.[96]

In 1952 Haiti and the Dominican Republic signed a recruitment treaty which was renewed in 1958.[97] Table 8.2 shows the number of workers who officially migrated during this period from the regions of Jacmel, Léogâne, Croix des Bouquets, Ouanaminthe, Hinche, Belladère, Cayes and Jérémie to work in Catarey, Río Haina and Central Romana in the 1950s.[98] Needless to say, all these figures (which are flows) are underestimates since they do not take illegal migration into account.

Between 1957 and 1963 an estimated 30,000 workers crossed the border each year.[99] Allegedly the flow was maintained by means of various payments to Haiti's president, François Duvalier. 'Dominican sugar mills . . . paid Duvalier's contractors first of all $15 per head for each cane cutter delivered. Half of each cane worker's wages was then paid to him in Dominican pesos and half was sent to Haiti in dollars.'[100] There, it was kept by the Duvalier officials.[101]

Table 8.2: Legal Migration of Haitian Sugar Workers to the Dominican Republic, 1952-8

Fiscal year*	Number of workers
1952-3	16,500
1953-4	9,800
1954-5	3,850
1955-6	2,800
1956-7	3,800
1957-8	3,500

*The Haitian fiscal year starts on 1 October.
Source: Edouard (1969), pp. 195-6.

The Duvalier labor racket was brought to an end in 1963, when relations between the two countries deteriorated drastically, almost to the point of open warfare, because of Duvalier's attempts to drag Haitian political refugees out of the Dominican embassy.[102] Crossing the border became difficult since Duvalier created a 'war' zone of three miles from which peasants, cattle and huts were removed and where subsequently anybody found there was simply shot.[103] It seems, however, that not even these drastic measures sufficed to bring migration to a standstill. Even during 1964, it is reported that some 3,000 Haitian sugarcane workers were brought into the Dominican Republic.[104]

Three years later, the traffic was again in full swing. In 1966 a contract had been signed by the Haitian and Dominican governments according to which the Duvalier government was paid 60 dollars per cane-worker provided.[105] The following year, the Central Romana, which at that time accounted for some 30 per cent of total employment in the sugar sector, employed 12,578 Haitians. Altogether, some 30,000 Haitian cane-cutters were estimated to be employed by Dominican firms.[106] In 1970 42,142 Haitians lived legally in Dominican territory, but in addition some 45,000 are believed to have been in the country illegally, bringing the total to almost 90,000 people.[107] This figure may, however, be an underestimate. The *Oficina Nacional de Planificación* estimated that the true number was 100,000 in 1968 and the Dominican Border Commission gave a figure that was even higher: 200,000.[108] However, this figure presumably includes people of Haitian descent born in the Dominican Republic.[109] A third figure, of 300,000, estimated by Robert Rotberg, appears to be on the high side.[110]

Table 8.3 shows the number of Haitian cane-cutters who immigrated legally under contracts supervised by the *Consejo Estatal de Azúcar* (CEA) between 1966-7 and 1979-80.[111] Table 8.3 is based on information from the CEA itself. Only during the 1977-8 *zafra* was the work carried out exclusively by means of clandestine workers.[112] At that time, the Haitian government raised the price of Haitian cane-workers to 70 dollars, and as a result President Balaguer refused to allow any recruitment of Haitians and called upon the Dominicans to work in the harvest.[113] This temporary disagreement was, however, soon forgotten. The Haitian government received US$82 per worker supplied for the 1978-9 *zafra* and US$173 per head the following year. For 1980-1, some US$182 was paid for each of the 16,000 workers imported by agreement with the Haitian government.[114]

Table 8.3: Legal Immigration of Haitian Sugar Workers, 1966/7-1979/80

Year of *zafra*	Number of legal immigrants
1966-7	14,000
1967-8	10,000
1968-9	n.a.
1969-70	12,000
1970-1	n.a.
1971-2	12,000
1972-3	12,000
1973-4	12,000
1974-5	n.a.
1975-6	12,000
1976-7	12,000
1977-8	0
1978-9	15,000
1979-80	16,000

n.a.: information not available
Source: Veras (1981:1), p. 63.

In 1975 some 100,000 Haitians who had emigrated since 1950 were estimated to live permanently in the Dominican Republic.[115] This figure, however, appears to be an underestimate when seen in the light of what is by far the most reliable investigation of the quantitative aspects of Haitian immigration, undertaken by the *Oficina Nacional de Planificación* in 1980.[116] This survey included those sugar-workers who lived in the *bateyes*[117] of the CEA and of the private *ingenios*, as well as those working on coffee *fincas* who did not also take part in the sugar harvest and, finally, those working elsewhere in Dominican agriculture. The distribution is shown in Table 8.4. The *Oficina* arrived at a total number of Haitians in the Dominican *countryside* of 113,150; 40,140 of whom were workers, the rest being family members. The survey did not include the urban districts but since it is well known that substantial numbers of Haitians lived in Santo Domingo, La Romana, Higuey, San Pedro de Macorís, Santiago de los Caballeros, Barahona and other cities, it was concluded that the number of Haitians in the country as a whole was not lower than 200,000, with some 70,000 in the labor force.

Table 8.4: Haitians Residing in Rural Areas of the Dominican Republic in 1980

	Total	In the labor force
In the *bateyes* of the CEA	54,020	14,600
In the *bateyes* of private *ingenios*	31,050	11,500
Coffee workers not taking part in the sugar harvest	9,380	4,690
Workers in other *fincas*	18,700	9,350
Total in rural areas:	113,150	40,140

Source: Veras (1981:1), p. 64.

Living Conditions of Haitian *Braceros* in the Dominican Republic

Now that we have some idea regarding the historical pattern and the magnitude of Haitian migration to the Dominican Republic, we may go on to analyze the causes in economic terms. As a starting point, we will give an account of the conditions meeting the migrants once they have crossed the border and of the Dominican attitudes towards Haitian migrants.

The majority of the Haitian immigrants in the Dominican Republic are *braceros* who work in the sugar sector. The living conditions meeting these people in the Dominican side of the border are extremely onerous. In 1979, the Working Group on Slavery of the United Nations Commission on Human Rights, on the basis of a report on migrant workers in the Dominican Republic submitted by the Anti-Slavery Society for the Protection of Human Rights,[118] recommended that the Commission 'should bring the report . . . to the attention of the Governments of Haiti, the Dominican Republic and the United States and to the attention of the Organization of American States and the relevant United Nations specialized agencies for comment'.[119] The conclusions drawn by the Anti-Slavery Society after the visit of 'a responsible observer' to the Dominican Republic in 1978 was that 'the conditions of Haitian migrant workers could be compared only with slavery'.[120]

The issue was also brought up in the Haitian parliament, by the only Deputy of the opposition, Alexandre Lerouge, who demanded the formation of a parliamentary commission to investigate the violation of human rights against Haitian workers in the Dominican Republic, but this proposition was turned down.[121] The official reaction to the United Nations investigation both on the Haitian and on the Dominican side was one of 'surprise' and the Dominican Press Secretary of the President, Nelson William Méndez concluded that 'Never in the history of the country has an inhuman treatment been given to Haitians'.[122]

Such evidence is, however, not new in the history of Haitian migration to the Dominican Republic. The living conditions facing the Haitians once they have crossed the border have never been good. Writing in the early 1950s, Jean Price-Mars gave the following description of the situation:

The mills employing them provided a *sui generis* statute which meant that they belonged to the enterprise. Thereafter they no longer had the right or the freedom to leave the place to which they were attached and even less could they steal away from the task that had been assigned to them. The police took them as soon as they were found outside their sugar mill territory because they could not present the national *cédula* (their identity card), being equipped only with a residence permit delivered by the director of the enterprise to which they were attached.

They were paid according to the whims of the employer and, when the cutting season had ended, the employer could stop all wage payments. Then the poor immigrant was obliged to accept any task at any wage in order not to perish by hunger, and if, by chance, he did not find anything to do, he was forced to become a beggar, led astray into plundering. If the heavy arm of the law did not send him to jail, then the all too fast revolver sent him to join his equals in the cemetery of unknown tombs.[123]

Later observers give similar accounts. Roland Wingfield describes the scene in the early 1960s:

> Already at registration the prospective migrants are treated like chattel. Closely packed for hours in the broiling sun, stealing each other's place in line, the tempers of the men often flare up and occasionally fighting results. The rough treatment of officials makes this anarchic scene even more lacking in human dignity. Those who come from distant rural sections sleep in the public square in order to be the first in line the next morning. During that period, the streets of Jacmel become veritable public dormitories.
>
> The Dominican companies provide the transportation and give a dollar to every migrant for food on the trip. Then they are packed in trucks and taken to various parts of the neighboring republic. The trip takes from two to four days depending on the location of the Dominican sugar plantation to which they are assigned. It is a sight to behold, according to a Dominican informant, to see these men arrive at their ultimate destination. Tired, dusty and hungry after several days of traveling, guarded by soldiers, they look more like the inmates of a concentration camp than voluntary workers . . .
>
> The life of the Haitian migrant worker in the Dominican Republic is reminiscent of slavery days. Their work consists of cutting or carting cane from dawn to dusk. The companies provide them shacks and hammocks but they have to shift for themselves for food. It is incredible how they subsist on a meager diet of a little rice and beans which they cook themselves on open-fires with occasionally some bread and very rarely some meat. They get their energy from the cane that they chew all day long while working. They are intent on saving money on a salary of a few dollars a week. They generally keep to themselves, gamble or play cards with each other. Some manage to cohabit with Dominican women but in this case they generally return to Haiti empty-handed or don't return at all . . . The return trip is at the expense of the worker and sometimes uses up half of his savings. Some actually walk all the way back. Since the

majority are illiterate, they are occasionally short-changed when converting their Dominican pesos into Haitian gourdes . . .[124]

In 1973, Fanny Sánchez made a survey of the conditions of the sugar workers employed by the leading mills in the Dominican Republic.[125] She then found that only 58 per cent of the houses inhabited by the workers (67 per cent of whom were Haitian) had wooden floors, that only 56 per cent of all the houses used gas lighting and only 57 per cent possessed any latrines. Altogether 36 per cent of the people living under these conditions had to use the cane fields or other open fields instead. In addition, no clean drinking water was provided but the workers had to use a public trough which was also employed for washing animals.

As for the contemporary situation, this is described in the report of the Anti-Slavery Society:

At the border they are put on trucks and taken to a fenced staging post where they wait to be purchased either by colonos (Dominican private landowners) or by the representatives of the three main sugar producers . . . En route the only nourishment provided is cane juice or brown sugar. At the staging post the Haitian workers are sold for 10 pesos . . . each and taken by truck to the purchaser's farm.

On the farms the workers live in camps under conditions of extreme squalor, deprivation and danger to health. A family of five will share a 12' x 12' room furnished with a large bed, a table and a coal burner on the floor for cooking. There is neither electricity nor running water. Water for drinking is often from a polluted stream and a single latrine must suffice for forty people.

Wages are paid not by the hour but by the weight of cane cut and loaded. The rate is $1.30 per ton. A very strong, skilled cutter can cut three tons in a day but this does not guarantee the wage he will earn. The cutter is illiterate and cannot verify that the weigher's receipt is correct and the weigher is out to make a profit. A weigher who does not regularly send more cane to the mill than cutters are paid for will lose his job. As the cane dries it loses weight. This is not only an inducement to the weigher to cheat but also handicaps the cutter when he has to wait for transport to load his cane. The receipts can only be cashed fortnightly and the family needs money more often and so must borrow. They can sell their receipts but at a loss of 10% of their value. Every worker interviewed in a particular sample said this was a common occurrence . . .

The average cane cutter's family consists of his wife and five children.[126] If he cuts a ton of cane a day he earns $1.30 a day but he can get work for only six months in the year. Flour costs 21 cents a pound. His family consumes three pounds each morning, meat and even beans are out of the question. Add the cost of cooking oil and it is clear what the result must be. A Jesuit priest researching this situation was told by a cane cutter: 'My children wake me each morning, crying from hunger'.

Conditions in the work-camps throughout the country are uniformly characterized by the gross overcrowding and, though a few of the State Sugar Council (CEA) estates do have lavatories, the absence of hygiene and sanitation is otherwise pervasive. These conditions, coupled with poor clothing and malnutrition induced by an insufficient and unbalanced diet, result in the permanent existence and spread of acute and chronic diseases, most of which could be avoided or brought under control. These include diarrhoea, intestinal parasitism, tetanus, tuberculosis, syphilis and other venereal diseases, diphtheria, whooping cough, measles, poliomyelitis, scarlet fever, typhoid, hepatitis and dysentery. Maternal and child care are embryonic.[127]

Dominican Attitudes towards Haitians

The conclusion to be drawn from the descriptions in the previous section is that the Haitian cane-workers have had to work and live under conditions that have made it completely impossible to meet any 'basic' needs in terms of food, clothes, shelter or otherwise. In addition, we must take into account the treatment accorded the Haitians from the point of view of human relations.

The Haitian immigrants, apart from confronting the difficult living and working conditions to which they are submitted, have to endure the scorn and humiliation of a society which considers itself different and superior. For many Dominicans, Haitians are inferior beings: ugly, dirty, barbaric, corrupt and superstitious. Through generations, this view of the Haitian has been nourished through hearsay and by literature based on a racist conception of history. These beliefs are widely held by the Dominican population, encouraged by mass media and by the consent of the authorities.

The Dominican prejudices concerning the Haitians are based upon, among other things, misinterpretations of Haitian religious beliefs (voodoo) which in themselves contain many traces of the African heritage. The old racist clichés of Africa mix with the Dominican beliefs. Thus, the Haitian is seen as a cannibal, whose life is immersed in witchcraft. He is endowed with supernatural powers and has relations with the devil. Rich, upper-class Haitians who do not practice voodoo are consequently seen as decent and well educated.

In accordance with the view of the Haitian as a savage from the jungle his culture is also considered as inferior. The destiny of the Haitian is to disappear. His way of life, his conformity, his acceptance of his destiny, all this shows that he does not have any aspiration in life and the root of this evil is sought in his racial inferiority.[128] According to Marcio Veloz Maggiolo, there is an oral tradition behind all these beliefs, cultivated with a certain sadism.[129]

The attitudes of Dominicans towards Haitians must be seen in a historical perspective. They have their origin in the continuous Haitian invasions during the nineteenth century, especially the occupation of 1822-44. The mistrust and hatred that Dominicans felt at that time was nourished and increased by rational ideologists who preached nationalism with racist overtones. Dominican nationality was synonymous with white race, Spanish culture and Christianity, while the Haitians represented the black race, Africa, voodooism and superstition.

This racist ideology has contributed to perpetuate alienation among the non-white population in the country. Although the majority of the Dominican population are blacks and mulattoes, the African inheritance is usually rejected. They are Dominicans, and only the Haitian can be identified as a real *Negro*. There is a deliberate confusion of racial definitions in the Dominican Republic. No one is considered as black. People are either white, light Indian, dark Indian, *mestizo* or *moreno*, but never black.

The African ancestry, and the centuries of slavery to which the blacks were submitted, is a forgotten chapter in Dominican history. The Dominican population knows very little about its African origins. Only the European and Indian influences are recognized. Slavery is generally ignored and so are the circumstances under which it was abolished in the country. Dominican historians, in general, do not acknowledge that it was the Haitians who put an end to slavery in the Dominican Republic. Instead they stress the brutality of the Haitian army and indulge in descriptions of Haitian 'cruelties' towards the Dominican population. Thus the Dominicans are ignorant of the role of the Haitians in the liberation of the slaves.[130]

The contemptuous attitude towards Haitians is deeply rooted in the 'haitiphobia' which developed during the different Haitian raids in the nineteenth century, but its modern version was created during the Trujillo era. During this period, most Dominican writers and intellectuals saw a potential enemy in the Haitians. The continuous Haitian migration was seen as a permanent threat for the 'preservation of the race', morality, language and customs of the Dominican people: 'This immigrant is of the worst kind. Totally black, almost naked, nearly always hungry and sick, nomadic tribes deprived of everything, dark caravans bringing misery, superstition, immorality, voodoo, africanization . . .'[131] The quotation is from a well-known Dominican historian. Another prominent colleague of his presents an identical view:

This type is frankly undesirable. Being of a purely African race, he cannot represent any ethnic incentive at all to us . . . [he is] a badly nourished and worse clad man; he is feeble, although very prolific, given his low level of living. For this very reason, the Haitian who encroaches upon us lives contaminated by numerous and capital vices and is necessarily affected by sickness and physiological deficiencies which are endemic at the bottom of that society.[132]

Anti-haitianism was preached loudly during the Trujillo era and the massacre of 1937 can be interpreted as an attempt to put an end to the Haitian presence in the country. This incident was hailed by Trujillist ideologists. Joaquín Balaguer, later president of the Dominican Republic, approved of Trujillo's action with the following words:

The problem of the race is the principal problem of the Dominican Republic . . . If the nationalization of the border is implemented as planned by President Trujillo, then the future of the Dominican Republic has been ensured. The glory that Trujillo shall receive by initiating, conducting and bringing the process of nationalization to a fortunate end will not be inferior to the glory corresponding to that of the creators of the Republic.[133]

The obscure tradition of prejudices against the Haitian immigrants is carried on today as well, as Haitians continue to work in sugarcane cutting and other agricultural activities. It is kept alive by politicians who try to blame the high levels of unemployment persisting in the country on the presence of Haitian nationals in the country. A good case in point is Elías Wessin y Wessin, leader of a right-wing party, who, using an exaggerated estimate of the number of Haitians living in the Dominican Republic — 500,000 — stated that action ought to be taken to stop this 'pacific invasion'.[134] It is not at all uncommon to find anti-Haitian 'news' in the newspapers which keeps the prejudices alive.[135] Naturally, the situation under which the Haitian cane-workers are forced to live and work in the Dominican Republic, helps to preserve and encourage prejudices Dominicans have about the culture and way of life of the Haitian people in general.

The Economics of Migration

Equipped with knowledge of the living conditions confronting the Haitians in the Dominican Republic and of the Dominican attitudes towards Haitians we go on to provide an explanation of migration.[136] In this context, two questions are of interest:

1. Why are Haitians, in spite of the bad living conditions and the often hostile attitudes they meet, attracted to the Dominican Republic?
2. Why are Haitians, and not Dominicans, hired if the Dominican attitude towards Haitians is negative?

To answer these questions, we must look at what determines the supply of Haitian and Dominican sugar-workers.

The Supply of Haitian Migrants

The most elaborate explanation of why Haitians are willing to migrate to the Dominican Republic has been given by André Corten.[137] According to Corten, the supply of Haitian cane-cutters cannot be explained in terms of traditional labor market analysis, since the latter assumes 'a certain mercantilization of social relations'.[138] In underdeveloped societies of the Haitian type no such mercantilization exists. By this argument, Corten obviously implies that there is no labor market in the normal sense, where the labor supply depends on the wage rate offered, because Haiti does not possess a class of wage laborers. Most of the rural economy in Haiti does not work on a cash or wage basis, but barter is a much more important form, when commercial transactions are undertaken at all.

The part of the Haitian economy where, according to Corten, cash transactions assume most importance is in the land market. The Haitian inheritance laws are based on the *Code Napoléon*, according to which all children inherit equal amounts when their parents die. Consequently, there is a tendency for the peasants' plots to become successively smaller over time. Sooner or later the peasant is faced with the choice of whether he should buy more land or sell what he already has and stop being a peasant. However, Corten maintains, the land is then bought or sold for reasons of *necessity*, for example to construct a house, buy a car or go abroad, not as a result of economic calculations.[139]

Thus, states Corten, rural Haiti is characterized by a contradiction between the weak commercialization of agriculture on the one hand and the inheritance principles in the land market on the other. The former prevents the accumulation of the necessary funds to buy land (or other assets). One way of providing a partial solution to this dilemma is to migrate to an environment where there is abundant circulation of money that may be saved and brought home. One such environment is the Dominican Republic.

It is difficult to see the justification for Corten's analysis. The core of this argument is that Haitians offer their services not primarily as a function of the wage level, since cash is not needed in everyday life, but only when a 'need' for other outlays arises. This argument hardly stands up when confronted with the institutional realities. Rural Haiti is a *market* economy.[140] It is true that to a varying degree the agricultural products are consumed by those who produce them but substantial proportions are sold in local, regional or inter-regional marketplaces. The base of these transactions is virtually always *cash*, i.e. the peasant needs cash in his daily transactions.

Corten even alleges that the sale of the Haitian cash crop *par excellence*, coffee, essentially entails a barter transaction between the peasant and the *spéculateur* (intermediary) to whom the coffee is sold. The reason, according to Corten, is that the peasants store the coffee, sometimes for several months, before they dispose of it. Sales only take place when the need arises. Generally, this need can be satisfied by barter with the *spéculateur*, since the latter as a rule also owns a store from which he sells to the peasants.

This part of the argument is also incorrect, since coffee sales often take place on an advance basis. The peasant obtains money from the coffee intermediaries against the future crop but then has to part with the crop as soon as the harvest comes.

Thus, it must be concluded that the Haitian peasant employs cash in all types of daily transactions. By the same token, he is prepared to take a job outside his farmstead when he can do so without jeopardizing his own production. Corten points out that the 1950 census revealed that only 12 per cent of the labor force were wage laborers. Consequently, the remainder ought to work outside the cash economy. This argument is misleading, since it does not take into account that those classified as having a personal enterprise without employees frequently obtained cash at the same time from outside work.[141] They were classified as non-wage laborers because their *main* economic activity was farming on land that they owned or leased.[142] This, however, does not mean that they were not prepared to respond to wage incentives in the outside labor market.

Corten's argument is an indirect one in that it does not depart from an analysis of the rural *labor* market in Haiti. He derives his conclusions by looking at the produce and land markets. However, not only the land market but the rural produce markets as well function mainly on a cash basis. The Haitian peasant has a demand for cash for *all* types of transactions and one way for him to satisfy this demand is by taking a job outside his farmstead. This tendency to supply work against cash should have become more pronounced over time, since the Haitian population has been growing continuously, while at the same time the natural resources, notably the land, has been shrinking.[143] One way of alleviating the increased population pressure is by means of temporary or permanent migration. We should thus conclude that, contrary to what Corten maintains, there are no good reasons precluding a 'traditional' analysis of the supply of Haitian workers to Dominican agriculture. The higher the wage rate offered, *ceteris paribus*, the larger the supply of Haitians ought to be.[144]

In traditional labor market analysis, migration takes place when wage differences are sufficiently large to outweigh the costs connected with migration between two areas. In the well-known Harris-Todaro model of rural-urban migration, for example, movement takes place when the expected urban wage (the wage rate in formal employment weighed by the probability of getting a job) exceeds what the migrant earns at his place of origin.[145] The same should apply in the present case. As long as a Haitian perceives that he can earn more during the relevant time period in the Dominican Republic than at home, and this difference is not outweighed by the costs he incurs by migrating, we should expect him to move. As we have seen in the foregoing, these costs are not only pecuniary (e.g. transport costs) but also of a social kind. The migrant has to break up from his customary environment and go to live for longer or shorter periods under difficult conditions where discrimination against his nationality is widespread.

How large are the wage or income differentials that induce Haitians to move across the border? Unfortunately, little is known in quantitative terms, but it is possible to arrive at some approximations of the relevant figures. Around 1973, the average daily wage for a sugarcane cutter in the Dominican Republic was 2 pesos. During a good sugar year the *zafra* lasts for some 200 days.[146] Thus, the annual income in 1973 for a cutter who did not undertake any other work amounted to 400 pesos, or as many US dollars at the official exchange rate. If instead the black market exchange rate (assumed to represent the equilibrium rate), of 1.20 pesos per dollar is used, the figure becomes US$333.

For Haiti, the data are not as good. Clarence Zuvekas has provided what appears to be the best estimate (based on World Bank data).[147] According to this, per capita personal income in rural districts lay around US$96 in 1975. Assuming, as the World Bank does, in its calculations of income distribution figures for 1970, that the ratio between personal income per capita and income per person employed in agriculture is approximately 1 to 3,[148] this gives us a figure of US$288 per *worker* for the entire year. Adjusting for inflation between 1973 and 1975, assuming that no other changes took place,[149] we arrive at a 1973 figure for Haiti of US$203 for the *average* member of the rural labor force in Haiti. The poorer sections naturally earned even less, and it is precisely these sections that we would expect to emigrate.[150] Thus, traditional economic theory can explain why there is a supply of Haitians willing to work in Dominican sugar production.

The Supply of Dominicans

The second question posed at the beginning of the present section was why Haitian and not Dominican workers are hired by the sugar producers.[151] The employment situation in the Dominican Republic is characterized by substantial underemployment in rural areas.[152] Of course, the level of underemployment varies throughout the year depending on the season, but even so it does not disappear completely even during the month of December (the busiest month of the year).[153] Consequently, one would expect that the sugar industry would be able to procure workers within the Dominican Republic itself without having to resort to Haitian immigrants. However, this is not the case. The Haitians have played a very important role in Dominican sugar production for a full century and continue to do so today. The inquiry undertaken by the *Oficina Nacional de Planificación*, referred to above, found that more than 75 per cent of the labor force in the sugar industry consisted of Haitians in 1980.[154] The Dominicans are found mainly in supervisory positions and positions requiring special skills.

To explain this extensive use of Haitians we must look not only at the supply of Haitian workers, but also at that of Dominicans. It is well known that it is difficult to recruit Dominicans to the sugar industry. The survey of the Dominican labor market undertaken by the International Labor Office in the early 1970s offers some reflexions on this subject. In the first place, it was found that more than 80 per cent of the rural labor force consisted of people who owned some land. Only 20 per cent were landless. Of those owning land some 60 per cent were cultivating 2 hectares or less. This group supplemented their incomes with work outside their farmsteads. Such work could be found for example in the sugar industry, although these minifundistas are not as a rule particularly interested in that type of work. They work instead on the farms of those who have more land. In this way, they manage to keep busy for six months only per year. The remainder of the time they are idle.[155]

This period of idleness coincides to some extent with the period during which the sugar harvest takes place. Nevertheless, the minifundistas are not particularly eager to work on the sugar estates. According to the ILO mission, the reason for this decision is that the minifundistas cannot leave their farms for any great length of time if they are simultaneously to work on the sugar estates. Moreover, the minifundistas live in regions other than those where the sugar estates are located. The highest rural population densities are found in the Cibao Valley and in the Valle del Yaque del Sur but the sugar estates are in the eastern parts of the country where the population density is low.[156] At the same time, the Haitians provide efficient competition in the rural labor market. They are willing to work long hours for low wages and to live under the conditions described above.

The ILO mission sums up the situation by referring to the existence of a vicious circle in the sugar labor market:

> The import of Haitian braceros and the resistance of the small farmers of other regions to abandon their own cultivations during five or six months reinforce and influence each other reciprocally. The sugar enterprises bring foreign braceros because of their — justified — fear that the Dominicans will not come from the zones where they live and the Dominicans manifest strong resistance and strong prejudices against cutting cane because they know that the enterprises have imported braceros and that, consequently, no vacant jobs exist.

The Dominicans do not come to the cane cutting because of the low wages that are paid and the bad living conditions that are offered, and wages remain low and living conditions bad because the imports of cutters continue. The original circumstances and factors reinforce each other in this manner, reciprocally, in a vicious circle.[157]

The situation may also be illustrated with the aid of Figure 8.1. On the horizontal axis we measure the demand and supply in the sugar labor market. On the vertical axis we have the wage rate and the marginal revenue product of labor to the sugar industry (the demand curve for labor). If only Dominicans had been employed in the sector, with given inputs of land and capital E_A workers would have been employed at a wage rate of w_A. However, in addition to the supply of Dominican workers (given by the S_D curve) we also have a supply curve for Haitian workers (S_H). This curve starts at a point on the vertical axis which lies below the corresponding point of the S_D curve. In addition, the S_H curve is less steep than the S_D curve which indicates that it takes a smaller wage increase to obtain a given number of Haitians at the margin than it takes to obtain the same number of Dominicans. Adding the two supply curves horizontally gives the total supply of labor (S_{TOT}). The intersection of the latter curve with the demand (marginal revenue product) curve gives the total employment E_B which is higher than when no Haitians are allowed, and the wage rate w_B, which is lower. By recruiting Haitians, the sugar companies can increase their surplus over wages from DFG in the figure to HIG, and with given inputs of land and capital also their profits. By moving leftwards from the intersection point H until we reach the S_H and S_D curves respectively, we also find that a comparatively large number of Haitians (E_H) and few Dominicans (E_D) are employed. At least in the short run, when the possibilities of substituting capital for labor are limited, we should expect the demand curve to be very steep, demand being highly inelastic. In this perspective, low wages appear to be mainly a supply-side phenomenon.

Figure 8.1.

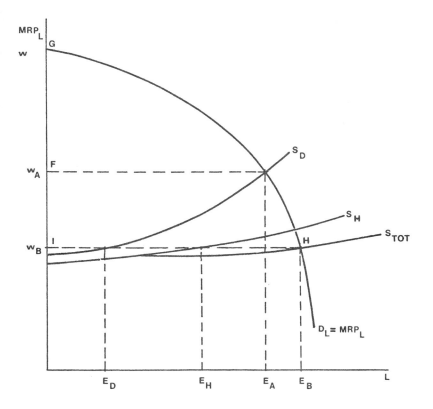

Conclusions

Migration from the western to the eastern part of Hispaniola has taken place at least since the two areas were politically separated in 1697. The first phase of this migration consisted of the escape of slaves from the French sugar plantations. The slaves fled to the Spanish part of the island where they stood a good chance of being manumitted. After the liberation of Haiti from the French a series of Haitian incursions into Spanish, and later Dominican, territory took place through the first two-thirds of the nineteenth century, with the occupation of the Spanish part between 1822 and 1844 as the crowning achievement. During this period, the eastern part of the island was underpopulated as a result of the turmoil in connection with the Haitian wars of liberation. Consequently, it proved easy for the Haitians to penetrate into Dominican territory.

The 'modern' phase of Haitian migration to the Dominican Republic began with the rise of the sugar *ingenios* during the last third of the nineteenth century. The substitution of *ingenios* for the small *trapiches* that had traditionally been used for the production of sugar led to an increased demand for labor. The Dominican supply of labor was inadequate. However, large numbers of Haitians were recruited, legally or illegally. This pattern has persisted ever since. Deterioration of political relations between Haiti and the Dominican Republic as well as fluctuations in world market sugar prices have influenced the magnitude of the migration, but the flow has never been completely stopped. It is estimated that a minimum 200,000 Haitians were residing, permanently or temporarily, in the Dominican Republic in 1980.

The living conditions confronting the Haitians in the Dominican Republic are extremely onerous most of the time. Various observers have classified them as reminiscent of slavery. The living quarters are utterly primitive. Sanitary facilities are lacking and drinking water is difficult to obtain. The cane-cutters work long days for low wages. All kinds of diseases are common. The Haitian immigrants also have to contend with the attitude of the Dominicans who consider Haitians to be inferior beings, different in color and culture, utterly alien and a negative influence on Dominican society.

In spite of these facts Haitians continue to migrate to the Dominican Republic. Attracted by the difference in earnings between the two countries, thousands of Haitians every year cross the border, legally or illegally. These people manage to outcompete the Dominicans for jobs especially in the sugar industry, but also in other branches of agriculture. Most of the Dominican rural labor force consists of people who have some land to cultivate and who therefore, given the low wages in the sugar industry and the living conditions prevailing there, prefer to stay on their farms. For these reasons, the majority of the sugar-workers in the Dominican Republic are Haitians.

Notes

Thanks are due to Frank Kirwan for constructive comments on a draft version.
1. World Bank (1980), p. 110.
2. A description of the techniques of sugar production is given in Lundahl (1979), pp. 256-8.
3. Victor (1944), p. 24. This is a very uncertain figure, however. (Cf. Debien, 1974, p. 339.)

4. Lundahl (1979), p. 259.
5. Moreau de Saint-Méry (1958), p. 28.
6. Moya Pons (1980), p. 108; Deive (1980), pp. 532-6. The vast majority of maroons remained in Saint-Domingue, however. (Debien, 1974, p. 456.)
7. Debbasch (1961), p. 54, for the 1720 figure, Debien (1974), p. 445 for that of 1751. Cf. also Vissière (1909), p. 235.
8. Debbasch (1961), pp. 52-3.
9. Cf. the description in Lundahl (1979), pp. 257-8.
10. Leyburn (1966), pp. 18-20 gives an account of the increasing discrimination against the *affranchis* when the latter became economically too powerful. The desire to limit their numbers should be viewed in the same light.
11. Debbasch (1961), p. 54. Cf. also Fouchard (1972), pp. 165, 427-9; Debien (1974), pp. 445-6; and Deive (1980), pp. 502-4.
12. Quoted by Debbasch (1961), p. 52.
13. Ibid., p. 54.
14. Moreau de Saint-Méry (1796), vol. 1, p. 255.
15. Palmer (1976), p. 47.
16. Details regarding the border conflict and the negotiations are found in Moya Pons (1980), Chapters 12-13.
17. Cf. Lundahl (1979), pp. 256-9.
18. Quoted by Debbasch (1961), pp. 72-3.
19. The most famous of these communities, in the Bahoruco mountains, was that of Le Maniel, which existed for more than 85 years before the French and Spanish authorities managed to negotiate a peaceful agreement with it in 1785, after several abortive attempts to take it by force. (For details regarding Le Maniel, see e.g. Moreau de Saint-Méry (1958), pp. 1131-6; Brown (1837), pp. 120-8; Debbasch (1962), pp. 185-8).
20. Debien (1974), pp. 429-30; Deive (1980), pp. 519-20.
21. Debbasch (1962), p. 148; Moya Pons (1980), p. 141. Cf. also Deive (1980), pp. 525-7, for some more details.
22. Debbasch (1962), note, p. 142.
23. Quoted by ibid., p. 149.
24. For details, see ibid., note, p. 149.
25. Quoted by ibid., p. 150.
26. Palmer (1976), p. 62.
27. Leyburn (1966), pp. 33-4.
28. Palmer (1976), p. 62.
29. Murray (1977), p. 410.
30. Hoetink (1971), p. 43.
31. Heredia y Mieses (1955), p. 162.
32. For details see Moya Pons (1972), esp. Chapter 2.
33. Quoted by Moya Pons (1980), p. 257.
34. Candler (1842), p. 132.
35. Palmer (1976), pp. 67, 69.
36. Bonó (1968), p. 280.
37. Hoetink (1971), pp. 14ff.
38. Ibid., p. 44.
39. Around Baní at the beginning of the 1870s some 100 of these *trapiches* were to be seen and around Azua some 100-200 (ibid., p. 19.) Samuel Hazard, who visited the Dominican Republic in 1871 mentions on the subject of the *trapiches* that 'these were actually the only kind of sugar-mills I saw in operation in any part of my journeyings in St Domingo' (Hazard, 1873, p. 370).
40. Hoetink (1971), p. 44.
41. For details regarding this war, see e.g. Thomas (1971), Chapters 20-22.
42. Quoted by Hoetink (1971), p. 60.

43. Moya Pons (1980), pp. 407-8.
44. Ibid., p. 409.
45. Knight (1928), p. 25.
46. Eugenio María de Hostos, quoted by Hoetink (1971), p. 33.
47. As a result, a lack of fruits, vegetables and other food crops was observed for example in the capital (ibid., pp. 33-5).
48. Ibid., p. 44.
49. This is, however, not to say that the sugar industry did not attract domestic workers.
50. During the last quarter of the nineteenth century, land had clearly become a scarce factor in Haiti, as a result of the population growth. (Cf. Lundahl (1982), where the determinants of Haitian migration to Cuba during the 1890-1934 period are discussed. On the supply or push side, the same factors were active in promoting migration to the Dominican Republic.)
51. Hoetink (1971), p. 64.
52. Quoted by ibid., p. 31.
53. Ibid., p. 64.
54. The publication of these *Memorias de la Secretaría de Estado de Agricultura e Inmigración* was discontinued in 1926.
55. Acosta (1981), p. 136 and *Primer censo nacional* (1923), p. 147, respectively.
56. Lundahl (1982), p. 28.
57. Ibid., p. 29.
58. Castor (1971), p. 84 quotes a confidential note from the United States consul in Cap-Haïtien to the State Department, dated 22 March 1924 (US Department of State, Document 838.504) which contains this opinion. Cf. also Moral (1959), p. 41.
59. Moral (1959), p. 41. Cf. also Balch (1927), pp. 76-8.
60. Hernández (1973), p. 52. Knight (1928), p. 158, estimated the yearly flow to be around 100,000, but this is likely to be an exaggeration. A report from the US legation in the Dominican Republic, from 1926, gave a minimum of 60,000 and a maximum of 'perhaps' 100,000. (Quoted by Castillo, 1981, p. 185.)
61. Moya Pons (1980), p. 480.
62. Ibid.
63. Spitzer (1972), p. 331.
64. Knight (1928), pp. 47-8. Ibid., Chapter 12 gives details regarding the expansion.
65. Munro (1964), p. 318.
66. Spitzer (1972), pp. 253-4.
67. Jimenes Grullón (1965), p. 168.
68. Knight (1928), p. 350.
69. Lundahl (1982). For details regarding the American debt policy, see Lundahl (1979), pp. 370-2.
70. Hernández (1973), pp. 56-61.
71. Quoted by ibid., p. 61.
72. Knight (1928), p. 158.
73. Millspaugh (1931), p. 143.
74. Moya Pons (1980), p. 494.
75. Palmer (1976), pp. 84-6.
76. Ibid., p. 85.
77. Moya Pons (1980), p. 519.
78. Hernández (1973), pp. 53-4. The absolute figures are probably not too reliable.

79. Machado Báez (1955), pp. 230-1.
80. Lundahl (1979), pp. 281-2.
81. Hicks (1946), p. 104 estimates that more than 200,000 Haitians were at this time living in the Dominican Republic. This figure appears to be exaggerated, however.
82. Heinl and Heinl (1978), p. 528.
83. Explicit orders had been given not to use firearms so that the killings, which were carried out by Dominican soldiers, could later be blamed on 'angry Dominican farmers'. (Hicks, 1946, p. 113.)
84. For details regarding the massacre see e.g. Hicks (1946), Chapter 12; Galíndez (1962), pp. 196-201; Crassweller (1966), pp. 149-64; Heinl and Heinl (1978), pp. 525-30.
85. Thus, the British minister in Ciudad Trujillo reported that 'care was taken not to molest Haitians working or living on foreign-owned property or in towns where foreign witnesses might be'. Quoted by Heinl and Heinl (1978), p. 528.)
86. Vincent (1938), pp. 219-25; Pierre-Charles (1965), pp. 111-12.
87. Palmer (1976), p. 88.
88. Ibid., p. 90.
89. Ibid., p. 91.
90. Ibid.; Moya Pons (1980), p. 520.
91. Wingfield (1966), p. 97.
92. Hernández (1973), p. 56.
93. The former figure derives from Bosch (1979), p. 259. The latter, which is probably an overstatement (Corten, 1970, p. 714) comes from Romain (1959), p. 33.
94. Jimenes Grullón (1943), p. 22.
95. Moya Pons (1980), p. 517.
96. Franco (1967), p. 76.
97. Veras (1981:2)
98. Edouard (1969), p. 195.
99. Gingras (1967), p. 115.
100. Ibid., p. 115.
101. Ibid., pp. 115-16.
102. For details, see e.g. Diederich and Burt (1972), Chapters 13-14 and Heinl and Heinl (1978), Chapter 14. An account of the events on the Dominican side is given by John Bartlow Martin (1966), Chapter 18. Martin was at the time United States Ambassador to the Dominican Republic.
103. Heinl and Heinl (1978), p. 638.
104. Gingras (1967), p. 115.
105. Veras (1981:2); Anti-Slavery Society (1979), p. 4. Cf. also Pierre-Charles (1969), pp. 120-1.
106. Corten (1970), p. 716.
107. Díaz Santana (1976), p. 129.
108. Ibid.
109. Segal (1975), p. 212.
110. Rotberg with Clague (1971), p. 249. Cf. Segal (1975), p. 212.
111. The 1966 agreement between the Haitian and Dominican governments expired in 1971 and was never renewed, but both governments have continued to act according to it (Veras, 1981:2).
112. It was stated officially that the *zafra* had been 'dominicanized' but this was not true. Finally it was recognized that more than 16,000 Haitians were working in the seven *centrales* of Romana, Caei, Colón, Angelina, Barahona, Monte Llano and Amistad. (The daily newspaper *El Caribe* on 30 July 1971

provided a figure of 16,288 Haitians. Hernández, 1973, p. 65.)
113. Anti-Slavery Society (1979), p. 4.
114. Veras (1982:1), pp. 40, 41.
115. Segal (1975), p. 198.
116. *Participación de la mano de obra haitiana en el mercado laboral; el caso de la caña y el café*, summarized in Veras (1981:1).
117. A *batey* is a small community located in the neighborhood of a sugar mill.
118. Anti-Slavery Society (1979).
119. United Nations (1979), p. 14.
120. Anti-Slavery Society (1979), p. 1.
121. *Haití Información*, No. 23, Octubre de 1980, p. 2.
122. *Haití Información*, No. 13, Septiembre de 1979, p. 4.
123. Price-Mars (1953), pp. 329-30.
124. Wingfield (1966), pp. 98-9, 100.
125. Sánchez (1973).
126. This figure is probably too high. The average number of people in a Haitian family is around five or six, including the parents (Moral (1961), p. 176.). Cf. also Veras (1981:1), p. 63, where a range of 2.5-3.7 dependants per worker is given.
127. Anti-Slavery Society (1979), pp. 4-7. The same picture in much more detail emerges from the description in Lemoine (1981). Cf. also the documents contained in World Council of Churches (1980).
128. Veloz Maggiolo (1977), pp. 105-6.
129. Ibid., p. 106.
130. Deive (1979), pp. 67-73.
131. Rodríguez Demorizi (1955), p. 46.
132. Peña Batlle (1954), pp. 67-8.
133. Balaguer (1947), pp. 124-5.
134. Quoted by *Haití Información*, No. 18, Enero de 1980, p. 2.
135. For example, the front page of *El Nacional* (2 February 1981) relates under the heading of *¡Haitianos!* an incident when one hundred Haitian nationals were rounded up by Dominican troops in the northern part of the country. One of the Haitians was said to have a 'human head' and 'other articles for the practice of witchcraft' among his belongings. After the incident, the prisoners were brought to the sugarcane fields in the eastern part of the country.
136. An alternative analysis, in Marxist terms, is offered by Díaz Santana (1976).
137. Corten (1970).
138. Ibid., p. 722.
139. It is not clear what Corten means, but it can be conjectured that he does not regard the supply of labor in rural Haiti as a function of the wage rate, as is the case in the standard neo-classical economic models.
140. Cf. Lundahl (1979), Chapter 4.
141. Cf. Zuvekas (1978), p. 91.
142. Cf. Départment de l'Economie Nationale (1950), pp. 15-16.
143. Cf. Lundahl (1979), Chapter 5.
144. Corten (1970), pp. 728ff. and Díaz Santana (1976), pp. 130-1, both note that the Dominican government and sugar factories have always favored the clandestine migration of Haitians over the legal one. The reason is that workers who have entered the Dominican Republic without legal permission are obtained at a lower cost than those who have been recruited openly, since no medical examination has to be undertaken, no official papers have to be signed, and no

truck fare has to be paid for the workers, which (around 1970) meant a saving of up to 30 pesos per worker. Even more important, however, is the fact that the illegal status of clandestine immigrants puts these in a much weaker bargaining position than those who have come with their papers in order. (Since 1971 no legally valid agreement exists between Haiti and the Dominican Republic regarding imports of cane-workers, but the governments of both countries act as if the 1966 agreement, which expired in 1971 were still valid. See Veras, 1981:2) for details.)

145. Harris and Todaro (1970).

146. Oficina Internacional del Trabajo (1975), p. 136. Figures for 1980 are given in Veras (1982:2).

147. Zuvekas (1978), p. 123.

148. International Bank for Reconstruction and Development (1976), Table 1.4.

149. Institut Haïtien de Statistique (1976), p. 32, gives the cost of living index for Port-au-Prince as 187.6 in 1973 and 265.8 in 1975.

150. Corten (1970), pp. 720-2 attempts a similar conclusion based on data for the 1950s and early 1960s and arrives at the conclusion that the difference in what a Haitian could earn at home and by cutting cane in the Dominican Republic may be grossly exaggerated. His conclusion must be taken *cum grano salis*, however, since at least the Haitian figures used for the comparison are extremely shaky. It should be noted that these figures (in so far as they are reasonably correct) are *equilibrium* figures which take the existence of migration into account. Had no migration taken place, the difference would of course have been even greater.

151. It is important to note that the Dominican employers do not seem to let whatever prejudices they may hold against Haitians influence their decision to hire them.

152. Oficina Internacional del Trabajo (1975), pp. 130-4.

153. Ibid., p. 133.

154. Veras (1981:1), p. 61.

155. Oficina Internacional del Trabajo (1975), pp. 131-43.

156. Ibid., p. 136. The alternative for those who leave their farms is not primarily work in the sugar industry, but migration to urban areas. Cf. Vargas (1981).

157. Oficina Internacional del Trabajo (1975), p. 137.

Bibliography

Acosta, Mercedes. 'Azúcar e inmigración haitiana', in *Azúcar y política en la República Dominicana*. Second edition. Santo Domingo, 1981

Anti-Slavery Society For the Protection of Human Rights. 'Migrant Workers in the Dominican Republic', Report for 1979 to The United Nations Working Group of Experts on Slavery, 1979

Balaguer, Joaquín. *La realidad dominicana*. Buenos Aires, 1947

Balch, Emily Greene. 'Notes on the Land Situation in Haiti', in Emily Greene Balch (ed.). *Occupied Haiti*. New York, 1927

Bonó, Pedro F. *El montero*. Santo Domingo, 1968

Bosch, Juan. *Composición social dominicana. Historia e interpretación*. Santo Domingo, 1979.

Brown, Jonathan. *The History and Present Condition of St. Domingo*. Volume I. Philadelphia, 1837

Candler, John. *Brief Notice of Hayti with its Conditions, Resources and Prospects.* London, 1842
Castillo, José del. *Ensayos de sociología dominicana.* Santo Domingo, 1981
Castor, Suzy. *La ocupación norteamericana de Haití y sus consecuencias.* México, D.F., 1971
Corten, André. 'La migration des travailleurs haïtiens vers les centrales sucrières dominicaines', *Cultures et Développement*, vol. 2, 1970
Crassweller, Robert D. *Trujillo, The Life and Times of a Caribbean Dictator.* New York, 1966
Debbasch, Yvan, 'Le marronage: essai sur la désertion de l'esclave antillais', *L'Année Sociologique*, vol. 3, 1961, 1962
Debien, Gabriel. *Les esclaves aux Antilles Françaises (XVIIe-XVIIIe siècles).* Basse-Terre and Fort de France, 1974
Deive, Carlos Esteban. *Vodú y mágia en Santo Domingo.* Santo Domingo, 1979
Deive, Carlos Esteban. *La esclavitud del negro en Santo Domingo (1492-1844).* Tomo II. Santo Domingo, 1980
Département de l'Economie Nationale. Bureau de Recensement. *Recensement géneral de la République d'Haïti (Population, habitation, agriculture) août 1950. Instructions aux énumérateurs.* Port-au-Prince, 1950
Díaz Santana, Arismendi. 'The Role of Haitian Braceros in Dominican Sugar Production', *Latin American Perspectives*, vol. 3, 1976
Diederich, Bernard and Burt, Al. *Papa Doc. Haiti and its Dictator.* Harmondsworth, 1972
Edouard, Bertholand. 'Les migrations de travailleurs', in Secrétairerie d'Etat des Affairs Sociales, *Actes du IIème Congrès National du Travail.* Port-au-Prince, 1969
Fouchard, Jean. *Les marrons de la liberté*, Paris, 1972
Franco, Franklin J. *República Dominicana. Clases, crisis y comandos.* Santo Domingo, 1967
Galíndez, Jesús de. *La era de Trujillo.* Buenos Aires, 1962
Gingras, Jean-Pierre O. *Duvalier, Caribbean Cyclone. The History of Haiti and Its Present Government.* New York, 1967
Haiti Información. Organo del Comité Democrático Haitiano, no. 13, Sept. 1979, no. 18, Feb. 1980, no. 23, Oct. 1980. México, D.F
Harris, John R. and Todaro, Michael P. 'Migration, Unemployment and Development: A Two-Sector Analysis', *American Economic Review*, vol. 60, 1970
Hazard, Samuel. *Santo Domingo, Past and Present; with a Glance at Hayti.* New York, 1873
Heinl, Robert Debs Jr. and Heinl, Nancy Gordon. *Written in Blood. The Story of the Haitian People 1492-1971.* Boston, 1978
Heredia y Mieses, José Francisco de. 'Informe presentado al muy ilustrísimo ayuntamiento de Santo Domingo, capital de la Isla Espanola', in Rodríguez Demorizi (1955)
Hernández, Frank Marino. *La inmigración haitiana.* Santo Domingo, 1973
Hicks, Albert C. *Blood in the Streets. The Life and Rule of Trujillo.* New York, 1946
Hoetink, Harmannus. *El pueblo dominicano: 1850-1900. Apuntes para su sociología histórica.* Santiago de los Caballeros, 1971
Institut Haïtien de Statistique. Département des Finances et des Affaires Economiques. *L'économie haïtienne, son évolution récente.* Port-au-Prince, 1976
International Bank for Reconstruction and Development. *Current Economic Position and Prospects of Haiti. Volume II: Statistical Appendix.* Washington, DC, 1976

Jimenes Grullón, Juan I. *El contrasentido de una política*. La Habana, 1943
Jimenes Grullón, Juan I. *La República Dominicana. Una ficción*. Mérida,
    Venezuela, 1965
Knight, Melvin H. *The Americans in Santo Domingo*. New York, 1928
Leyburn, James G. *The Haitian People*. Revised edition. New Haven, 1966
Lundahl, Mats. *Peasants and Poverty: A Study of Haiti*. London, 1979
Lundahl, Mats. 'A Note on Haitian Migration to Cuba, 1890-1934', *Cuban
    Studies*, vol. 12, 1982
Machado Báez, Manuel A. *La dominicanización fronteriza*. Ciudad Trujillo, 1955
Martin, John Bartlow. *Overtaken by Events. The Dominican Crisis from the Fall
    of Trujillo to the Civil War*. Garden City, 1966
Millspaugh, Arthur C. *Haiti under American Control 1915-1930*. Boston, 1931
Moral, Paul. *L'économie haitienne*. Port-au-Prince, 1959
Moral, Paul. *Le paysan haïtien (Etude sur la vie rurale en Haïti)*. Paris, 1961.
Moreau de Saint-Méry, Médéric-Louis-Elie. *A Topographical and Political
    Description of the Spanish Part of Saint Domingue*. 2 volumes. Philadelphia, 1796
Moreau de Saint-Méry, Médéric-Louis-Elie. *Description topographique, physique,
    civile, politique et historique de la partie Française de l'Isle Saint-Domingue*.
    New edition, 3 volumes. Paris, 1958
Moya Pons, Frank. *La dominación haitiana 1822-1844*. Santiago de los Caballeros,
    1972
Moya Pons, Frank. *Manual de historia dominicana*. Fifth edition. Santiago de los
    Caballeros, 1980
Munro, Dana G. *Intervention and Dollar Diplomacy in the Caribbean 1900-1921*.
    Princeton, 1964
Murray, Gerald, F. 'The Evolution of Haitian Peasant Land Tenure: A Case Study
    in Agrarian Adaptation to Population Growth', PhD thesis, Columbia
    University, New York, 1977
El Nacional de Ahora, Santo Domingo, 11 February 1981
Oficina International del Trabajo. *Generación de empleo productivo y crecimiento
    económico. El caso de la República Dominicana*. Geneva, 1975
Palmer, Ernest Charles. 'Land Use and Landscape Change along the Dominican-
    Haitian Border', PhD thesis, University of Florida, Gainesville, 1976
Peña Batlle, Manuel. A. *Política de Trujillo*. Ciudad Trujillo, 1954
Pierre-Charles, Gérard. *La economía haitiana y su vía de desarrollo*. México, D.F.,
    1965
Pierre-Charles, Gérard. *Haití: radiografía de una dictadura—Haití bajo el régimen
    del doctor Duvalier*. México, D.F., 1969
Price-Mars, Jean. *La République d'Haïti et la République Dominicaine*. Port-au-
    Prince, 1953
Primer censo nacional de la República Dominicana, 1920. Santo Domingo, 1923
Rodríguez Demorizi, Emilio (ed.). *Invasiones haitianas de 1801, 1805 y 1822*.
    Ciudad Trujillo, 1955
Romain, Jean-Baptiste. *Quelques moeurs et coutumes des paysans haïtiens*.
    Port-au-Prince, 1959
Rotberg, Robert I. with Clague, Christopher K. *Haiti: The Politics of Squalor*.
    Boston, 1971
Sánchez de Bonilla, Fanny. 'Los problemas de los negros en la industria azucarera'.
    Mimeo, Coloquio sobre la presencia de Africa en las Antillas y el Caribe,
    Santo Domingo, 1973
Segal, Aaron Lee, 'Haiti', in Aaron Lee Segal (ed.), *Population Policies in the
    Caribbean*. Lexington, Mass., 1975
Spitzer, Daniel Charles. 'A Contemporary Political and Socio-Economic History
    of Haiti and the Dominican Republic', PhD thesis, University of Michigan,
    1972

Thomas, Hugh. *Cuba. The Pursuit of Freedom*. New York, 1971
United Nations Economic and Social Council. Commission on Human Rights.
Sub-Commission on Prevention of Discrimination and Protection of
Minorities. 'Question of Slavery and the Slave Trade in All Their Practices
and Manifestations, including the Slavery-like Practices of *Apartheid* and
Colonialism. Report of the Working Group on Slavery on its Fifth Session'.
Mimeo, New York, 1979
Vaissière, Pierre de. *Saint-Domingue. La société et la vie créoles sous l'ancien
régime (1629-1789)*. Paris, 1909
Vargas, G., Rosemary. 'Unemployment, Underemployment and Labor Inputs in
the Dominican Republic: A Sketch of Some Problems', *Ibero-Americana*,
vol. 10, 1981
Veloz Maggiolo, Marcio. *Sobre cultura dominicana . . . y otras culturas*. Santo
Domingo, 1977
Veras, Ramón Antonio. '¿Cuántos haitianos hay aquí?', *Ahora*, no. 942,
1981:1
Veras, Ramón Antonio. 'Legalidad e ilegalidad de los inmigrantes haitianos en
R.D.', *Ahora*, no. 943, 1981:2
Veras, Ramón Antonio. 'El tráfico de braceros; forma de enriquecimiento
oficial', *Ahora*, no. 945, 1982:1
Veras, Ramón Antonio. 'Algunas consecuencias del estado de ilegalidad de los
habitanos', *Ahora*, no. 947, 1982:2
Victor, René. *Recensement et démographie*. Port-au-Prince, 1944
Vincent, Sténio. *Efforts et résultats*. Port-au-Prince, 1938
Wingfield, Roland. 'Haiti. A Case Study of an Underdeveloped Area', PhD thesis,
Louisiana State University, Baton Rouge, 1966
World Bank, *World Development Report, 1980*. Washington, DC, 1980
World Council of Churches, Migration Secretariat. *'Sold Like Cattle', Haitian
Workers in the Dominican Republic*. Genève, 1980
Zuvekas, Clarence Jr. 'Land Tenure, Income, and Employment in Rural Haiti: A
Survey', Mimeo, US/AID, Washington, DC, 1978

III. SPACE AND MARKETS

9 THE STATE OF SPATIAL ECONOMIC RESEARCH ON HAITI: A SELECTIVE SURVEY*

During the past few years, two excellent little books by Georges Anglade (1974, 1977), which deal with the economic geography of Haiti, written for use in Haitian schools, have appeared. These books constitute the only attempt to date to summarize and synthesize some of the information regarding the spatial features of Haiti's economy. This is a non-satisfactory state of affairs, for however excellent and useful Anglade's books may be (and they very definitely are), the fact that they are schoolbooks necessarily puts a limit to the type of material which can be presented. Thus, the spatial dimension of the Haitian economy remains one of the least known. So far, little systematic research on spatial and regional problems has seen the light of day. This is not, of course, to say that no information on the regional dimension exists, but that the problem is that this information is hopelessly scattered in an enormous number of documents which are in turn scattered themselves among a host of official and unofficial organizations and libraries inside and outside Haiti.

One possible reason for the neglect of the regional/spatial dimension is the presumption that such a small country would display relatively little regional variation. However, this presumption is likely to prove incorrect in the case of Haiti. A second and perhaps more important explanation may be found in the degree of centralization of the 'Republic of Port-au-Prince', as the country is sometimes jokingly labeled. Virtually everything of importance to the ruling parties is concentrated in the capital: governmental institutions, higher education, communications, the bulk of industry, the bulk of the urban population and last, but not least, the elite themselves. The capital has always come first in Haitian life, and the rest of the country, including the secondary cities, appears much as a hinterland in comparison to Port-au-Prince and its suburbs.

Whether this situation continues or is changed remains to be seen. One cannot exclude the latter alternative, however. It ought to be pointed out that when the second five-year plan for national development was formulated in the mid-seventies, regional problems were given

*Source: *Anthropologica*, NS, vol. 22, no. 1, 1980

much more consideration at the highest level than at any time hitherto, and the President, during the preparation of the plan, in a speech to the officials of CONADEP (the national planning body), repeatedly pointed to decentralization as a cornerstone in government development policy (Donner, 1977: 10-11).

A serious attempt to decentralize government and to foster regional economic development instead of concentrating on the capital and its surroundings requires economic information, however, and it is the purpose of the present essay to survey some of the existing works which deal specifically with regional and spatial problems. The essay is divided into four different parts, covering (1) studies dealing with all of Haiti's regions, (2) studies of particular regions, (3) studies of spatial aspects of the agricultural marketing system and, finally, (4) studies of external and internal migration. No attempt at completeness will be made. The intention is only to point to the major achievements in each of the four areas.

Studies Dealing with the Entire Country

The first modern, somewhat unsystematic, attempt to deal with regional economic problems in a comparative fashion was made by Paul Moral, who devoted a chapter of *Le paysan haïtien* (Moral, 1961) to such issues. Moral wrote during a period when the relative isolation of the countryside was being eroded by the gradual penetration of the *camion* to hitherto more or less inaccessible districts. Still, he felt that the peasants by and large 'remained locked up within their familiar horizons' (Moral, 1961: 123), their main contact with the outside being via the local market-places. Thus, regional differences could be important, and Moral proceeded to describe these. He identified nine different geographical regions, described their topographic and climatic characteristics, attempted to determine some of their more important economic differences, and gave a summary account of the adaptation of farming to population and natural resources. His perspective was partly historic – often extending all the way back to the colonial period.

Judged with the wisdom of hindsight, the main deficiency of Moral's work on the regional economy is that the emphasis is too much on description, while few analytical points are made. The same type of criticism may be directed against another monograph which appeared in 1962: Richard Schaedel's *An Essay on the Human Resources of Haiti*. Schaedel (who did not deal exclusively with regional matters) chose a somewhat different approach. Instead of attempting to cover entire regions in general terms, he picked particular communities in each of Haiti's five traditional *départements* and assumed that these represented 'typically distinct cultural adaptions and adjustments' (Schaedel, 1962:III).

Such an approach can be defended basically in terms of research economy, and provided that the communities chosen may actually be considered as 'typical' for each particular region, some interesting differences and similarities may very well be uncovered. In Schaedel's case, the method does not work, however. Schaedel, while providing some interesting information, failed to select the communities studied carefully, i.e. in a way which allows comparisons to be made, both from the point of view of the communities picked and when it comes to the matters analyzed. Thus, his discussion of the Artibonite Valley, for example, is heavily concentrated on a description of a rural *lakou*,[1] while in the south and north, a social survey was made of two small *towns*. The discussion of the northwest, again, centers upon a rural *commune*,[2] while in the case of the west, finally, the *arrondissement*[3] of Belle Anse is dealt with in very general terms, and a very brief comparison is made of contemporary Mirebalais with the same community as described by Herskovits in the latter's classic study from the 1930s (Herskovits, 1971). Finally, an appendix presents tables of average cash farm incomes and outlays for four of the five *départements*, unfortunately without giving any details regarding the method for constructing the series.

In addition to the arguments already advanced, Moral and Schaedel may be criticized for another weakness: their failure to ask sufficiently specific questions. Narrowing the scope of the investigation is frequently a good strategy, as exemplified by Wolf Donner's attempt (1975) at regionalization of the Haitian territory. Donner's approach resulted from an appreciation that erosion was the major problem of Haitian agriculture. The task of agricultural planning, according to Donner, should be the physical defense and development of the territory, i.e. protection and controlled use of the natural resources. This, in turn, necessitated a 'synopsis' of the items generally known as 'land': soil, soil fertility, soil chemistry and physics, manipulation of soil fertility, natural vegetation, crops grown, and the whole hydrological and climatological complex. 'These single phenomena have to be seen in their inter-relation. They may be studied separately, but in nature they all interact within the framework of a *watershed* or a *hydrological basin*' (Donner, 1975 : 44).

Hence, Donner chose to base his regionalization on the concept of watershed. A catchment area should be conceived of as an entity 'because of the close interdependence between soil and water, slopes and plains, natural vegetation and crops grown' (Donner, 1975:49). Seven agricultural regions were identified according to two criteria:

1. Extensive watershed areas could be regarded as agricultural regions.
2. So could extensive plains which with their adjacent bordering slopes and their catchment areas would permit the establishment of integrated development plans.[4]

From here, Donner could go on to outline a regional development strategy for each of these regions.

The importance of asking specific questions is also clearly brought out in the study by Clarence Zuvekas (1978:124-31) which is much more restricted in scope than those discussed hitherto. Zuvekas surveys the available data with respect to the regional distribution of income in Haiti. From the point of view of statistical accuracy, the material leaves a lot to be desired. It is patchy, unsystematically collected, and is not homogeneous with respect to the date of collection. Individual margins of error are necessarily large. Still, by concentrating on one particular problem and by casting the analysis within a strictly comparative framework, Zuvekas manages to 'confirm' some of the impressionistic views generally held as to which areas are the wealthiest ones (mainly the fertile plains) and the poorest (the northwest and the adjacent islands). This is an important step in the right direction, for it allows the formulation of hypotheses which can be made subject to more rigorous testing at a later stage.

To sum up: the comparative study of Haitian regions has barely started. Naturally, in the beginning, we should, perhaps, expect much of the work to be of a fairly descriptive nature, but even so, it is surprising to learn that there have been so few attempts at spatially disaggregated *analysis*. It is futile to attempt to arrive at meaningful regionalization schemes without at the same time identifying the objectives of such disaggregation. Future comparative regional research in Haiti should begin by clearly specifying those objectives.

Studies of Particular Regions

One year before the publication of Moral's book, the first detailed study of a particular region, the southern peninsula, by John Street (1960), appeared. Street's neglected contribution, which includes natural and economic (historical and contemporary) geography, primarily aims to 'describe the agriculture of the peasants of southern Haiti and to determine its origins and its relationship to the physical environment' (Street, 1960 : 10).

Street spans a wide variety of issues. Geology, climate, soils and vegetation are all dealt with in the section on natural geography, and the contemporary (1952 and 1953) economic geography of Haiti south of the Cul-de-Sac plain is presented. The physical setting is described as are techniques for planting, crop protection and harvesting, the methods of growing and uses of no less than 95 different plants, from abricotier to vetiver, and the domestic animals and their use. Street's monograph also deals with small-scale industries (including crafts), forestry, fishing, transportation, stores and market-places, housing, settlement patterns, malnutrition, disease, literacy, land tenure (unfortunately far too briefly) and co-operative labor. Some of the best parts of Street's work are to be found in the historical sections in which he traces the island's history back to the Indian and Spanish periods and deals extensively with the French colonial period with good descriptions of technology and production methods which reveal a thorough familiarity with the historical material. It is also in the historical section of analysis that Street makes his major contribution. He shows that little from the pre-Columbian period or the Spanish period remains in today's rural Haiti, an exception being the livestock introduced by the Spanish. The French influence, on the other hand, is evident everywhere. All but a few of the crops cultivated by today's peasants were introduced by the French, and so were many of the production techniques. In principle, the contemporary peasant cultivates the same crops as he did in 1790, employing the same methods.

The breakdown of the plantation system during the nineteenth century is described, and an account of the changes in technology is given, pointing towards technological retrogression in certain cases.[5] Street also describes the changes brought by the American occupation (especially in communications, where a vastly improved road network led to less isolation in the countryside) but also the decay after the departure of the Americans. He attempts to trace certain agricultural practices to West Africa and compares Haiti with the Dominican Republic in terms of population and farm size (cf. Palmer, 1976).

Another study of a particular region — in this case the *Département du Nord* — was reported in 1961 and 1963 by Harold Wood: of 'something very close to the maximum productivity possible, in a variety of types of land' (Wood, 1963:XI) (the North being the most densely populated department of the most densely populated country of Latin America). Thus, Wood in a different way deals with the same problem as Street: that of obtaining a picture of man and his economic activities in relation to natural resources.

His main point here deserves to be stressed: whatever differences that we are likely to find in the utilization of the natural resources by the human element derive from differences in the former – *not* the latter. On the regional level, the observable differences are not large. Peasant cultivation dominates the scene, with plantation agriculture constituting an exception. As we focus on the local level, however, differences in cropping patterns emerge, and to explain these adequately, reference must be made to 'variations in elements of the physical environment, such as the texture, fertility, and drainage of soils, the depth of the overburden, the gradients, and the amount and seasonal distribution of precipitation' (Wood, 1963:126). The human factor, on the other hand, is comparatively constant: 'In few parts of the world will one find so homogeneous a culture and so classless a society as in rural Haiti' (Wood, 1963:22).

Thus an important hypothesis emerges: 'It is possible to appreciate the relations between the land and its people both qualitatively and quantitatively. Rock, soil, months of wet weather, and months of drought can be expressed in terms of the crops which will grow, the proportion of the land which can be cultivated, the number of people who are able to gain their livelihood from each square mile, and the occurrence of seasonal food shortages' (Wood, 1963:141). Wood goes on to detail such differences. This is his main contribution to the regional economic geography of Haiti.

The third detailed regional study differs from the two previous ones in the sense that it was undertaken with a practical purpose in mind. In 1977, Wolf Donner completed a survey of the Northwest (including the Gonaïves area). This survey, which covered one of the seven agricultural regions identified by Donner in 1975, was to serve as a factual basis for agricultural planning in the region. Here, as in the studies of the southwest and the north, emphasis is on descriptive economic geography while no economic analysis is made.

Basically, Donner divides his study into three different parts: physical, social and economic. The first one involves topography, climate, geology and soils, hydrography and, finally, vegetation. The social description deals with population (especially the economically active population and internal and external migration), education, health, family planning (one of Donner's favorite topics), and peasant community organization. The economic section leans heavily towards a physical interpretation of the economy (while the tools of economics are not used). Under the heading of agriculture, the situation with respect to arable land, land tenure and agricultural production is described, and livestock, forestry, fishing, industry, transport and communication, trade and energy all receive treatments of varying length.

The Northwest study constitutes a formidable catalogue of information regarding that area. It should be mentioned that the purpose is not only to study a particular area of Haiti, but also to provide a methodology which can be used for regional studies in the rest of the country. It is only to be hoped that such studies will actually be undertaken in the future, since careful descriptive studies of each of Donner's seven regions along the lines sketched by him would organize the material which is now scattered among a multitude of national and international organizations. The Northwest study should be an indispensable tool in any planning situation, with the shortcut it provides to information which is otherwise difficult and time-consuming to get access to.

Summing up: When we move from comparative regional studies to monographs dealing with one particular Haitian region, the few studies undertaken appear more meaningful. The emphasis continues to be on detailed description of the regions under study, but one can at least see the beginnings of regional analysis here. It is quite possible and perhaps even probable that no meaningful comparative work will be undertaken until the separate building blocks, in the form of studies of all the particular regions, are available. It may very well be that one of the most important questions to be asked is to what extent it is really warranted to cast the analysis of the Haitian economy in regional terms. Are the existing regional differences important, or is it generally sufficient to deal with the country as an entity?

Spatial Aspects of the Agricultural Marketing System

The best documented spatial aspect of the Haitian economy is the system of agricultural commercialization. A major survey made by the *Institut Interaméricain des Sciences Agricoles* (IICA) in 1975 identified 519 state-controlled market-places (La Gra, Fanfan and Charleston, 1975:3). These regular markets have been extensively described in the literature on Haiti, and several attempts of classification have been made. Officially, a distinction is upheld between *urban* and *rural* market-places. To be classified as urban, a market must be located in a community where there is a communal magistrate (La Gra, Fanfan and Charleston, 1975:10). Only urban markets are officially allowed to stay open more than one day a week (Moral, 1959:74), and only urban markets may possess warehouses and speculation posts (Moral, 1961:240). In 1954, there were 106 urban and 188 rural markets in Haiti (Moral, 1959:74), and in 1975, the corresponding figures were 152 and 367, respectively (La Gra, Fanfan and Charleston, 1975:7).

The theoretical differences between urban and rural markets are not observed in practice. Of the 188 supposedly rural markets in 1954, 35 were open more than one day every week, and seven of them every day (Moral, 1959:74). Such discrepancies have led various authors to propose other classifications that better correspond to reality. These according to various criteria establish a hierarchical order of markets. Table 9.1 shows five such classifications. On the lowest level we find what has been termed local, intraregional or semi-rural markets. This is the most common type of organized market in Haiti. No less than 426 of the markets in the IICA survey were classified as semi-rural (La Gra, Fanfan and Charleston, 1975:7).

Although the characteristics of the local or semi-rural market-place vary somewhat from author to author, some common characteristics emerge. Hence, the local market only touches the locality where it is situated. Its radius of action is limited to one or two kilometers. The trade that takes place there is either between peasant women from the local community or between peasant women and traveling intermediaries (*Madam Sara*) that are bulking foodstuffs to be brought into urban areas. The latter also dispose of peasant necessities of urban or imported origin in these markets.

Table 9.1: Classifications of the Haitian Market-place System

Author	1 (highest)	2	3	4 (lowest)
Paul Moral	sea coast	regional	town	local
Sidney W. Mintz	–	strategic	captured	local
Harold A. Wood	port	inter-regional	–	intraregional
E.A.J. Johnson	port city	major inland assembly and wholesale	–	local
Jerry La Gra *et al.*	urban	regional	–	semi-rural

Sources: Moral (1959:74-8) (1961:241-7); Mintz (1960:51-3); Wood (1963: 130-40); Johnson (1970:83-92); La Gra, Fanfan and Charleston (1975:10-13).

On the next level we find Moral's town markets, and Mintz's captured markets. The main difference between this type of market and the purely local markets is that more bulking appears to go on on the former level. These markets are also somewhat more advantageously situated than the local markets (which are either points of origin or termini in the marketing process) in that they join plains and mountains or two different mountain ranges, i.e. they join producers and consumers from different economic environments.

Yet another step up the ladder are the regional or inter-regional market-places ('strategic' market-places in Mintz's terminology). Their influence extends over a wider area than that of the town markets, in extreme cases across almost the entire country. Larger and more varied quantities of good are bought and sold here. Staples come in from different regions, some of which are bulked by the large number of *Madam Sara* usually present to be taken into the largest cities, and yet another part is subdivided to be distributed and sold to the local communities in town markets and local markets. Some consumers may also buy directly in these markets to take advantage of the wide range of goods displayed there.

On the highest level in the hierarchy of market-places, finally, are the urban markets — the large sea ports and the department capitals. These are the points of final consumption for much of the peasant produce. The transactions that take place in this type of market are mostly between consumers and middlemen and between different categories of middlemen before the goods reach the final consumer. These markets, if situated on the sea, are also the points where imported peasant necessities reach the country and undergo the first bulk-breaking operations.

The picture that emerges from the above classification of market-places is one of an essentially hierarchical system.[6] Most of the trade in this system is *vertical* in nature, i.e. the goods move between different categories of markets rather than between markets belonging to the same category. This of course is not to deny that goods move also horizontally, but in principle for an item to move between two markets on the same level of the hierarchy, especially on the lowest level, it must also pass a market which is 'above' or 'below' these two markets. This, in turn, may be interpreted largely as a consequence of the geographical specialization of the intermediaries.

The *Madam Sara*, in order to develop as tight-knit a network of reliable trading partners as possible, tend to stick to a given geographic route, moving upwards and downwards in the hierarchy of marketplaces

rather than sideways or in circles. This usually gives them more opportunities of using the same contacts both as buyers and sellers than
would horizontal or circular movements that always entail a certain
amount of horizontal movements between markets supplying the same
type of goods and with consumers with essentially the same needs.

Also when it comes to the special features of the marketing system,
our knowledge is rather good. Thus, a great deal of information with
respect to regional variation in the prices of different agricultural
products exists, though until fairly recently it has not been made
available to researchers. For many years data have remained more or
less buried in the government organizations which have collected them,
but due to the efforts of the IICA project, the best of these price data
for the 1965-74 period have been published together with a discussion
of their reliability (La Gra, Charleston and Fanfan, 1975; IICA, 1975:a,
1975:b).

Very little has been done to analyze this price information though.
Only a rudimentary beginning has been made by James Johnson and
Jerry La Gra (1975), who made use of six products for the 1971-4
period. Their main conclusions were that no significant price differences seem to exist between the three types of market-places defined by
IICA, and that for each product the geographical price differences were
large. Johnson and La Gra finally also identified which market-places
and regions generally had the higher prices. It must be pointed out,
however, that their study is severely limited by the fact that only
average (yearly) prices were used in the analysis. It is therefore possible
that their conclusions need to be revised, or at least qualified, when a
more detailed analysis, involving seasonal patterns as well, has been
made.

Related to the compilation of price data is also an analysis of the
taxation of market-places which was carried out by Verdy Duplan and
Jerry La Gra (1974), who checked how agricultural goods were taxed in
Port-au-Prince. Not surprisingly, their main finding was that the
taxation system was totally arbitrary, and that it led to abuses by the
tax collectors in the form of highly unequal levies on the intermediaries
in a way which created manifest inefficiencies in the marketing system.
This study was highly successful in the sense that it led to the suppres-
sion of these taxes by presidential decree in 1974.

The physical movement of goods has been subject to fairly detailed
scrutiny, with emphasis, however, on movements to Port-au-Prince,
and to a lesser degree, to Cap-Haïtien. Thus, Duplan and La Gra have
undertaken two studies of transportation of agricultural products into

the two largest cities, Port-au-Prince and Cap-Haïtien. The authors provide information on the mode of transportation used to bring the products into the cities (generally motor vehicles when the distance traveled was large, while the merchandise was as a rule carried on the head when it came from the immediate surroundings), where the products go once inside the urban areas, and during which week-days most intermediaries enter.

Two papers, by Locher (1974) and by Werleigh and Duplan (1975) respectively, discuss in detail how the goods move inside the cities before they reach the final consumer. Murray and Alvarez (1973) analyze the commercialization chain of a particular commodity – beans from the producers in a community in the Cul-de-Sac plain to the consumers in Port-au-Prince, and René Dorville (1975:a) has made a similar effort with respect to vegetables (produced in a zone near the capital). Girault and La Gra (1975) discuss marketing chains for various products, Verdy Duplan (1975) surveys the marketing system for agricultural inputs, Fatton (1975) covers sisal, and a team from the JWK International Corporation does the same for coffee (1976). None of these studies, however, is concerned mainly with spatial issues. Ira Lowenthal (1974) has checked how different actors involved in marketing understand and utilize the internal marketing system. Lundahl (1979), finally, provides an overall evaluation of the economic efficiency of the commercialization of coffee and subsistence crops as well as a short account of the transportation system as an obstacle to increased competition in the marketing system.

It is not as easy to sum up the results of the research on the market systems as it is to provide an evaluation of most other spatial aspects of Haiti's economy. One should, however, not lament this, since the reason simply is that our knowledge with regard to markets is greater than with respect to other areas. The main market-places have been identified, and their relationships have been described, even if we do not yet know in detail how and in what quantities goods move from market to market within and between particular regions. What we do have is a good grasp of the competitive aspects of marketing, although existing price data have not yet been analyzed in detail. We also know with some accuracy how the physical distribution of goods takes place, and what the commercialization chains for a number of important goods look like. Thus, in a sense, the topics for future research differ here from what we found in the first two sections. While in the latter, research is still very preliminary and exploratory in nature, when it comes to the marketing system we have often reached a stage where main hypotheses are already formulated and where future research will be able to yield also systematic quantitative data of the sort economists generally prefer to work with.

External and Internal Migration

The last spatial aspect of the Haitian economy to be dealt with in the present survey is migration, which in Haiti takes two forms. On the one hand, people migrate from the countryside to urban areas and in particular to Port-au-Prince. On the other hand, a steady flow of Haitians leave the country permanently or temporarily to make a living abroad

The directions of the migratory currents are known with a fair degree of accuracy. Migration is not a phenomenon which is new to the country. Georges Anglade (1972, 1974) has described the earliest migratory movements: those taking place in the wake of the independence from French sovereignty in 1804. During the Spanish and French colonial periods, the best areas in terms of soil fertility had been occupied: the coastal plains, the river plains and the mountain flanks surrounding these plains − basically the Northeast, the plains around Port-au-Prince and Léogâne, and the Cayes area, respectively, all of which were excellently suited to cultivations of sugar and coffee (the latter on the mountain slopes).

After independence, the population of Haiti slowly expanded and established new settlements in less fertile and less accessible areas. The Plateau Central and other districts which had not been occupied and cultivated to more than a limited extent were now incorporated into the economy. This movement continued through most of the nineteenth century, until during the last quarter of the latter virtually all the arable land was either cultivated or claimed by some owner (Murray, 1977:410). At this point, new migratory currents were triggered off. While some poor peasants pressed on to marginal lands, others turned back to the areas which had been populated during the days of the colony − to look for jobs in urban areas. Finally, a number of Haitians for the first time began to look for opportunities abroad.

Temporary or permanent emigration has become a major characteristic of contemporary Haitian life. The rise of American domination in Cuban sugar cultivation after 1898 and the subsequent displacement of some Cuban sugar interests to the Dominican Republic created a need for cheap labor during the sugar harvest in these countries, and this demand to a large extent was satisfied by organized or unorganized migration of Haitians for longer or shorter periods.[7] While the exodus of Haitians towards Cuba practically came to a standstill after Castro's rise to power, emigration to the Dominican Republic has continued more or less uninterrupted since the beginning of the present century, in spite of Trujillo's massacre of up to 25,000 Haitians in 1937 and in spite of the fact that the border between Haiti and the Dominican Republic has been officially closed most of the time.

In the 1950s, the Bahamas became a third important recipient of Haitian emigrants (Wingfield, 1966:101-9; Segal, 1975). To serve the rising number of tourists to the Bahamas in the 1950s, unskilled labor was in great demand, and Haitians willingly rushed in to meet this demand. The last two decades have seen a further enlargement of the area of inmigration of Haitians. A number of other Caribbean islands now regularly receive Haitian immigrants (mainly illegally), but also, and perhaps more importantly, the United States and Canada are turning into important endpoints for Haitian migrants. It is thus fairly certain that after Port-au-Prince, New York is the largest 'Haitian' city in the world.

Altogether, an estimated 0.4 per cent of the total Haitian population migrate abroad every year (Lundahl, 1979:628), though this is believed by some authors to be a gross underestimate. In fact, the

Table 9.2: Estimates of Haitians Residing outside the Country

| Source of estimate | Country and year | | | | |
	Dominican Republic	Bahamas	Cuba	United States	Canada
Schaedel (1962)	18,772 (1950)	–	27,543 (1953)	–	–
Rotberg (1971)	300,000 (1968)	11,000-20,000 (1968)	50,000 (1968)	75,000 (1968)	10,000 (1968)
Díaz Santana (1976)	42,142-200,000 (1970)	–	–	–	–
Dorville (1975:b)	–	38,000 (197?)	–	–	–
Segal (1975)	100,000 (1975)	20,000 (1975)	–	200,000 (1975)	15,000 (1975)
Palmer (1976)	–	–	–	21,466 (1970)[a]	–
Joseph (1976)	300,000-500,000 (1976)	–	–	–	–

Note: a New York City only
Source: Zuvekas (1978), p. 75.

magnitudes involved in the migration currents are not known accurately. Estimates of their geographical distribution (summarized in Table 9.2) are subject to particularly wide margins of error.

Our knowledge of internal migration currents is not quite as good as that of movements abroad. Thus, the census figures for 1950 and 1971 indicate that the urban population grew at approximately 4 per cent during the 1950s and 1960s, with the capital displaying a growth rate of more than 6 per cent per annum (Ahlers, 1978: 2). It also appears as if this high rate of migration into urban districts is a fairly recent phenomenon, while before the 1950s, and especially before 1920, the rural population was much less mobile (Lundahl, 1979: 629).

In examining the motivation for external and internal migration, presumably a distinction must be made between different categories. It has been estimated that some 80 per cent of all Haitian professionals were living abroad in the mid-1960s (Rotberg with Clague 1971: 243) due to an oversupply of qualified manpower, a previous decline in real salaries for professionals and the unattractive political conditions prevailing in Haiti at the time (Zuvekas, 1978: 73-4). These conditions have, however, subsequently improved, so that today the share of Haitian professionals residing abroad ought to be lower (Zuvekas, 1978: 74).

The great majority of the emigrants and *a fortiori* the migrants from rural to urban districts within the country are, however, not professionals, but rather people with their roots in the peasant community. What causes this group to migrate? Most explanations, or rather hypotheses, offered, one way or another center upon the poverty of rural areas as the main determinant of migration (Lundahl, 1979:625-34). The existing evidence is, however, not so simple to interpret. Thus, while it appears plausible that perceived differences in incomes between rural and urban districts *à la* Harris and Todaro (1970) should play an important (perhaps the *most* important) role, one important group of migrants may be those who move to town to get an education, and these elements in turn, frequently come from the better off parts of the rural population (Moral, 1959:34; Ahlers, 1978).

Another interesting question in relation to migration which so far has not received any satisfactory answer is whether migration from rural areas to Port-au-Prince takes place in steps or directly. A pattern thought to be common is that of a person first moving from the countryside into the nearest town, thereafter to the province capital, and finally to Port-au-Prince. However, the most ambitious study of rural-urban migration so far undertaken, that of Theodore Ahlers, failed to provide definite support for the hypothesis. It rather appears as if the poorer migrants have to bypass the small towns entirely, since they are in immediate need of employment, and this they will probably not find, unless they move to the capital (Ahlers, 1978).

A final topic connected with migration, and one which has received hardly any attention at all, is what impact migration has on the areas left by the migrants and on the urban districts where they end up (except for the highly visible creation of vast slum areas). Of special interest here are the remittances from Haitians abroad, which are believed to be somewhere in the order of 5 per cent of the gross national product − a figure which should be sufficient to help ensure the subsistence of hundreds of thousands of Haitians (Segal, 1975).

Conclusions

Our survey of spatial economic research on Haiti conclusively shows that we really know very little of the regional and other spatial dimensions of the Haitian economy. In the field of regional economics proper hardly anything − with the exception of three geographical monographs on particular regions − has so far been achieved. The marketing system has been far better researched, although quantitative data to permit tests of the main hypotheses are often lacking. In the field of external and internal migration, finally, we are in an 'intermediate' position. Many of the patterns are known (while others have hardly been researched), but not in much detail, and all attempts at quantification remain utterly uncertain.

There remain many issues which we have not dealt with at all. The most important of these is concerned with systematization of the patchy information on spatial problems hidden in general works on Haiti. Something of this kind has been started in the two works of Anglade cited at the beginning of the present survey. May we hope for a continuation in the future, but on a more ambitious scale?

Notes

1. 'The *lakou* or yard is used to describe the members of one large extended family (usually including 3 or 4 generations), having a common physically demarcated residence' (Schaedel, 1962: 25).
2. There were 116 *communes* in Haiti at this time.
3. Haiti contained 27 *arrondissements* in 1962.
4. These physiographic criteria constitute the cornerstone of the approach, but certain criteria of magnitude were applied as well to ensure that the regions demarcated did not turn out to be too large or too small (Donner, 1975: 50). Finally, for practical reasons, an adjustment to the boundaries of the existing *arrondissements* had to be made.

5. This issue is discussed in some detail in Lundahl (1979), Chapter 12.

6. E.A.J. Johnson calls this type of market system a *dendritic* system. (Dendrites are processes of a nerve cell extending from the cell body that transmit incoming impulses to the cell body.)

7. See Lundahl (1979), Epilogue, for a summary view. Migration to the Dominican Republic is discussed by Moral (1959: 40-1), Wingfield (1966: 96-101). Hernández (1973), Segal (1975), Palmer (1976: 136-44), Díaz Santana (1976) and Zuvekas (1978: 75-6). As of recently, the living conditions of the Haitian cane-cutters in the Dominican Republic have been brought to the attention of the UN. (See Anti-Slavery Society (1979).) Studies of the migration to Cuba are scarce. Moral (1961) devotes less than three pages to the issue, and Castor (1971) gives us about as much. Cf. also Wingfield (1966: 93-6).

Bibliography

Ahlers, Theodore H. *Haitian Rural-Urban Migration: A Case Study of Four Small Towns*. Mimeo. Institut Interaméricain des Sciences Agricoles (IICA), Port-au-Prince, 1978

Anglade, Georges. *Las variaciones regionales de población en Haití*. Mexico City, 1972

Anglade, Georges. *L'espace haïtien* Montréal, 1974

Anglade, Georges. *Mon pays d'Haïti*. Port-au-Prince, 1977

Anti-Slavery Society for the Protection of Human Rights. *Report for 1979 to the United Nations Working Group of Experts on Slavery: Migrant Workers in the Dominican Republic*. Mimeo, 1979

Castor, Suzy. *La ocupación norteamericana de Haití y sus consecuencias*. Mexico City, 1971

Díaz Santana, Arismendi. 'The Role of Haitian Braceros in Dominican Sugar Production', *Latin American Perspectives*, vol. 3, 1976

Donner, Wolf. *Agricultural Development Regions as Instruments for Spatial Agricultural Planning*. Mimeo. Département de l'Agriculture, des Resources Naturelles et du Développement Rural, Port-au-Prince, 1975

Donner, Wolf. *The Reduced, Action-Oriented Approach in Regional Agricultural Programming under Haitian Conditions*. Mimeo. Département de l'Agriculture, des Ressources Naturelles et du Développement Rural, Port-au-Prince, 1977

Donner, Wolf in collaboration with Dorville, René; Moise, Martiel; Nonez, Jean Edner and St-Fleur, Gabriel. *Région agricóle du Nord-Ouest. Programme de Développement Rural*. Département de l'Agriculture, des Ressources Naturelles et du Développement Rural, Port-au-Prince, 1977

Dorville, René. *Production et commercialisation des légumes en Haïti*. Mimeo. Institut Interaméricain des Sciences Agricoles, Port-au-Prince, 1975:a

Dorville, René. *Perspectives d'une politique de l'emploi dans le secteur rural d'Haïti*. Mimeo. Département de l'Agriculture, des Resources Naturelles et du Développement Rural, Port-au-Prince, 1975:b

Duplan, Verdy. *Commercialisation des intrants agricoles en Haïti*. Mimeo. Institut Interaméricain des Sciences Agricoles, Port-au-Prince, 1975

Duplan, Verdy and La Gra, Jerry. *Analyse du système de taxation des produits agricoles dans les marchés haïtiens*. Mimeo. Institut Interaméricain des Sciences Agricoles, Port-au-Prince, 1974

Duplan, Verdy and La Gra, Jerry. *Transport des produits agricoles vers Port-au-Prince*. Mimeo. Institut Interaméricain des Sciences Agricoles, Port-au-Prince, 1975

Fatton, Bernard. *Eléments d'information sur la production et la commercialisation du sisal en Haïti.* Mimeo. Institute Interaméricain des Sciences Agricoles, Port-au-Prince, 1975

Girault, Christian and La Gra, Jerry. *Caractéristiques structurelles de la commercialisation interne des produits agricoles en Haïti.* Mimeo. Institut Interaméricain des Sciences Agricoles, Port-au-Prince, 1975

Harris, John R. and Todaro, Michael P. 'Migration, Unemployment and Development: A Two-Sector Analysis', *American Economic Review*, vol. 60, 1970

Hernández, Frank Marino. *La inmigración haitiana.* Santo Domingo, 1973

Herskovits, Melville J. *Life in a Haitian Valley.* New York, 1971

IICA (Institut Interaméricain des Sciences Agricoles). *Agricultural Product Prices in Haitian Marketplaces. Annex 3.* Mimeo. Port-au-Prince, 1975:a

IICA. *Agricultural Product Prices in Haitian Marketplaces. Annex 4.* Mimeo. Port-au-Prince, 1975:b

Johnson, E.A.J. *The Organization of Space in Developing Countries.* Cambridge, Mass., 1970

Johnson, James L. and La Gra, Jerry. *The Internal Agricultural Marketing System of Haiti: A Price Analysis.* Mimeo. Institut Interaméricain des Sciences Agricoles, Port-au-Prince, 1975

Joseph, Raymond A. 'Haitian Peons and Dominican Sugar: Border Strife in Hispaniola', *The Nation*, 27 November 1976

JWK International Corporation. *Agricultural Policy Studies in Haiti: Coffee.* Mimeo. Département de l'Agriculture des Ressources Naturelles et du Développement Rural, Port-au-Prince, 1976

La Gra, Jerry, Charleston, Wesner and Fanfan, Guy. *Prix des produits agricoles dans les marchés haïtiens.* Mimeo. Institut Interaméricain des Sciences Agricoles, Port-au-Prince, 1975

La Gra, Jerry and Duplan, Verdy. *Enquête sur le transport des produits agricoles à l'entrée et à la sortie du Cap-Haïtien.* Mimeo. Institut Interaméricain des Sciences Agricoles, Port-au-Prince, 1975

La Gra, Jerry. Fanfan, Guy and Charleston, Wesner. *Les marchés publics d'Haïti.* Mimeo. Institut Interaméricain des Sciences Agricoles, Port-au-Prince, 1975

Locher, Uli. *The Internal Market System for Agricultural Produce in Port-au-Prince.* Mimeo. Institut Interaméricain des Sciences Agricoles, Port-au-Prince, 1974

Lowenthal, Ira. *Commercial Activities in Rural Haiti: A Community-Centered Approach.* Mimeo. Institut Interaméricain des Sciences Agricoles, Port-au-Prince, 1974

Lundahl, Mats. *Peasants and Poverty: A Study of Haiti.* London and New York, 1979

Mintz, Sidney W. 'A Tentative Typology of Eight Haitian Marketplaces', *Revista de Ciencias Sociales*, vol. 4, 1960

Moral, Paul. *L'économie haïtienne.* Port-au-Prince, 1959

Moral, Paul. *Le paysan haïtien (Etude sur la vie rural en Haïti).* Paris, 1961

Murray, Gerald F. 'The Evolution of Haitian Peasant Land Tenure: A Case Study in Agrarian Adaptation to Population Growth', PhD thesis, Columbia University, New York, 1977

Murray, Gerald F. and Alvarez, Maria D. *The Marketing of Beans in Haiti. An Exploratory Study.* Mimeo. Institut Interaméricain des Sciences Agricoles, Port-au-Prince, 1972

Palmer, Ernest Charles. 'Land Use and Landscape Change along the Dominican-Haitian Border', PhD thesis, University of Florida, Gainesville, 1976

Rotberg, Robert I. with Clague, Christopher K. *Haiti: The Politics of Squalor.* Boston, 1971

Schaedel, Richard P. *An Essay on the Human Resources of Haiti.* Mimeo. US/
AID, Port-au-Prince, 1962
Segal, Aaron Lee, 'Haiti' in Aaron Lee Segal (ed.), *Population Policies in the
Caribbean.* Lexington, Mass., 1975
Street, John M. *Historical and Economic Geography of the Southwest Peninsula
of Haiti.* Mimeo. University of California, Berkeley, 1960
Werleigh, Georges-Emmanuel and Duplan, Verdy. *Système de commercialisation
interne des produits agricoles au Cap-Haïtien, Haïti.* Mimeo. Institut Inter-
américain des Sciences Agricoles, Port-au-Prince, 1975
Wingfield, Roland. 'Haiti. A Case Study of an Underdeveloped Area', PhD thesis,
Louisiana State University, Baton Rouge, 1966
Wood, Harold A. 'Physical Influences on Peasant Agriculture in Northern Haiti',
Canadian Geographer, vol. 5, 1961
Wood, Harold A. *Northern Haiti: Land, Land Use and Settlement.* Toronto, 1963
Zuvekas, Clarence, Jr. *Agricultural Development in Haiti. An Assessment of
Sector Problems, Policies, and Prospects under Conditions of Severe Soil
Erosion.* Mimeo. US/AID, Washington, DC, 1978

10 IMPERFECT COMPETITION IN HAITIAN COFFEE MARKETING

A widely discussed theme in studies of the Haitian economy is whether or not the marketing of agricultural produce is characterized by imperfect competition.[1] As a result of the Haitian peasant's strong market orientation, i.e. he produces first and foremost with the market in mind and, conversely, is dependent on the market for his own supply not only of 'city goods' but also to get a number of staple foods, imperfect competition among the intermediaries could easily do severe damage to his standard of living. This consideration is of great importance since in most cases the Haitian peasants have only a very slim margin — if any at all — between the incomes they regularly receive from their plots and hunger or even outright starvation. Monopsonistic or monopolistic exploitation by the middlemen could thus place the peasants in a directly precarious position.

Opinions have differed widely over the past 30 years regarding the degree of competition among the intermediaries both in the internal system of market-places which handles the sales of food crops and in the chain of *spéculateurs* and exporters who buy coffee from the peasants and sell it outside the country. For a long time the most disturbing feature of this debate was the lack of systematic information that could be used for reliable generalizations. During the past couple of decades, however, a sufficient number of empirical studies have been made to allow a more accurate picture of the marketing process to be drawn.

This picture is not uniform. In the case of food crops a consensus has gradually emerged as to the genuinely competitive nature of the system. Marketing is carried out by a large number of intermediaries whose profits are so small that they should hardly be considered as profits in the standard sense of the word but rather as a return to the labor effort expended. This applies to all levels of the system.

In the case of coffee such a consensus has not yet emerged. The two hitherto most important empirical studies of the coffee marketing system, those by William Gates in the late 1950s and JWK Corporation in the mid-1970s,[2] both indicated that coffee marketing was a competitive industry.[3] Recently, however, an excellent study by Christian Girault,[4] that provides by far the most comprehensive coverage so far

171

of the entire coffee marketing chain from producer to exporter, has strongly challenged this view. In the pages that follow we will examine the new evidence presented by Girault and see to what extent his findings modify the conventional wisdom regarding competition in the coffee industry.

The Organization of the Coffee Industry

The marketing system for coffee contains three essential links: producers, *spéculateurs* and exporters. Figure 10.1 presents this chain.

Figure 10.1: The Coffee Marketing Chain

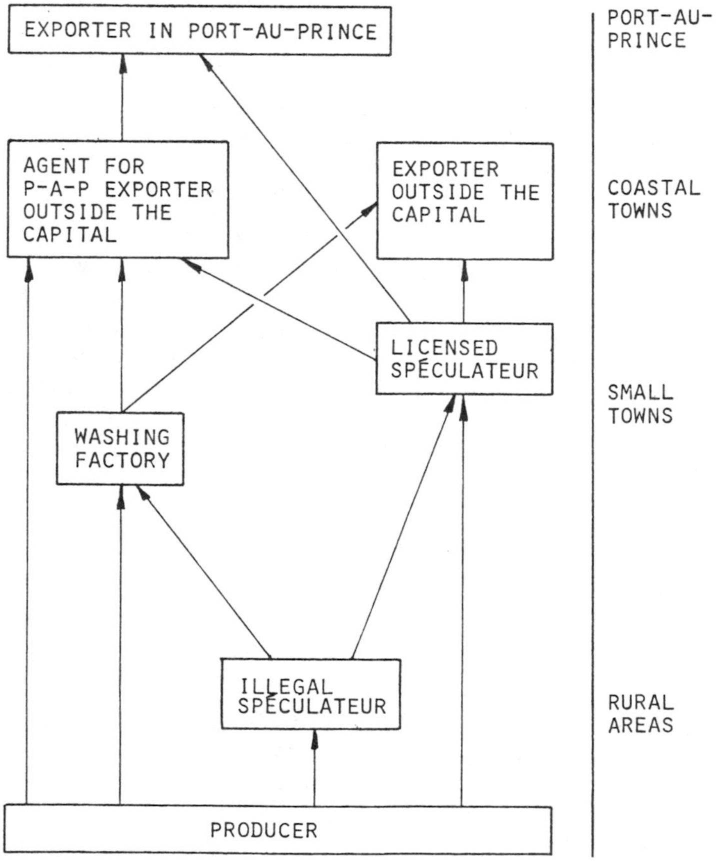

Source: Based on Girault (1981:1), p. 128.

According to the JWK Corporation study there were some 384,000 coffee-growing peasants in Haiti around 1975.[5] However, the figure given by Girault — 180,000 for the same period[6] — suggests that the JWK estimate is a gross exaggeration. Girault's figure confirms an earlier one, given by Paul Moral, of 150,000 growers at the beginning of the 1960s.[7] Hence out of a total of more than 600,000 farms in Haiti in 1971,[8] no less than one-third of all Haitian peasants produced coffee. The remainder concentrate on other crops.

Girault also shows that the average coffee grower has a farm which is slightly larger than the average Haitian farm in general. According to the 1971 census, the average size of Haitian farms was 1.4 hectares,[9] while Girault gives an average for coffee farms of 1.5-2 hectares. More than 65 per cent of all farms where coffee was grown contained more than 1.3 hectares.[10]

Figure 10.1 shows that at all stages of the marketing chain there are options as to the channel through which the produce could flow.[11] Thus, a coffee producer may sell either to a *spéculateur* (licensed or unlicensed), to a washing factory, to an exporter, or to an agent employed by any of these categories. It should, however, be noted in this context that only a minor proportion of the coffee is washed in washing factories (mostly owned by exporters) to obtain a higher quality, while most of it is prepared simply by drying the beans in the sun.[12] Also, the agents involved in the marketing chain act only on behalf of the middlemen by whom they are hired. Thus, disregarding agents and washing factories, we are basically left with a system that contains two (or three) levels: exporters and (legal and illegal) *spéculateurs*. In the remainder of this essay we will concentrate on the competitive situation at these two levels. Let us begin at the top, with the exporters.

The Exporters

The number of coffee exporters has remained low at least since the early 1950s. William Gates lists 28 companies for 1951-2 and 25 for 1957-8,[13] the JWK Corporation enumerates 28 for 1972-3,[14] and Girault, finally, presents the names of 27 exporters in 1976-7.[15] Of these companies, most of the important ones have their principal offices in Port-au-Prince.[16]

The degree of concentration among exporters, however, is higher than the mere listing of numbers indicates, and this concentration has by and large remained unchanged during the past 30 years. Figure 10.2 shows Lorenz curves for the concentration of exports for four years: 1951-2, 1957-8, 1972-3 and 1976-7. The differences between the curves are minimal. The degree of exporter concentration changed very marginally from the early 1950s to the late 1970s.

Figure 10.2 also shows that exports are strongly concentrated in a handful of firms. Their shares of total exports are shown in Table 10.1. The table indicates that the four largest exporters together have accounted for more than 50 per cent of total coffee exports. At times, the figure has been even higher, as for example during the mid-1950s when the share of the first four firms was over 60 per cent.[17] The six firms ranking fifth to tenth in importance, in turn, have accounted for between 20 and 30 per cent of total export sales during the same period.[18]

Table 10.1: Export Shares of the Four Largest Coffee Exporters, 1951/2-1976/7

| | | 1951/2 | | 1957/8 | | 1972/3 | | 1976/7 |
Rank	Firm	% of tot. exp.	Firm	% of tot. exp.	Firm	% of tot. exp.	Firm	% of tot. exp.
1	Mantèque	16.7	Reinbold	16.2	Mantèque	18.2	Madsen	17.3
2	Madsen	14.7	Madsen	15.1	Wiener	15.4	Mantèque	15.8
3	Wiener	14.0	Wiener	14.6	Madsen	13.1	Wiener	11.0
4	Blanchet	8.5	Mantèque	10.0	J. Dufort	7.0	Jacomin	7.6
First four		53.9	First four	55.9	First four	53.7	First four	51.7

Sources: See Figure 10.2.

The high degree of sales concentration does not mean that the market structure has been completely frozen. Table 10.2 contains a comparison between the relative positions of the ten most important firms in 1956-7 and 1976-7. The pattern of stability is represented mainly by three firms: Madsen, Mantèque and Wiener, which are found among the first four during the entire period (as well as in 1951-2 for that matter). Of the remainder only Novella is represented at both dates.

During shorter periods, the degree of stability is naturally higher. Table 10.2 also contains a comparison between 1972-3 and 1976-7. Here, eight of the top ten firms from the former date remain on the list four years later as well. Note, however, that a new firm, Jacomin,

Figure 10.2: Concentration of Coffee Exports, 1951/2-1976/7

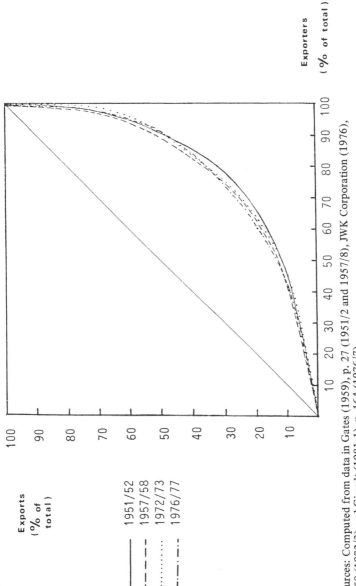

Exports
(% of
total)

——— 1951/52
– – – 1957/58
·········· 1972/73
–·–·– 1976/77

Exporters
(% of total)

Sources: Computed from data in Gates (1959), p. 27 (1951/2 and 1957/8), JWK Corporation (1976),
p. 50 (1972/3) and Girault (1981:1), p. 164 (1976/7).

managed to move from outside the list (rank 13)[19] to fourth place in four years. A second interesting observation is that the leading firm in 1956-7, Reinbold, had disappeared completely by the early seventies.[20]

Table 10.2: The Ten Largest Coffee Exporters and their Market Shares, 1956-7, 1972-3 and 1976-7

| | | 1956-7 | | 1972-3 | | 1976-7 |
| | | % of tot. | | % of tot. | | % of tot. |
Rank	Firm	exp.	Firm	exp.	Firm	exp.
1	Reinbold	16.2	Mantèque	18.2	Madsen	17.3
2	Madsen	15.1	Wiener	15.4	Mantèque	15.8
3	Wiener	14.6	Madsen	13.1	Wiener	11.0
4	Mantèque	10.0	J. Dufort	7.0	Jacomin	7.6
5	J. Dufort	6.2	Kersaint	5.7	Kersaint	6.2
6	Blanchet	5.9	Novella	5.4	Novella	5.8
7	Vital	4.7	Baptiste	5.2	Copexim	4.8
8	Berne	3.6	Vital	3.9	J. Dufort	4.6
9	Oliver	3.0	Berne	3.2	Baptiste	4.5
10	Novella	2.6	Copexim	2.9	Duvernaud	3.4

Sources: See Figure 10.2.

However, the changes shown in Table 10.2 should not be interpreted as a sign of intense competition. The fact that for example Jacomin (and Kersaint before that)[21] has been able to rise to relative prominence in a few years' time does not mean that there were no barriers to entry or that collusion did not exist among the exporters.

Some of these barriers can best be understood in a historical perspective. The history of the large coffee exporters goes back to the nineteenth century. Foreign merchants began to establish themselves in Haiti as soon as the country had broken with France. These merchants had good reasons for concentrating their activities in the export and import trade.[22] By law, their activities were restricted to wholesale trade. They had to be located in the export-import ports. Finally, they could not legally acquire land or real estate. These rules were codified in the 1804 constitution and later constitutions reconfirmed this legislation.

Naturally, the foreigners attempted to circumvent these restrictions in various ways, by association with Haitian partners or by marrying Haitian women and registering their businesses in the names of the latter. Nevertheless, a majority of the foreign merchants were limited to the largest cities. They could not open any branches in the interior of the country which by law was reserved for Haitian nationals (who in addition were free to start whatever businesses they liked in the ports).

In this way a division has grown up between the large-scale export-import commerce, dominated by foreigners, and the retail operations, handled by Haitians. The foreigners gradually acquired a comparative advantage in exports and imports. The tendency was to specialize in one type of operation, and specialization entails certain economies of scale. This was the case especially during the 1920s. The operations of the foreign traders were furthered by the 1918 American-penned constitution which did away with the ban on foreign ownership of real estate and land to pave the way for American investment. Subsequently, the exporters, and among them the coffee exporters, generally withdrew from the import business. At this point, a large number of foreigners had also been naturalized and could in this way branch into the *arrière-pays* with offices and agents.

The established exporters are in a good situation, fairly sheltered from entrants in the market. Girault calculates that it takes something like US$1 million to enter the coffee export trade successfully.[23] Thus, barriers to entry do exist at the exporter level. However, as historical experience shows, they are not completely unsurmountable. New firms have appeared since the 1950s and will presumably continue to appear in the future. The coffee export industry works under oligopolistic conditions, which means that there is always the possibility of stiff competition. Indeed competition has also been reported to be cutthroat at times.[24] New entrants can always upset the existing equilibrium.

Competition, however, does not appear to be the most salient characteristic of coffee exporting. Rather, there seems to exist a tendency for the dominant firms in the market to co-opt the stronger new firms and accommodate them within the rules set by the already established network. The instrument for this is the *Association des Exportateurs de Café* (ASDEC) which was founded in 1960, as it seems to solve some of the problems of the oligopsonistic situation.

Writing in 1959, William Gates concluded that 'The coffee industry in Haiti is organized on a thoroughgoing competitive basis'.[25] This, among other things, meant that 'The margin received by exporters tends to be narrow and *at best* gives them a return on their investment and skills over a period of time no greater than the return they might receive in other lines of enterprise'.[26] According to Gates, 'careful study' did not reveal any joint action among exporters to fix the price paid to the peasants for their coffee. Whatever agreements that existed in the 1950s were 'temporary' and 'fleeting' and broke up 'into strong competitive bidding for the crop almost immediately'.[27] The main reason for this, as Gates saw it, was that coffee-exporting in the fifties was subject to certain disadvantages of large scale:

> My impression is that a small to medium sized exporter can compete effectively with the larger houses and that, in fact, past 90,000 bags or so, there are substantial administrative and supervisory difficulties for a single firm — at least as the companies are organized today.
>
> Success and growth of a firm seems to depend upon building up a network of personal contacts and financial ties back in the hinterland of the spéculateur; availability of a modest amount of credit facilities or working capital; and the detailed attention to supervision to eliminate waste, minimize theft and bad advances to spéculateurs, and to maintain quality of final product. Finally, it seems to take some speculative ability, strong nerves and a dash of luck in the marketing end of business.[28]

To this, Gates adds 'the aggressive and successful efforts of one of the big four to reestablish its position in the industry' is 'a major factor in the competitive picture throughout the past decade'.[29]

Girault strongly challenges the view that holds coffee-exporting to be competitive. We will soon return to his evidence. Let us first, however, note that his thesis is not incompatible with that of Gates. The case appears to be that the degree of competition has decreased since the fifties, after the formation of ASDEC. In a 1976 report, a US consultancy firm, the JWK Corporation, while maintaining that coffee marketing was still competitive, noted that 'Competition among coffee exporters reportedly is not as strong as it was a few years ago. Competition then was such that most of them lost money and several were on the verge of bankruptcy.'[30]

The solution to this dilemma, as we have already noted, was the formation of ASDEC in 1960. Before that date no formal exporter association existed in the country, but when in the late fifties the market began to shrink as coffee prices fell in international markets, the exporters felt the need for co-operation to prevent competition from driving some of them out of the market. This need has increased drastically since then. The number of bags per exporter fell from some 23,000 in 1957-8 to less than 10,000 in 1976-7. This makes for a potentially explosive situation where a war could easily break out among the exporters if all of them act independently.[31]

However, in view of the way ASDEC operates, this does not appear to be a very probable course of events. ASDEC controls some 98 to 99 per cent of all coffee exports, i.e. it has virtually perfect control over the market. Its members meet regularly, every Wednesday, to discuss pricing and other matters of common interest.[32] The association is run by a bureau with a president, a vice president, a secretary and a treasurer. Two of the three largest firms are always represented on the bureau.

In this way, ASDEC fixes both prices and, since 1977, quotas, for its members, in relation to the respective members' past export performance. An exporter who sells more than is permitted by his quota has to pay to ASDEC a sum equal to the difference between his actual sales and his quota. An exporter who does not manage to fill his quota is entitled to receive money from the organization. In this way, export incomes are stabilized and competition is minimized.

The best way to obtain a check on the efficiency of the oligopolistic collusion within ASDEC is to examine profit margins. Girault considers that the profit margin estimates made by the JWK Corporation in 1976[33] are biased downwards and instead presents his own figures, based on actual buying and selling for the year 1974-5. His figures are somewhat difficult to interpret, since the calculations are not shown explicitly. Still the main conclusions are clear. In 1974-5 exporters earned a gross profit (after deduction of some marketing costs but before deducting overheads) of some 16 per cent of the f.o.b. price of coffee.[34] If export profits are instead calculated as a percentage of the *price paid by the exporter* plus his direct marketing costs, we arrive at a gross margin of 27.5 per cent.[35] This figure appears too high to be solely a result of competition. It undoubtedly reflects the collusion taking place among exporters.

An important question at this stage is the strength of the oligopsony power of the exporters. Terry Roe regressed monthly farm level prices of coffee on the f.o.b. price for the 1970-4 period and found that virtually the entire variation in the latter was forwarded to the producers ($R^2 = 0.994$).[36] This appears to indicate that the middlemen, including the exporters, must follow variations in the world market. On the other hand, Roe worked with official figures, not field data, which are known sometimes to be subject to considerable error.[37] Thus, his correlation figure may be largely spurious and biased upwards. It may, however, also indicate (at least to some extent) that the market situation is potentially explosive. Competitive forces may reassert themselves if the oligopsonistic price established by ASDEC is allowed to diverge substantially from the competitive level.

In support of the latter argument, it can be adduced that the coffee-growing peasants are as a rule not monocultivators. When the relative price of coffee and other products, notably food crops sold via the internal marketing system, changes in favor of the latter, the peasants react by reallocating land and labor away from coffee production.[38] This in turn means that if ASDEC attempts to exert excessive pressure on the peasants, the response of the latter may simply be to drop out of the coffee market. Substantial price cuts could have repercussions on the supply of coffee and hence trigger off competitive forces that would otherwise have remained dormant.

The situation is analogous to the one when a sales tax is imposed. Some of this tax will fall on the producer, but if the tax is too high at least part of it may be avoided by shifting into other crops which then appear to be relatively more profitable. The peasants may also protect themselves in other manners. Some 40 per cent of all Haitian coffee (legally sold) is not exported but traded by the channels used to sell food crops,[39] and these channels, as we noted initially, are competitive. Thus only 60 per cent of the legally sold coffee is subject to oligopsonistic pricing. In addition, an unknown amount is smuggled across the border, to the Dominican Republic. Very little is known about this traffic, but it could well be the case that one of the reasons for preferring contraband trade to the legal Haitian circuits is the wish to avoid oligopsonistic exploitation from the exporters. It should, however, be noted that the coffee sold outside the regular *spéculateur*-exporter network as a rule is of inferior quality.

The *Spéculateurs*

Girault suggests that not only is competition imperfect among the exporters but there is collusive oligopsony also on the *spéculateur* level. This argument is, however, much more difficult to accept than the one holding competition among exporters to be limited.

In the first place, the number of *spéculateurs* is quite high, as shown by Table 10.3. The table reveals that in the mid-seventies there were 859 licensed *spéculateurs* in a total of 101 speculation centers, i.e. an average of 8.5 *spéculateurs* per center. With the exception of Saint-Marc, which handled less than 1 per cent of total sales, no center had fewer than 28 *spéculateurs*.

Table 10.3: Number of Coffee *Spéculateurs* and Volume of Coffee Sold by District, 1974-5

District	Speculation centers	Spéculateurs		Volume of coffee sold	
		Number	Average per center	No. of 60 kg sacks	Average no. of sacks per *spéculateur*
Port-au-Prince	10	106	10.6	39,258	370
Croix-des-Bouquets	10	48	4.8	8,765	183
Cap-Haïtien	24	110	4.5	72,840	662
Port-de-Paix	5	57	11.4	17,745	311
Gonaïves	4	28	7	8,305	297
Saint-Marc	4	6	1.5	2,516	419
Jacmel	5	79	15.8	37,244	771
Petit-Goâve	9	133	14.8	14,316	108
Jérémie	18	207	11.5	85,893	415
Cayes	12	85	7.1	42,219	497
Total	101	859	8.5	329,101	383

Source: Girault (1981:1), pp. 142, 146

The conventional wisdom is that most of the *spéculateurs* are mere agents for the exporters, lacking the capital necessary to carry out purchase operations on their own behalf, the exporters paying their legal fees.[40] Girault questions this view, pointing out that agents represent only a smaller percentage of the total. Between 720 and 750 of the 859 licensed *spéculateurs* fall outside this category.[41] The *spéculateurs* have been comparatively successful in retaining their right to buy from the peasants.

According to Girault, *spéculateurs* employ different fraudulent practices when carrying out transactions with the peasants.[42] The quality of Haitian agricultural produce is often highly uneven. This creates a problem in the process of weighing and deciding the price. In addition, the peasants are not used to calculating in terms of weight but in terms of volume measures. Coffee, on the other hand, must be bought and sold by weight, if the transaction is to be legal. Here, the *spéculateurs* attempt to cheat the peasants by weighing in a fashion that leaves the latter at a disadvantage. Cheating is possible, especially with the modern type of scales, where the weight is given as a figure which the peasants often cannot read and where weighing is carried out very quickly. Sometimes scales are also fixed to yield figures that are lower than the correct ones.

However, there is presumably a limit to the extent of cheating that can be carried out in this way. It appears somewhat improbable that the peasants should not have an approximate idea of how much coffee they bring to the *spéculateurs*. The peasants themselves are sometimes also doing their best to bias the weighing in their own favor, by adding water, stones, etc. to the produce. Finally, if a *spéculateur* cheats peasants too obviously the word will get around and the *spéculateur* is then likely to lose business.

Thus, there should be a limit to the extent of cheating that is possible. There are also problems connected with the interpretation of cheating. Girault views it as a means of exploiting the peasants. This is of course to some extent true, but there is at least one other aspect to be noted as well. It may easily be the case that the *spéculateurs* resort to cheating as a means of competing in a situation where profit margins are slim. If collusion had been effective, there would not have been any need to resort to that kind of trick.

This interpretation receives some support when we look at *spéculateur* profit margins. These appear to be very modest. The average quoted by Girault amounts to 1.3 per cent of the f.o.b. price, or 2.7 per cent of the purchase price (including marketing costs) that is paid by the *spéculateurs* themselves.[43]

Girault also argues that the peasants are subject to usurious exploitation by the *spéculateurs* in the credit market, so that even if profits on coffee appear to be small, the peasants end up by being squeezed when they sell their coffee to these intermediaries. In Figure 10.3, the flow of credit involved in coffee marketing, as Girault sees it, is depicted.

Frequently the procedure for a peasant is to obtain an advance from a *spéculateur* against the future harvest. The thin arrows denote loans at zero interest. These are given by the exporters or their agents to the *spéculateurs*. The thick arrows represent allegedly usurious credit given to illegal *spéculateurs* and producers by licensed *spéculateurs* and washing factories and by illegal *spéculateurs* to producers.

However, the figure contains some strange discrepancies. In the first place, it is difficult to understand how the illegal *spéculateurs* could be in a position where they can extract a rate of interest from the peasants which is above that given by opportunity costs, risk premia and transaction costs. The illicit *spéculateurs* are poor peasants or peasant women who enter the coffee trade mainly at the beginning of the harvest when the produce is abundant. According to the figure, they are themselves victims of exploitation from *spéculateurs* and washing factories. They travel in the countryside and buy directly from the peasants at low prices, and the peasants respond by giving them a product of correspondingly low quality.[44] When there is scarcity in the coffee market, the illegal *spéculateurs* are pushed out of the market. Thus, they apparently have no hold whatsoever over the peasants. It also becomes difficult to understand how they could simultaneously be in a position where they are able to extract a monopoly profit on credit provided to the same peasants.

Figure 10.3: Credit Flows in Coffee Marketing

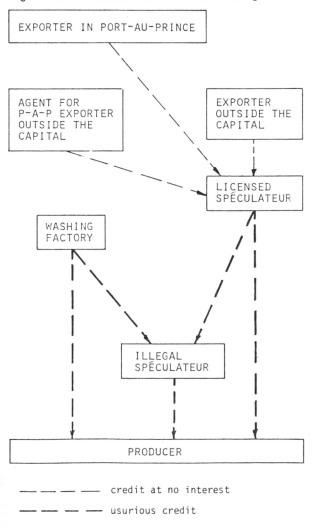

EXPORTER IN PORT-AU-PRINCE

AGENT FOR P-A-P EXPORTER OUTSIDE THE CAPITAL

EXPORTER OUTSIDE THE CAPITAL

LICENSED SPÉCULATEUR

WASHING FACTORY

ILLEGAL SPÉCULATEUR

PRODUCER

— — — — credit at no interest

— — — — usurious credit

Source: Based on Girault (1981:1), p. 128.

It is also difficult to see why the exporters, who are after all much more concentrated than the *spéculateurs*, should be giving loans to the latter category at zero interest instead of attempting to bind the *spéculateurs* to them in the same way as the *spéculateurs* are alleged to tie the peasants. There is no doubt as to the fact that the real power in the marketing system for coffee resides with the exporters and not with the *spéculateurs*, but if this is so, why do the exporters not use it to their advantage in the credit market?

This question brings us directly into the operation of the rural credit market. It is well known that interest rates can often be quite substantial. However, do these rates indicate exploitation or are they a result of other forces? This is not such an easy question to answer. No systematic empirical research has ever been done on rural credit in Haiti. Thus the evidence we have to fall back upon is indirect.

I have examined elsewhere the rural credit markets in Haiti.[45] Virtually the only disposable credit comes from informal sources. Government-sponsored credit has been extremely inefficient and extremely rare. Only a minute fraction of the peasants have been reached by such efforts. What the peasants generally do whenever they need a loan is either to join forces or to approach an informal lender.

The supply of non-institutional credit comes from a variety of sources. Interest-free loans are obtained from friends and relatives whenever such a possibility exists. A second source consists of the spontaneously formed *sangues*, rotating credit associations where the members save and lend to each member in turn.[46] Finally, loans are obtained from the intermediaries in the marketing chains for both food crops and coffee, i.e. from the *Madam Sara* (the wholesale food merchants) and from the *spéculateurs*. Those loans belonging to the latter category that are given as part of a *pratik* relationship[47] should normally not carry any interest. However, other loans do, including the loans advanced by *spéculateurs* to coffee-growing peasants.

Exceptionally high interest rates have sometimes been reported.[48] This, however, does not necessarily mean that the loans in question are usurious. On the demand side, high interest rates may be explained by strong preferences for additions to present income held, for example, by peasants who are running short of cash for consumption purposes immediately before the arrival of the coffee harvest. In this situation, the alternative to a short-term loan may be to sell and repurchase assets, notably land. However, that alternative is subject to transaction costs both when selling and when repurchasing and with earnings forgone on the asset in the meantime. It can then be shown that loans with an interest rate of, say, 50 to 100 per cent on a yearly basis, may easily become an alternative which is superior to parting with assets for, say, a month even with very modest asset yields and transaction costs.[49]

On the supply side, considerations of risks are presumably very important. My guess is that it is mainly in cases where the risk of default on the part of the borrower is high that we find the higher interest rates. The argument in favor of the existence of monopoly profits requires that we must somehow show that entry is restricted on the supply side. However, it is difficult to come up with convincing reasons for any such restrictions.[50] Until carefully designed field studies prove the opposite, the working hypothesis, I think, should be that monopoly is the exception rather than the rule in Haiti's rural credit markets.[51] By the same token it is difficult to see how e.g. the *spéculateurs*, except under special circumstances, would be able to exploit the peasants in the credit market.

The above should not be interpreted to mean that circumstances conducive to exploitation of coffee-growing peasants by the *spécula-teurs* are never available. In cases where the *spéculateurs* are simultaneously the sole sellers of prime necessities to the peasants and where, in addition, by Haitian standards, they could be termed 'large' landowners, leasing some of their land to coffee-growing peasants, the latter may become dependent on selling to a particular *spéculateur*. Furthermore, in the situation where the *spéculateur* is a local level Duvalierist politician who possesses some degree of administrative control and power in his area, it may not be easy for the peasants to venture to sell to his competitors.[52] It is, however, very difficult to know how general this type of situation is.

New Channels: Co-operatives

The conclusion to be drawn from the comments above is that power in the marketing chain for coffee resides with the exporters (and not so much with the *spéculateurs*), who by means of oligopsonistic pricing make peasant coffee incomes fall to a level which is lower than would otherwise have been the case in a purely competitive situation. Hence, the question arises whether there are no alternative channels whereby the peasants could avoid going through the traditional export merchants.

Such channels do exist: coffee co-operatives. The purpose of most of these has been to make a short-cut in the traditional marketing chain.

Some exports of coffee have been made directly by the co-operatives, but only four units have been involved, and the amounts exported only constitute some 0.1 per cent of the total.[53] The co-operatives face four difficult problems here. They have to handle the technical preparation of the beans (mainly washing, which is normally not done by peasant producers) well enough to obtain an exportable quality. Secondly, they must handle the administrative paperwork required to obtain an export license as well as pay export duties. Thirdly, they must find an overseas market. Finally, all these ventures must somehow be financed.

It would seem that coffee-marketing co-operatives have sufficient problems even without venturing into exports. The tax advantages envisaged for co-operatives in the *Code Rural* can be obtained only after registration with the *Conseil National de la Coopération*, but registration has proved to be a very difficult affair in practice.[54] The CNC operates very slowly and bureaucratically.

The financial outlook of many coffee-marketing co-operatives appears not to be promising. Technically and financially, the most successful ones have been able to draw on outside assistance, either from the Catholic clergy, including whatever infrastructure the Church has been able to provide, or from international organizations in the form of grants. Quite probably, they would not survive without this assistance.[55]

In some instances, according to Girault, the *spéculateurs* have been able to infiltrate and paralyze the co-operatives. In other instances, threats of political action have contributed to making the co-operatives less active. In this context it must be stressed that the government has not lent other than nominal support to the coffee-marketing co-operatives.[56]

Finally, the co-operatives have also been plagued by all sorts of conflicts: between members of the same unit and between co-operatives and sponsor organizations. Girault concludes that the coffee-marketing co-operatives are not democratic organizations, but that their functioning accurately reflects the stratification of rural Haitian society, in that the co-operatives mainly operate to the benefit of large and middle-sized coffee growers while the smaller producers do not at all benefit to the same extent.[57]

Conclusions

Christian Girault's *Le commerce du café en Haïti* has provided us with a host of new insights into how the marketing chain for coffee operates in Haiti, from the producer to the exporter. The case of exporters is especially well penetrated and Girault manages to dispel a number of false notions regarding competition at this stage. His sections on the *spéculateurs* are somewhat less convincing. It appears that he attributes rather too much power to this group, a contention which is not quite borne out by his own evidence.

However, this should not obscure the fact that what Girault has produced is without doubt the most authoritative work on Haitian coffee marketing so far. He shows that the marketing system works very much to the disadvantage of the basic link in the chain, the peasants, and that, unfortunately, few alternatives to marketing through this chain exist. The co-operative movement has failed to become a viable alternative. The option for the peasant is to move instead into food crops and sell these in the domestic markets.

Notes

Thanks are due to Christian Girault for open-minded and constructive comments on a draft version. Naturally, however, the opinion expressed in the present essay is my own.

1. See Lundahl (1979), Chapter 4 and the literature referred to there for a sample of views.
2. Gates (1959); JWK Corporation (1976).
3. The evidence is summarized in Lundahl (1979), Chapter 4.
4. Girault (1981:1). The study is summarized briefly in Girault (1981:2).
5. JWK Corporation (1976), p. 44.
6. Girault (1981:1), p. 92.
7. Moral (1961), p. 261.
8. Institut Haïtien de Statistique (1973), p. 37.
9. Lundahl (1979), p. 51.
10. Girault (1981:1), p. 92.
11. Note, that the freedom of choice of marketing channel varies depending on geographic location, e.g. on whether a washing factory exists in the neighborhood.
12. Girault (1981:1), p. 197. For a brief description of the drying process, see Lundahl (1979), note, pp. 133-4.
13. Gates (1959), p. 27.
14. JWK Corporation (1976), p. 50.
15. Girault (1981:1), p. 164.
16. Ibid., p. 165.
17. Gates (1959), p. 27.
18. For evidence, see the sources indicated in Figure 10.2.

19. JWK Corporation (1976), p. 50.
20. The circumstances are given in Girault (1981:1), p. 170.
21. Ibid., p. 174.
22. Cf. Joachim (1971) and Girault (1981:1), Chapter 8.
23. Girault (1981:1), p. 217.
24. JWK Corporation (1976), p. 51.
25. Gates (1959), p. 26.
26. Ibid.
27. Ibid.
28. Ibid., p. 28.
29. Ibid.
30. JWK Corporation (1976), p. 51.
31. Girault (1981:1), p. 218. Girault also points out that ASDEC to some extent was formed to strengthen the traditional exporter class politically in the face of the Duvalierist repression.
32. Ibid., p. 219.
33. JWK Corporation (1976), pp. 56-9.
34. Girault (1981:1), p. 195.
35. The producer price used in the calculation is US$39.60 per 60 kilo sack (ibid., p. 193).
36. Roe (1978), p. 71.
37. Christian A. Girault, personal communication, 29 January 1983.
38. Cf. Lundahl (1979), Chapter 5 and Appendix 2 to Chapter 5.
39. Girault (1981:1), p. 103.
40. Ibid., p. 152.
41. Ibid., p. 140.
42. Ibid., pp. 200-2.
43. Ibid., p. 195. The latter figure has been calculated on the basis of this information, plus a producer price equal to the one given in note 35.
44. Ibid., p. 153.
45. Lundahl (1979), Chapter 11.
46. A description of these is given in Laguerre (1976).
47. *Pratik* is an institutionalized personal secret relationship between two parties involved in the marketing process and entails mutual concessions. The system is described in Mintz (1961).
48. Lundahl (1979), pp. 511-13 gives some details.
49. See ibid., pp. 517-18 for details.
50. Ibid., pp. 529-34.
51. It is, however, not possible to discard the monopoly hypothesis completely, this being a persistent theme in Haitian literature, folklore, proverbs, etc.
52. Girault (1981:1), pp. 233-6.
53. Ibid., p. 242.
54. The *Pères Oblats* in 1977-8 had to call a 'sacramental strike' to obtain legal recognition of two co-operatives. (Ibid., p. 240.)
55. Ibid., pp. 243-4.
56. Ibid.
57. Ibid., p. 244. It should be noted that coffee growing is the area of peasant production in Haiti where the differences are largest between small and large producers, both economically and socially.

Bibliography

Gates, William B., Jr. *The Haitian Coffee Industry*. Mimeo, Williams College, Williamstown, 1959

Girault, Christian A. *Le commerce du café en Haïti. Habitants, spéculateurs et exportateurs.* Paris, 1981:1

Girault, Christian A. 'Habitants, spéculateurs et exportateurs. Le commerce du café en Haïti', *Revue de la Société Haïtienne de Géographie et de Géologie*, vol. 39, 1981:2

Institut Haïtien de Statistique. Département des Finances et des Affaires Economiques. *Résultats préliminaires du recensement général de la population, du logement et de l'agriculture (septembre 1971).* Port-au-Prince, 1973

Joachim, Benoît. 'La bourgeoisie d'affaires en Haïti de l'independance à l'occupation américaine', *Nouvelle Optique*, vol. 1, 1971

JWK International Corporation. *Agricultural Policy Studies in Haiti: Coffee.* Mimeo, Département de l'Agriculture, des Resources Naturelles et du Développement Rural, Damien, 1976

Laguerre, Michel S. *Le sangue haïtien: un système de crédit rotatoire.* Mimeo, Institut Interaméricain des Sciences Agricoles (IICA), Port-au-Prince, 1976

Lundahl, Mats. *Peasants and Poverty: A Study of Haiti.* London, 1979

Mintz, Sidney W. 'Pratik: Haitian Personal Economic Relationships', in *Proceedings of the 1961 Annual Spring Meeting of the American Ethnological Society.* Seattle, 1961

Moral, Paul. *Le paysan haïtien (Etude sur la vie rurale en Haïti).* Paris, 1961

Roe, Terry. *An Economic Evaluation of the Haitian Agricultural Marketing System.* Mimeo, US/AID, Port-au-Prince, 1978

11 PRICE SERIES CORRELATION AND MARKET INTEGRATION: SOME EVIDENCE FROM HAITI*

A commonly employed method for measuring the integration between agricultural markets in developing countries is that of correlating time series of price data for different market-places and products. This procedure builds on the rationale that if markets are perfectly competitive and spatially well integrated, differences in prices between markets will reflect transport and processing costs only and the bivariate correlation coefficient between a pair of such time series of prices will be equal to one. A lower correlation, according to this reasoning, will reflect bottlenecks arising e.g. from lack of market information, lack of product homogeneity or monopoly power.

The studies that have been undertaken with this method have yielded very different results. Such studies have been undertaken mainly in two areas: India and West Africa.[1] The 'best' results have been obtained for India. Thus, Ralph Cummings presents a modal correlation coefficient of 0.85 for 27 wheat markets in Northern India (1956-64)[2] and Uma Lele reports that *all* coefficients calculated for Delhi and five Punjab wheat markets lay above 0.90 (1955-65).[3] R.C. Gupta gives the following modal coefficients for Uttar Pradesh markets: rice: 0.79, wheat: 0.71, jowar: 0.85, peanuts: 0.91.[4] D.S. Thakur found that 71 per cent of all correlations between seven Gujarat wheat markets exceeded 0.75 (1965-71).[5] Lower figures have, however, also been reported. Thus, Lele found the number of correlation coefficients for Tamil Nadu rice and paddy markets that exceeded 0.8 to be as low as three (out of 507).[6]

West African studies generally give much lower figures. Thus, William Jones in 1968 reported from Nigeria that out of 4,836 correlation coefficients computed for seven products only 19 reached the 0.90 level or more while 424 were zero or negative. The product showing the best correlation was gari, where more than one-third of the coefficients were 0.80 or higher. For cowpeas, some 30 per cent were equal to 0.70 or more. No yam coefficient was as high as 0.80 and a maximum of 1 per cent of the coefficients for the remaining

*This chapter was written together with Erling Petersson
Source: *Ibero-Americana, 12*, no. 1, 1983. Shorter version in *Indian Journal of Agricultural Economics*, vol. 37, no. 2, 1982

products (rice, sorghum, millet and corn) reached this level.[7] Alan Thodey reports better figures for cowpeas in Western Nigeria (almost all coefficients above 0.80) but equally low ones for rice and corn (almost all below 0.70)[8] and Elon Gilbert in Northern Nigeria found the modal coefficient for cowpeas to be 0.65, for rice 0.55, for sorghum 0.45 and for millet 0.35.[9] H.M. Hays likewise reports that correlation coefficients for sorghum and millet in Northern Nigeria in only 1 per cent of the cases exceed 0.80.[10] D. Kohlers in a study of Niger for single years (1971, 1973 and 1975) mostly arrived at statistically insignificant coefficients during the first and last years but for 1973 found that most coefficients were significant and that half of them exceeded 0.80.[11] Elliot Berg for Upper Volta analyzed the three years 1962, 1963 and 1976. For the early years he found only 20 per cent of his coefficients were significant at the 0.05 level but for 1976 90 per cent of the coefficients exceeded 0.90 and were significant.[12] Southworth, Jones and Pearson, finally, analyzed 16 markets in the Atebubu District of Ghana (1965-72) and found that in the case of corn 88 per cent of all coefficients were 0.75 or higher but that for rice, yams and kokonte the figures were significantly lower: 31, 21 and 15 per cent, respectively.[13]

The interpretation of correlation coefficients calculated in this manner, from raw price data, is not without problems, however. In some of the aforementioned studies, correlation was found to be highest between markets which had no physical contact or during periods when one should expect contacts to be less intense. Hence, criticism of the calculations has not been lacking. George Blyn[14] has pointed out that there may be common, underlying trends in the series which bias the results upwards. Inflation or population growth, for example, may give rise to linear trends, and such trends show perfect correlation even if the markets in question are not at all integrated. Also, seasonal variations may be synchronized, for example due to a common climatic pattern with planting and harvesting taking place at the same time near all the markets included in the sample. This would lead to high (spurious) correlation, even when there is no or little contact between markets. As a remedy Blyn suggests that the data should instead be grouped into twelve groups, one for each month, that a trend should be fitted to each of the thus obtained series and that the residuals within each group should thereafter be correlated. He has also undertaken to calculate monthly coefficients from Cummings's data, showing that this produced an average which lay below the Cummings (modal) 0.85: 0.68.

The correlation method has also been criticized by Barbara Harriss on the grounds that a high correlation between two markets does not necessarily mean that these two markets are well integrated in the sense that a competitive network of traders exists which ensures that agricultural goods move between market-places in swift response to price differences that exceed transport costs.[15] High correlation could just as easily indicate stable margins and monopolistic imperfections in the marketing system as competitive conditions and efficiency. Also, low correlation does not have to be an indication that markets are not well integrated. We will come back to this below.

The purpose of the present essay is to use price data from an economy where, on other grounds, an efficiently integrated marketing system for agricultural products is believed to exist, that of Haiti, to calculate monthly correlation coefficients in the same manner as done by Blyn with Cummings's data, to show that coefficients of about the same size emerge, that a seasonal pattern which resembles the one found by Blyn is present and, finally, to discuss what these patterns may indicate with respect to the structure of the marketing network. Before we do that, however, we will give a brief overview of the Haitian marketing system and the indications for efficiency in this.

The Haitian Agricultural Marketing System

Between 1973 and 1975, the Interamerican Institute of Agricultural Sciences (IICA) carried out a major project entitled 'Analysis and Diagnosis of the Internal Marketing System for Agricultural Produce in Haiti' in collaboration with the Canadian Embassy and a number of Haitian public agencies. The IICA project for 1975 identified a total of 519 market-places in Haiti with a presence of 50 persons or more on a normal market day.[16] IICA classified all market-places in three different categories: urban, regional and semi-rural.

The urban market-places are those found in the largest ports and the *département* capitals. Before the products reach these markets, they have passed through a chain of intermediaries. The market women who buy produce from the producers rarely themselves resell the goods to the consumers in urban markets but dispose of the goods to retail vendors. Thirty-four of the 519 markets covered by the IICA survey were classified as urban.

The regional market-places serve a large geographical area — in extreme cases almost the entire country. The sellers bring to these markets staples from different regions in order for them to be redistributed, partly to the cities and partly to local markets, i.e. many of the transactions taking place are transactions between intermediaries of various kinds. Consumers, however, frequently buy in the regional markets due to their large variety of goods. Fifty-nine of the markets of the IICA survey were of this kind.

Finally, we have the most common type of market: the semi-rural one. No less than 86 per cent of the 519 IICA markets, i.e. 426 marketplaces, belonged to this category. These markets only touch the immediate area where they are located. Peasant women bring in the goods from the surrounding countryside and sell to traveling intermediaries who bulk the produce in order to bring it to regional or urban marketplaces. The same intermediaries dispose of goods of urban origin in these markets. In the semi-rural market-places, local producers also sell directly to local consumers.

This network of public market-places handles the marketing of all subsistence crops in Haiti, i.e. of all the crops grown in the country that are cultivated for the domestic market. In addition, it ensures that products that the peasants themselves do not manufacture – often imported goods – reach rural districts. It has to serve a large number of households. Haiti had a rural population of some 3.4 million in 1971, or 760,000 households,[17] all of whom were dependent on this marketing system for disposing of farm products and for buying urban goods and agricultural commodities not grown on the farmstead.

The strategic person in the marketing system for agricultural products is *Madam Sara*,[18] who is the Haitian counterpart to the West African 'market mammy'. She is the traveling intermediary who connects the countryside with towns and cities. *Madam Sara* as a rule is a wholesale dealer who only carries retail trade as a wide activity if she bothers at all with the latter type of transactions. In most cases she follows a regular geographic route and deals with customers with whom she has established close and reliable contacts. Often she carries a limited number of products only, where one crop is the main item and the others are carried as sidelines which she can fall back upon, should something exceptional happen to the demand or supply of her regular staple. She usually employs the services of truckers who regularly go back and forth between determined geographic points in the country.

The retail level of the marketing system is represented by another group of women, the *revendeuses*. These either obtain their stock from the *Madam Sara*, from the family farm, or from other peasants. It should be noted that the division between *revendeuses* and *Madam Sara* is not a rigid one. We have already seen that under certain (exceptional) circumstances, the *Madam Sara* may turn to retailing, but it also occurs that certain *revendeuses* go on trips in the countryside, in the same manner as the wholesale dealers do — only on a more infrequent and irregular basis. Often the ambition of the retailers is to become wholesalers (which requires more capital).[19]

The Efficiency of the Marketing System

The Haitian marketing system for agricultural products has been the subject of a fairly large number of studies since the late 1950s. The opinion as to whether the system is an efficiently functioning one in the sense that it enables goods to flow from producers to final consumers at minimum cost varies from author to author. Thus, Paul Moral, in his standard work on the Haitian peasant, contends that the 'infinite number of small transactions' in the rural marketing system leaves the peasants with but 'a miserable benefit', that the smallness and frequency of the transactions (with goods sometimes passing through many hands before they reach the consumer) increases the price of urban goods to the peasants, that the intermediaries subject the peasants to all kinds of petty frauds both when buying and when selling, and that the peasants as a rule are forced to sell their commodities at the most unfavorable moment in time — at the beginning of the harvest, when prices are low.[20] In this view, the marketing system is characterized by imperfect competition, and the victim of these imperfections is the peasant.

Other observers, notably Sidney Mintz, who in the late fifties carried out a number of studies on the marketing system,[21] hold the opposite view and point to the economies involved in using large numbers of people with few alternative employment opportunities, investing human effort and time and economizing on scarce capital resources.[22] The system with this view is one which builds on stern competition between intermediaries at all levels and which does not contain any exploitative elements.

A detailed evaluation of the available information regarding the efficiency of the marketing system for agricultural products has been made by Mats Lundahl,[23] who concludes that the view which contends that the system is an efficient one and that exploitation of the peasants by the middlemen does not appear to take place is the one closest to the truth. Five types of evidence are discussed:

1. profit margins among intermediaries,
2. freedom of entry,
3. possibilities of making short-cuts in the marketing chain,
4. determination of prices, and
5. non-price competition.

The overall impression regarding profit margins is that these appear to be slim. It should be stated that no systematic evidence of the size of intermediary profits has been collected, but the available evidence shows that at the lowest levels of the trading hierarchy, the irregularly working *revendeuses*, the profits amassed yield only a small supplementary income to that generated by other livelihoods. Regular *revendeuses* appear to be a little better off, but not much. The evidence points to profit margins of perhaps 10 to 20 per cent per *gourde*[24] invested. The profit level of the *Madam Sara* seems to be in the same range. Even these figures are probably too high, however, since they presumably are not *net* figures, i.e. they do not for example take the value of the labor input into account. If a wage figure is imputed, the margins could be considerably lower.

There is enough freedom of entry in the marketing system to ensure that the system does not permit monopsony or oligopsony and hence inefficiency. Everybody cannot be a *Madam Sara*, since for this, a minimum capital is required, but the point to be noticed is that there are always enough *revendeuses* around who are prepared to enter wholesale trade, should the profit level there start to rise. In the same manner, *revendeuses* working on an irregular basis will start working full time if prospects in the retail sector look more promising than usual, and so on, all the way down the scale.

Ample opportunities exist for producers, intermediaries and consumers to make short-cuts at all steps in the commercialization chain. Consumers may buy both from intermediaries (at various levels) and from producers. The latter may sell both to the final consumers and to different types of intermediaries. The middlemen, finally, may sell either to other intermediaries (at many levels) or to the final consumers. This means that if middlemen, at any level in the system, attempt to fix prices to increase profits, they can be bypassed by simply avoiding that level, and proceeding to the next level instead.

The process whereby the price is set in a particular market-place bears a striking resemblance to the one described by economic textbooks when discussing free competition, i.e. it is set by the interaction of demand and supply. The existence of hundreds of different units of measurement which vary from place to place complicates the procedure, but haggling is always used for solving this problem. In any market, the equilibrium price is established within a couple of hours and thereafter varies very little during the day.

The final means whereby competition and efficiency are ensured is that of non-price competition. Price competition is quite intense in the marketing system for agricultural goods, but it is not the only form of competition prevailing. In their struggle to remain in business, the intermediaries attempt to form *pratik* relationships with the customers and sellers. Such relationships entail mutual concessions from the two parties entering the agreement, such as lower prices for a given quantity when selling or higher prices when buying. By doing so, the contracting parties attempt to neutralize extreme fluctuations in the market. The intermediary buys more than she would have done without *pratik* when there is a glut in the market, and in a situation when demand is high the seller does not sell scarce goods without first offering them to her *pratik*.

The *pratik* institution also saves some of the time normally involved in searching for goods. Finally, it should be mentioned that another form of non-price competition is that of trying to buy goods outside the market-places. Many *Madam Sara* employ agents who trace the produce among the peasants before it gets to the market to ensure that their employer is not without stock when leaving the market-place.

Thus, the conclusion to be drawn from this brief discussion is that the Haitian marketing system for agricultural goods appears to work smoothly and efficiently. Profit levels are not excessive. There is considerable freedom of entry. All parties involved have many opportunities to make short-cuts in the marketing chain. Prices are set by the forces of demand and supply. Non-price competition is used in addition to price competition.

Therefore, given the apparent efficiency of the Haitian marketing system, we would expect that the correlation analysis, as amended by Blyn, would apply throughout Haiti. However, the validity of these high correlation results are necessarily dependent upon the quality of the data. Let us then proceed with a discussion of the data base and its reliability.

The Data Base

During the course of the IICA marketing project, it was learned that four Haitian institutions, *Institut Haïtien de Statistique, Secrétairerie d'Etat du Commerce et de l'Industrie, Institut Haïtien de Promotion du Café et des Denrées d'Exportation* (IHPCADE) and *Institut de Développement Agricole et Industriel* (IDAI), were systematically collecting information regarding the prices of a number of agricultural products in a number of markets throughout the country.

The Secrétairerie did not start collecting data until 1974, and the data published by the *Institut Haïtien de Statistique* in its *Bulletin Trimestriel de Statistique* mostly turned out to be secondary data from IHPCADE, but the other two sets of price series contained enough information to warrant further analysis and publication by IICA.[25] Both IHPCADE and IDAI had collected daily data, the former since 1950 and the latter since 1965, and IHPCADE had in addition calculated weekly averages. With the aid of these series, IICA proceeded to calculate monthly averages by product and by market for the years 1965-74. This procedure yielded a total of 21 different crops and 49 different markets for which data were reasonably complete and where the units of measurement could be determined with some accuracy.[26]

James Johnson and Jerry La Gra point out that although time series exist for the entire 1965-74 period, these series are reasonably complete only for 1971-4.[27] This is not quite true, however. For some products it is possible to go back to 1969. We will therefore presently use the 1969-74 period. Furthermore, reasonably complete data exist only for a limited number of products. We have selected five commodities – rice, grain millet, grain corn, ground corn and red beans. Rex Oro rice was available for seven markets only. We therefore added other, coarser rice varieties as well. In this way, fourteen new series can be added to the original seven. This would, however, leave us with two overlaps, since for Cayes and Jacmel we have two series for each market. Since there are more non-Rex Oro series than Rex Oro series, we therefore dropped Rex Oro for these two markets. This procedure leaves a total of nineteen markets for rice of different quality. Assuming that the different varieties are fairly close substitutes, the procedure may be defended.

A remedy had to be found for the missing monthly data in many of the time series. Here, one could either omit those months where data were missing or try to fill in the gaps. The latter approach was chosen. We simply decided to follow Johnson and La Gra here:

A decision had to be reached as to which missing data could be effectively estimated and what was the best estimation procedure.

The prices for a number of products were plotted by month for each year that there was information and it was discovered that, in some cases, the patterns of price variation varied from year to year. A number of test estimates were performed on prices where the values were already known. These tests show that the estimates of prices based on the prices for the previous month and the following month in the same year were more accurate than estimates that included prices for the previous and following year for the same month. Thus, missing prices with adjacent prices for the same year were estimated by a simple average for the prices of the month preceding and the month following the missing price for that year.[28]

The upper limit for the number of consecutive observations to be filled in was arbitrarily put at four. Thus, linear interpolation was used for filling in missing observations which were not the last month of the year.[29] To obtain figures for those cases where the last or the last few (up to four) observations were missing, a different procedure was followed. We then used those observations for the remaining years which had *not* been filled in with the aid of linear interpolation, took the last month for which there was an observation in 1974 (the last year) and calculated the average price for the remaining (non-doctored) years. We repeated the procedure with the December observations, and thereafter assumed that the December value for 1974 followed this trend. (If September, October and November observations were also missing for 1974, these could subsequently be filled in with the aid of linear interpolation.) These two operations added 252 observations (out of a total of 5,256) to our data base.

Figure 11.1 shows the location of the markets included in the analysis, and Table 11.1 provides the key to the map. Altogether, series from 20 different markets could be used, although in only one case could use be made of all of them. The number used varied between 8 and 20; rice — 19, grain millet — 8, grain corn — 20, ground corn — 11, red beans — 15.

Figure 11.1

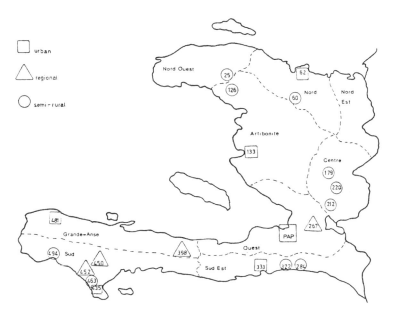

Table 11.1: Markets Used in the Analysis

IICA number *	Market	Source of data	Market type
PAP	Port-au-Prince**	IHPCADE	Urban
25	Bassin Bleu	IDAI	Semi-rural
60	Grison Garde	IDAI	Semi-rural
62	Cap-Haïtien	IHPCADE	Urban
126	Gros Morne	IDAI	Semi-rural
133	St-Marc	IHPCADE	Urban
179	Thomonde	IDAI	Semi-rural
212	Mirebalais	IDAI	Semi-rural
220	Lascahobas	IDAI	Semi-rural
267	Croix-des-Bouquets	IHPCADE	Regional
284	Marigot	IDAI	Semi-rural
322	Cayes-Jacmel	IDAI	Semi-rural
333	Jacmel	IDAI	Urban
398	St-Michel du Sud	IDAI	Regional
435	Les Cayes†	IHPCADE	Urban
450	Camp-Perrin	IDAI	Regional
452	Ducis	IDAI	Regional
463	Chantal	IDAI	Semi-rural
481	Jérémie	IHPCADE	Urban
494	Les Anglais	IDAI	Semi-rural

* According to the classification in La Gra, Fanfan and Charleston (1975).
This document also gives a description of each market-place.
** Not numbered in the IICA classification, since Port-au-Prince contains many
markets, each of which has a separate number.
† IDAI data for rice.

The Reliability of the Data

As we are already aware, our data are not perfect. Some observations were missing and had to be filled in. Other deficiencies in the data may also bias our results. One such source of errors has been encountered in the discussion of the rice series: different qualities of each product. In the case of rice, this source is presumably not a serious one, since we know what kind of quality has been measured in each market. The problem, however, also arises for the other products, but when the IICA personnel started to analyze the IHPCADE and IDAI price data, they tried to minimize this type of error. In the first place, IHPCADE and IDAI data were comparable for all the products included in the present study (and in the one by Johnson and La Gra).[30] Secondly, care was taken to include price data for one variety only of each product. In the case of corn, two varieties are reported: grain and ground, but the price of the ground variety is consistently higher due to the cost of processing.

The reported data could also be distorted by the fact that in Haiti the basic units for measurement are volume and not weight measures. Thus, all our six products are measured in *gros-marmites* (gro-mamit), but the *gros-marmite* is not a fully standardized measure:[31]

The size of the 'gro-mamit' is dependent upon the size of cans imported into Haiti or manufactured by Haiti Metal. These cans tend to be the standard No 10 can. One exception is when the gro-mamit is manually produced for enterprising intermediaries in which cases the weight of a product may vary by ½ pound in either direction depending upon whether the 'marchande' is buying or selling.[32]

When people refer to the *gros-marmite*, however, they often refer to a marmite of five, six, seven, eight or even ten, depending on the quantity equivalence in pounds. The latter of course differs from product to product. The IICA team collected *gros-marmite* measures from different regions of Haiti in an attempt to determine the average pound equivalent of a *gros-marmite* for a number of products. Their results are reproduced in Table 11.2. In no case did the *gros-marmite* measure for a particular product vary by more than 0.25 pound, and 'this variation was due to the fact that the mamit had had the bottom raised inside the can by an enterprising marchand (intermediary)',[33] which means that basically, the *gros-marmite* measures used for the same product are the same throughout the country.

Table 11.2: Average Weight Equivalent in Pounds of One *Gros-marmite* for Different Products

Product	Pound equivalent
Rice	6
Grain millet	5.75
Grain corn	5.75
Ground corn	5.25
Red beans	5.75

Source: La Gra, Charleston and Fanfan (1975), p. 32.

The practice of referring to marmite of seven, eight, etc., can instead be explained by the business practice prevailing:

> The fact that the 'gro-mamit' used throughout Haiti are of basically the same size leaves one with the question: What is a mamit of 7, of 8, or of 10, etc.? The answer is that in times of abundance of a specific crop or perhaps in a particular market, the marchand (intermediary) may use the term mamit but instead of a true mamit (equivalent to approximately six one-pound cups) she may sell the purchaser 7, 8, 9 or 10 of the smaller units (gobelets). Thus it seems that while the basic measuring unit (gro-mamit) is approximately the same size throughout Haiti, it is the terminology in reference to the 'mamit' which varies. When reference is made to a mamit of 8, one is referring to 8 gobelets (small tin cups).
> Depending on the region, 8 'gobelets' may vary in weight between 5.5 and 8 pounds. Thus 8 'gobelets' may be equal to or exceed the average weight of a standard gro-mamit.[34]

In the case of IDAI data, the pound equivalent of the *gros-marmites* were known, and for the IHPCADE data, *gros-marmite* prices were converted to pound prices with the aid of the conversion factors in Table 11.2.

A third weakness relates to the processing of the collected data. The collection itself appears to be fairly precise. Both IHPCADE and IDAI send agents to the market-places to interview the customers and to watch the transactions taking place, and this procedure, according to the IICA team who observed the collection in several instances, seems to be quite accurate.[35] It is when these data are processed at the respective regional offices or at the main IHPCADE office in the capital that errors may be introduced. In the calculation of the weekly averages, urban, regional and semi-rural market-places in some instances – presumably the larger urban concentrations – may be mixed. Moreover, the calculations are made by hand, which may be a source of further error. In the case of IDAI, no such errors should be present since the raw data are forwarded directly to the central office in Port-au-Prince and are filed there without having been processed.[36]

To conclude, our price data are not perfect, but on the other hand we have not found any deficiencies which are of such magnitude as to preclude their use for testing purposes. Most of the possible sources of error have been checked in one way or another.

Results

The average correlation coefficients for the 'raw' series were lower than those obtained by Cummings and Lele for Indian wheat but more or less of the same magnitude as those reported by Gupta and Thakur for other agricultural products in India and higher than the figures obtained in most of the African studies; rice: 0.82, grain millet: 0.72, grain corn: 0.77, ground corn: 0.83 and red beans: 0.77. Already this is a strong indication of the low reliability of 'raw' correlations. Provided that the Haitian marketing system is an efficient one, we would have expected higher figures.

The coefficients obtained after grouping and detrending data in the same manner as Blyn are shown in Table 11.3, where a comparison with Blyn's results is also made. It is immediately seen that the average coefficient for each of the products is approximately in the same range as the one calculated by Blyn for India. The supposedly well-integrated Haitian market system does not give rise to higher correlation between the residuals after removal of the trend for each month.[37]

The Haitian data also corroborate the finding by Blyn that correlation appears to be lower during the harvest months when most of the deliveries are made. For all the food grains there is a tendency for correlation to fall towards the end of the year (a little earlier for red beans). This is not what one would expect *a priori*:

> Viewed as a whole, trading activity in Haiti's rural market-places reaches its peak about December, declines very sharply in the first months of the year, climbs to a spring climax around Easter, and

then remains relatively stable (sometimes with a slight rise and fall in the late summer) until the November-December peak once more. This description is subject, of course, to variation and refinement, depending upon the region, the rainfall, the particular crops being considered, and so forth.[38]

Table 11.3: Average Correlation Coefficient for Given Months for Different Products. Haiti, 1969-74, Punjab and Delhi, 1956-64

Month	Rice	Grain millet	Grain corn	Ground corn	Red beans	Wheat
			Haiti			Nine Indian markets
January	0.55	0.44	0.65	0.46	0.74	0.95
February	0.52	0.85	0.64	0.54	0.72	0.88
March	0.56	0.92	0.78	0.70	0.73	0.94
April	0.70	0.95	0.80	0.75	0.73	0.68
May	0.78	0.96	0.79	0.71	0.71	0.42
June	0.76	0.96	0.74	0.68	0.66	0.44
July	0.68	0.94	0.83	0.81	0.65	0.50
August	0.71	0.90	0.81	0.84	0.25	0.71
September	0.61	0.87	0.66	0.77	0.15	0.30
October	0.50	0.48	0.34	0.34	0.28	0.56
November	0.43	0.28	0.15	0.21	0.32	0.80
December	0.41	0.11	0.19	0.22	0.43	0.95
Average	0.60	0.72	0.62	0.59	0.53	0.68

Sources: Haitian figures computed by the authors; Indian data: Blyn (1973), p. 57.

The picture conveyed by the present correlation series differs from the impression given by the quotation. One should *a priori* expect to find better correlation between market-places during periods of abundant supply of goods than when supply is scanty and erratic. In the former case, the itinerant traders should more easily be able to carry goods from one market-place to another so as to create a more uniform price picture, whereas when only smaller quantities are put on the market a split picture could arise. This is, however, not confirmed by the present findings. Neither can we explain the lower correlation during the winter months by the seasonal distribution of rain, since the winter is in general the period with *least* precipitation.

These findings are open to more than one interpretation. One explanation is that the Haitian internal marketing system for agricultural goods is not at all as efficient as commonly alleged. Other possibilities, however, appear to be more realistic. For correlation analysis to yield high coefficients when integration is high, trade must be unidirectional. Otherwise, the method breaks down. William Jones has constructed a 'gold point' model of trade where two markets, A and B, both produce and consume a particular commodity. Thus, trade in both directions between A and B is possible, and the price in market A may exceed or fall short of the price in B with an amount equal to the transport costs between the two markets, i.e. the price in A can vary with as much as twice the transport costs *without* affecting the price in B.[39] This is not accounted for in the correlation analysis which implicitly assumes that trade flows in only one direction between the two markets and that the range of possible price variation is limited to the transport costs between the two markets.

In Haiti, the situation appears even more complicated. The market system is basically vertical, i.e. a product does usually not travel between two markets at the same level in the market hierarchy. If it is to go from market C to market D on the same level, it usually does so only via market E on a higher or lower level. If then, in addition, there is (indirect) two-way trade between markets at the same level, the price in C may vary with twice the transport costs between C and E plus between E and D before affecting the price in D. In this situation, correlation coefficients do not provide any guidance as to the degree of integration between markets on the same hierarchical level. A very detailed knowledge of the trading patterns is needed before anything regarding the integration of the system can be inferred from our price data. During the non-harvest season, on the other hand, trade is more likely to be unidirectional with goods flowing from areas where storage takes place to deficit areas.

The reason for the mainly 'vertical' trade pattern is to be found in the behavior of the *Madam Sara*. These generally specialize in traveling along a *given* route which takes them upwards and downwards in the hierarchy of market-places rather than in horizontal or circular directions. In this way they keep coming back to the same markets and can therefore more easily establish lasting reliable contacts with customers and producers.[40]

This finding puts us in a rather unfortunate position regarding the possibilities of extracting information regarding market integration and competition from price data. Unless we have sufficient knowledge both of transport costs between different markets, of the structure (direction) of trade and of the share of different markets in the supply in a given market-place, there is not much we can do, especially not with correlation analysis. The conclusion reached by Barbara Harriss,

'Until the technique is greatly refined, its diagnostic use should be abandoned',[41] appears to be correct, not only as far as correlation of 'raw' price data is concerned, but also when it comes to correlating residuals after removing trend elements and seasonal factors.

Notes

1. An overall evaluation of most of these studies is made in Harriss (1979).
2. Cummings (1967), pp. 88, 95.
3. Lele (1971), p. 89.
4. Gupta (1973), pp. 118-25.
5. Thakur (1974).
6. Lele (1971), pp. 84-98, 245-6.
7. Jones (1968), pp. 110-11.
8. Thodey (1968).
9. Gilbert (1969), p. 249.
10. Hays (1975), p. 72.
11. Kohlers (1977), pp. 35-44.
12. Berg (1977).
13. Southworth, Jones and Pearson (1979), p. 189.
14. Blyn (1973).
15. Harriss (1979), pp. 202-3.
16. See La Gra, Fanfan and Charleston (1975).
17. Institut Haïtien de Statistique (1973), p. 1.
18. The name comes from that of a migratory bird that 'flies from place to place and never fails to find its food wherever it might be' (Murray and Alvarez (1973), p. 28), but the term also is somewhat derogatory, since this bird is known to pillage the peasants' crops.
19. For more details, see Lundahl (1979), pp. 145-9, and the literature cited there.
20. See Moral (1961), pp. 245-7. Cf. also Pierre-Charles (1965), pp. 154-5, and Brisson (1968), pp. 47-51.
21. See Mintz (1960:1. 1960:2, 1960:3, 1961:1, 1961:2 and 1964).
22. In addition to the Mintz works, see Métraux *et al.* (1951), p. 125; Underwood (1960), p. 32; and Rotberg with Clague (1971), p. 281.
23. Lundahl (1979), Chapter 4.
24. The Haitian currency unit, the *gourde*, equals 20 US cents since 1919.
25. See La Gra, Charleston and Fanfan (1975); IICA (1975:1, 1975:2).
26. These crops and markets are listed in La Gra, Charleston and Fanfan (1975).
27. Johnson and La Gra (1975), p. 5.
28. Ibid.
29. Even if the first observation in the series was missing, linear interpolation could be used, since in all cases data for December 1968 were available.
30. La Gra, Charleston and Fanfan (1975), p. 29. These products are the only ones for which this is true.
31. For a list of 160 different volume and weight measures employed in Haiti, see Moral (1959), pp. 79-81. Cf. also Duplan (1975), pp. 8-17; Murray and Alvarez (1973), pp. 22-5; and Mintz (1961:2), pp. 25-31.
32. La Gra, Charleston and Fanfan (1975), note, p. 33.
33. Ibid.
34. Ibid., pp. 33-4.
35. Ibid., pp. 11-16.

36. Ibid., pp. 39-40.
37. The coefficients in Table 11.3 come from a short time series of only six years, which means that for a coefficient to be significant at the 5 per cent level it has to equal at least 0.81. The percentage of coefficients of 0.80 or more for each product and month is shown in Table 11.4, which reveals the same type of seasonal pattern as that shown in Table 11.3.

Table 11.4: Percentage of Correlation Coefficients of 0.80 or More

Month	Rice	Grain millet	Grain corn	Ground corn	Red beans
January	23	29	38	18	54
February	23	79	41	33	43
March	23	89	63	49	48
April	46	100	57	58	51
May	68	100	64	47	42
June	51	100	58	56	33
July	64	96	71	67	33
August	57	86	62	75	19
September	42	79	32	53	10
October	22	29	20	16	10
November	23	14	18	13	12
December	24	7	14	15	24

38. Mintz (1964), pp. 271-2.
39. Jones (1968), pp. 116-17.
40. Cf. Lundahl (1980), p. 147.
41. Harriss (1979), p. 203.

Bibliography

Berg, Elliot, 'Upper Volta', in CILSS/Club du Sahel, *Marketing, Food Policy and Storage of Food Grains in the Sahel: A Survey, Vol. 2: Country Studies 1*, Center for Research on Economic Development, University of Michigan/US Agency for International Development, Ann Arbor, 1977

Blyn, George. 'Price Series Correlation as a Measure of Market Integration', *Indian Journal of Agricultural Economics*, vol. 28, 1973

Brisson, Gérald. *Les relations agraires dans l'Haïti contemporaine*. Mimeo. México, D.F. (?), 1968

Cummings, Ralph W. *Pricing Efficiency in the Indian Wheat Market*. New Delhi, 1967

Duplan, Verdy. *Equivalents des unités de mesure et emballages utilisés pour le transport des produits agricoles*. IICA, Port-au-Prince, 1975

Gilbert, Elon H. 'Marketing of Staple Foods in Northern Nigeria: A Study of Staple Food Marketing Systems Serving Kano City', PhD dissertation, Stanford University, Stanford, 1969

Gupta, R.C. *Agricultural Prices in a Backward Economy*. Delhi, 1973

Harriss, Barbara. 'There is Method in my Madness: Or Is It Vice Versa? Measuring Agricultural Market Performance', *Food Research Institute Studies*, vol. 17, 1979

Hays, H.M., Jr. *The Marketing and Storage of Food Grains in Northern Nigeria*. Samaru Miscellaneous Papers no. 50, Institute of Agricultural Research, Samaru, Zaria, 1975

IICA. *Les prix des produits agricoles dans les marchés haïtiens. Annexe 3*. IICA, Port-au-Prince, 1975:1

IICA. *Les prix des produits agricoles dans les marchés haïtiens. Annex 4*. IICA, Port-au-Prince, 1975:2

Institut Haïtien de Statistique. *Résultats préliminaires du recensement général de la population, du logement et de l'agriculture (septembre 1971)*. IHS, Port-au-Prince, 1973

Johnson, James L. and La Gra, Jerry. *The Internal Agricultural Marketing System of Haiti. A Price Analysis*. IICA, Port-au-Prince, 1975

Jones, William O. 'The Structure of Staple Food Marketing in Nigeria as Revealed by Price Analysis', *Food Research Institute Studies*, vol. 8, 1968

Kohlers, D. 'Niger', in CILSS/Club du Sahel, *Marketing, Food Policy and Storage of Food Grains in the Sahel: A Survey, Vol. 2: Country Studies 1*, Center for Research on Economic Development, University of Michigan/US Agency for International Development, Ann Arbor, 1977

La Gra, Jerry, Charleston, Wesner and Fanfan, Guy. *Prix des produits agricoles dans les marchés haïtiens*. IICA, Port-au-Prince, 1975

La Gra, Jerry, Fanfan, Guy and Charleston, Wesner. *Les marchés publics d'Haïti* IICA, Port-au-Prince, 1975

Lele, Uma J. *Food Grain Marketing in India. Private Performance and Public Policy*. Bombay, 1971

Lundahl, Mats. *Peasants and Poverty: A Study of Haiti*. London, 1979

Lundahl, Mats. 'The State of Spatial Economic Research on Haiti: A Selective Survey', *Anthropologica*, NS, vol. 22, 1980

Métraux, Alfred in collaboration with E. Berrouet and Jean and Suzanne Comhaire-Sylvain. *Making a Living in the Marbial Valley (Haiti)*. Paris, 1951

Mintz, Sidney W. 'Peasant Markets', *Scientific American*, vol. 203, 1960:1

Mintz, Sidney, W. 'A Tentative Typology of Eight Haitian Marketplaces', *Revista de Ciencias Sociales*, vol. 4, 1960:2

Mintz, Sidney W. 'Le systéme du marché rural dans l'économie haïtienne', *Bulletin du Bureau d'Ethnologie*, vol. 3, 1960:3

Mintz, Sidney W. 'Pratik: Haitian Personal Economic Relationships', in: *Proceedings of the 1961 Annual Spring Meeting of the American Ethnological Society*. Seattle, 1961:1

Mintz, Sidney W. 'Standards of Value and Units of Measure in the Fond-des-Nègres Market Place, Haiti', *Journal of the Royal Anthropological Institute*, vol. 91, 1961:2

Mintz, Sidney W. 'The Employment of Capital by Market Women in Haiti', in Raymond Firth and Basil S. Yamey (eds.). *Capital, Saving and Credit in Peasant Societies*. London, 1964

Moral, Paul. *L'économie haïtienne*. Port-au-Prince, 1959

Moral, Paul. *Le paysan haïtien (Etude sur la vie rurale en Haïti)*. Paris, 1961

Murray, Gerald F. and Alvarez, Maria D. *The Marketing of Beans in Haiti. An Exploratory Study*. IICA, Port-au-Prince, 1973

Pierre-Charles, Gérard. *La economía haïtiana y su vïa de desarrollo*. México, D.F., 1965

Rotberg, Robert I. with Clague, Christopher K. *Haiti: The Politics of Squalor*. Boston, 1971

Southworth, V. Roy, Jones, William O. and Pearson, Scott R. 'Food Crop Marketing in Atebubu District, Ghana', *Food Research Institute Studies*, vol. 17, 1979

Thakur, D.S. 'Foodgrain Marketing Efficiency: A Case Study of Gujarat', *Indian Journal of Agricultural Economics*, vol. 29, 1974

Thodey, Alan R. *Marketing of Staple Foods in Western Nigeria, Vol. 1: Summary*

and Conclusions. Stanford Research Institute, Menlo Park, 1968
Underwood, Frances W. 'The Marketing System in Peasant Haiti', in Sidney W. Mintz (ed.). *Papers in Caribbean Anthropology.* New Haven, 1960

IV. CHANGE AND STAGNATION

12 CO-OPERATIVE STRUCTURES IN THE HAITIAN ECONOMY

The Haitian peasant is usually pictured as an individualist and the Haitian economy is strongly pervaded by individualist features. Land is privately owned. Production of agricultural goods takes place on some 600,000 private farms.[1] The marketing of agricultural produce is carried out by middlemen who compete and work for their own individual benefit. Yet, co-operative structures have in the past played an important role in the economy and the remnants of these structures can still be found in contemporary Haitian society.

The importance of co-operative structures has, however, undergone a decline as compared to the situation a couple of generations ago. In spite of the manifest stagnation in the economy, particularly in the agricultural sector, Haiti has been subject to important economic and social changes during both the past and present centuries. Population has been growing while the natural resources have been shrinking, with a slow deterioration in the standard of living as the most visible result.[2] The extent of migration to both urban areas and abroad has increased which has led to the break up of the old family structure, based on the extended family system. As a result of these changes, collectivism and co-operation in economic life have gradually given way to individualism.

Today, many of the traditional forms of mutual aid and sharing of efforts and risks are in decline. At the same time, the problem of making a living assumes ever bigger proportions. Land is becoming increasingly scarce and the standard of living is being depressed towards the subsistence level. In an agricultural sector characterized by a low technological level, where the degree of control over nature is virtually zero, the ever-present risk of a harvest failure or a fall in agricultural prices becomes one of the greatest of all the worries of the peasants.

In facing this problem, the peasants receive very little help from their government. In contrast to both former times when the various risks were largely handled by means of co-operative efforts and to the fully modernized, industrial societies where elaborate social insurance schemes mitigate the impact of such adversities, the Haitian peasants find themselves in a precarious, intermediate or transitional position. The traditional structures are on their way out. However, no modern ones have been substituted for them, even though the need for mechanisms that reduce risks of all kinds continues to be present. A gap that has not yet been spanned has been created between the traditional and the modern in Haiti.

The purpose of the present essay is to discuss the role of co-operative structures in the Haitian economy. We will begin with an account of the traditional forms of co-operation and their economic functions. The gradual erosion of these co-operative structures as a result of the transformation of Haitian society will then be discussed in the light of the problems that have arisen when a modern social insurance system does not exist for the mass of the population. The second part of the essay deals with the possibility of developing the traditional co-operative structures in a fashion that makes it possible for them to fulfill, in today's Haiti, functions similar to those fulfilled in the past: social insurance and dampening of risks.

The *Lakou*

Life in the Haitian countryside during the latter half of the nineteenth century and the beginning of the present differed from life in contemporary rural Haiti in several respects. One of these was family organization. Today, the nuclear family of five or six people is the rule. A century ago, the extended family, headed by the oldest male, the *grandet*, *père* or *don*, grouped spatially in a *lakou*,[3] was the dominant unit.

The *lakou* is sometimes defined as 'the members of one large extended family (usually including 3 or 4 generations), having a common physically demarcated residence'.[4] Often, however, the term is reserved for the cluster of houses itself.[5] The number of houses varied considerably depending, for example, on the age of the establishment, with older *lakous* often, but not always, containing more buildings.[6] Ranges from five to nearly a hundred (in extreme cases) have been mentioned.[7] The *lakou* members as a rule also shared a common ancestral shrine and a burial ground on the *lakou*.

The origin of the *lakou* system is not well investigated, but quite probably, the system derives its roots from the time of the agrarian reform begun by Alexandre Pétion who in 1809 undertook to redistribute government lands.[8] Soldiers and officers in the Haitian army were given plots ranging from 5 *carreaux*,[9] in the case of non-commissioned officers and soldiers, to 25 *carreaux*, in the case of colonels,[10] to be held in perpetuity by the recipients and their offspring.[11] This process was continued by his successors, with few exceptions, until the end of the nineteenth century. As soon as this redistribution had begun, the plantation system began to crumble and an economy based on peasant ownership of the land was substituted for it.

Quite probably, it is in this process that we have to look for the origins of the *lakou*. Rémy Bastien, in his study of family life in the Marbial Valley in the late 1940s, traced the history of four *lakous* back to their foundation. All of them had been established during the 1830-45 period when a large number of people received grants of state land in the area or began to lease land from absentee owners. Two of these four *lakou* founders were army people.[12]

The first house of a *lakou* was naturally that of its founder and his family. Some years later, when the sons started to grow up, they built new houses, close to that of their father, and moved into these, alone or with a wife. In this way, increasing numbers of houses were added to the original one, to form finally the type of pattern referred to above.

This clustered pattern of settlement constituted a type of co-operative structure based on the extended family. It was an advantage to have one's kinsfolk nearby in case intruders had to be fended off. The co-operation, however, extended into the economic sphere as well. To understand how this worked it has to be kept in mind that Haiti before the mid-nineteenth century was a country where land was abundant in relation to labor, especially since the administrative apparatus was weak at all levels, which in turn made it difficult to prevent squatting. Thus, a person owning, say 25 *carreaux*, would have difficulties cultivating this area unless the necessary labor could be prevented from going into easily available land outside. Therefore, a pattern was established whereby a father by means of a pre-inheritance grant gave one-fourth of a *carreau* to each of his sons when they entered their teens or early twenties. The produce grown on this plot was the property of the young man who was free to dispose of it in whatever way he liked. In return, the youth had to provide labor for the cultivation of his father's land as well. Hereby, the father ensured that his sons would stay with him and not run off to work on somebody else's land or find a plot for themselves in some other district.[13] This contract also made it natural for the sons to live on their father's land, on the *lakou*, knowing that as the father died enough land would be inherited by each to make a decent living possible.

The *lakou* represented a mixture of patriarchate and co-operative. The need to keep the family labor force on the family land to a certain extent explains why discipline had to be exercised by the head of the *lakou*. The *père* made the decisions and his word was final. All the members of a *lakou* were subject to a code of conduct which in the ultimate instance was sanctioned by the authority of the head of the *lakou*.[14] Some of these obligations were strongly tied to the quest for survival of the *lakou* unit and its individual members. Thus, Bastien points out that one rule was to ensure that the members of the *lakou* saw to it that the individuals did not lose the esteem in which they were held by others, above all by not becoming involved in any scandals. This introduced a strong measure of social control which, however, also contributed to the cohesion of the *lakou*.

A second rule was that the extended family should act as a tight-knit unit towards the outside world. Thirdly, in case of contagious diseases, there was an obligation to isolate the individuals with the disease, so as not to jeopardize the health status of the group. Fourthly, and here a co-operative element enters the picture, the various family units that constituted the *lakou* should send some of the food they cooked to other units, receiving in their turn some of the meals prepared by others. These food exchanges could, however, be unilateral for long periods. No balanced obligations in the strict sense were present, but the reciprocity was rather of the generalized kind.[15] The obligation contracted upon the receipt of food was to return this gift some time in the future, when means were available and/or there was a need for a return gift. Finally, there was also a second obligation of a co-operative kind: to assist when something went wrong, as when somebody fell ill. It should be noted that there was a corresponding obligation on the part of the sick person to call upon the relatives for assistance.

Thus, the code of conduct of the *lakou* strongly emphasized both the subordination of the individual interest to that of the collective and the pooling of efforts in a co-operative fashion. Co-operation in combination with individual behavior that was geared to meeting the interests of the *lakou* as a whole was the rule. 'Mutual assistance in an infinite number of cases is the very essence of *lakou* life', writes Rémy Bastien.[16] This assistance was backed by the authority vested in the oldest male member of the collective, who was its undisputed leader.

When the founder of a *lakou* died, his authority passed on to the oldest of his male heirs. In economic matters, however, the latter had a less decisive voice than his father, simply because the Haitian inheritance laws followed the *Code Napoléon* with all children inheriting equal shares.[17] Thus the second-generation head of a *lakou* had less land than his father, unless he had acquired more in the market.

Still, Bastien calls the second generation of the *lakou* system the 'golden age'.[18] The reason for employing this label is that with a larger labor force at the disposal of the *lakou* than during the first generation, more of the total land could be cultivated, which meant a higher standard of living for everybody. It was for this situation that the *lakou* system was ideal. By imposing a co-operative spirit on its members, it extracted more work from them. In principle, everyone who had received a pre-inheritance grant or owned land by inheritance was responsible for feeding himself and his dependants. The best way to do so was by means of working the plot carefully.[19] In addition, labor was always provided for working the land of the fathers. The reciprocity principles, finally, ensured that the higher standard of living also became a safer one, by smoothing out to some extent individual differences in production:

> this was when every peasant with self esteem 'owned a good horse and a good saddle.' The families who today produce some two hundred kilos of coffee then harvested five hundred. Some bought houses in . . . town . . .[20]

The *Coumbite*

The co-operative spirit inherent in the *lakou* type of society has perhaps its most typical manifestation in the collective labor team that is traditionally employed in Haiti as soon as any agricultural or non-agricultural task of importance is to be carried out: the *coumbite.*[21]

The origin of the *coumbite* is not quite clear. The practice of co-operative work for mutual benefit did not exist during the colonial period and during the first 40 years of the post-independence period no foreign visitor to the country who has left a written record behind mentions it. Still, quite probably, the *coumbite* tradition was shaped between 1809, when the state patrimony was first redistributed, and the middle of the century. Similar practices exist in West Africa and Melville Herskovits maintains that these also constitute the origin of the Haitian labor team.[22] Collective work is, however, not a feature which is uniquely African: similar practices can be found in most parts of the world. In addition, the French planters used collective slave gangs on the plantations of Saint-Domingue before 1791. Hence, the *coumbite* appears to have a 'double' origin. Team or gang labor was most familiar to the Haitians from the slavery period and verbal traditions regarding West African practices ought to have been preserved well into the nineteenth century.[23]

Even though co-operative labor is resorted to for all tasks that require a concentrated work effort, its most important employment has been in agriculture. The combination of *lakous* with their concentrated settlement with family labor under immediate control and the organization of labor in teams provided a solution to the problem caused by the loss of some 150,000 souls during the wars of liberation.[24] By ensuring work discipline and a more or less steady rhythm of operations, economies of scale were obtained which would not otherwise have been realized if the lots had been cultivated on a nuclear family labor basis alone.

The need for co-operative efforts arises in agriculture because of the concentration in time of certain agricultural operations. The timing of the latter are determined mainly by the timing of the rainy seasons. Clearing, for example, cannot take place too early, since the weeds will then come back and the land will have to be cleared a second time. Nor can it be delayed too long, since in that case the heavy tropical rains will already have set in. Clearing will become a cumbersome affair and time will be lost during which the plants should have been in the ground to benefit from the rain needed to bring them to maturity in time.

Around 1850, the co-operative work force was an established feature of Haitian rural life. With time, the labor team developed into more sophisticated, sometimes quite elaborate, organizations on a permanent or semi-permanent basis where agricultural work was but one of many purposes. In the late 1920s one observer noted that: 'The purpose of these organizations is fourfold. First, they are cooperative labor groups; second, the members are afforded protection; third, they are mutual benefit societies; and fourth, they provide social entertainment.'[25]

Basically, three different types of co-operative labor team may be distinguished: the *coumbite* proper, the *escouade* and the *société de travail*.[26] The most loosely organized variety is the *coumbite*, with an average size of about 50 people. This team is based on reciprocity principles which are mainly of a balanced, *quid pro quo*, type. When there is a need for it, a group of peasants get together to do a determined job during one day, from approximately 10 a.m. to 4 p.m. (at the latest). An invitation has then to be made eight days before the *coumbite* is to take place. This invitation may be either closed or open, or it may take place via an intermediary. A closed invitation means that only those invited by the organizer of the *coumbite* may show up. An open invitation allows those invited to bring other people with them.

Finally, when the invitation is delegated to another person, the latter assumes the entire responsibility for bringing workers to the field on the agreed date.

There is no obligation to participate for a person who has been invited to join a *coumbite*, and many of those who show up may do little work, or even none at all. Still, they must be given food and drink. Meals and alcoholic beverages for the participants are one of the ways in which the organizer of the *coumbite* reciprocates the work carried out. (Money, on the other hand, is never exchanged unless an *escouade* is present simultaneously, and then only as payment for the services of that organization.) Furthermore, the organizer at a later point in time may participate in *coumbites* organized by people who have worked for him. When a *gros nèg* (a member of the rural upper class) extends an invitation to a *coumbite*, he does not, however, reciprocate by participating himself in other *coumbites*. Instead he resorts to other types of favors for those who have worked on his field or by a payment in kind.

The *escouade*[27] is the smallest of the three groupings – some 5 to 15 people.[28] It possesses much more stable features than the *coumbite*. It is also the most genuinely co-operative labor team in that it builds on strict reciprocity. All the members of an *escouade* must be capable of working and the work performed takes place on an egalitarian basis, although the exact organization principle differs from *escouade* to *escouade*. A member who does not show up for work either has to send a substitute or the money required to get one. Each member has a day which belongs to him, when the team works on his plot. Should the field not be ready for cultivation, the member can sell his turn to someone else. No member has the right to more than one day until all others have had theirs. The services of the *escouade* are also sold to people who do not participate in the labor team, and then most of the time against money (or in some cases goods).

The last, and largest, type of labor team is the *société de travail*. Instances of up to 180 members have been recorded.[29] Like the *escouade*, the *société* is based on a rotation principle and in the same manner, its services are sold to outsiders, but against food and drink, not against money. The *société* is not an egalitarian association, but it contains both working and non-working members (dignitaries). The non-working dignitaries have the right to a day's work by the *société* when they need it, but they are not included in the systematic rotation which the working members enjoy.

The *Sangue*

The third and last traditional co-operative structure that we will deal with is the *sangue* (*solde, associé, comblé*), a mutual rotating credit organization which is widespread in Haiti.[30] Even less is known about the origin of the *sangue* than of the origins of the *lakou* or the *coumbite*.[31] Presumably, however, it goes back to the nineteenth century and has developed along with the need for money in transactions as the cash nexus penetrated the countryside.

A *sangue* is born when a need for it arises and dies when the need is no longer there. Thus, in principle *sangues* are not permanent organizations. They may, however, show considerable constancy in situations where several consecutive ventures among the members are financed via them. The *sangue* is headed by a president, who is generally the person who took the initiative in the creation of the association. The common, rotating fund of the *sangue* is known as the *main*. The latter is paid by the members at regular intervals, generally each week, and is then handed out to each member in turn.

The structure of *sangues* varies in complexity, from the 'simple' *sangue* where all members have the same rights and obligations to more complex structures where, due to differences in member payments, rights and obligations differ in a corresponding way and *sangues-réseau* (net *sangues*) where one or more of the members are simultaneously involved in more than one *sangue* with a simpler structure. It may be open to new members or closed, if the members so choose.

The only guarantee for the efficient functioning of a *sangue* is the members themselves and their readiness to comply with the principles of payment and rotation. The organizer of a *sangue* as a rule is a reputable person who can be trusted by the members and he is generally careful to invite only such persons that can be trusted to pay their shares regularly. The president is the person who basically decides whether a particular person may join a *sangue* or not. In this matter, he may or may not consult the other members.

The Decline of the *Lakou*

Together, the *lakou* and the *coumbite* constituted a co-operative structure around which most rural activities revolved. The mutual aid in agricultural tasks in *coumbites*, *escouades* and *sociétés* was a corollary of the extended family with its tightly coherent social system. As we have seen, these structures served in various ways to stretch the available resources, mainly the human ones, in order to ensure as high and as secure a living standard as possible, given the natural resources. The *lakou* system ensured that labor was concentrated in the most efficient way, one which gave rise to some economies of scale, when the workers were organized in *coumbite* teams. This system allowed a greater amount of work to be done in a given time than would have been the case, had everyone worked the land with the aid of the immediate (nuclear) family only. In addition, the *lakou* acted as a social insurance system, by redistributing food between nuclear families and by providing a larger unit upon which the individuals could fall back in times of need. However, both the *lakou* and the collective labor team were soon to be placed under a heavy strain as a result of the increasing population pressure. (The *sangue*, on the other hand, as we will see later, continues to operate in the same fashion as before.)

At the beginning of the present century, the size of a *lakou* could be as large as some 25 to 40 hectares.[32] However, a process of decline and gradual disintegration of the extended family subsequently set in. Rémy Bastien reports that it was difficult to find *lakous* of eight or ten houses in the Marbial Valley in the late 1940s, whereas 'In the past these *lakous* were like little villages'.[33] Similar observations were made by Paul Moral a decade later. Only some vestiges remained, he states, in the plains (Cayes, Cul-de-Sac, Artibonite and Cap-Haïtien) or in places where local circumstances were favorable to the preservation of the *lakou* structure.[34] In 1962 and 1976 Richard Schaedel and Ramiro Domínguez, respectively, found several instances of *lakous*, but those *lakous* appeared to be simplified units as compared to the earlier ones.[35] 'The family gradually leaves the tribal scheme [the extended family] to adapt to the nuclear system', writes Domínguez and concludes that 'the *lakou* hardly persists as a scheme of urbanization'.[36] The original *lakou* had been converted into a village and dispersed settlement had come instead of the extended family cluster. Even the term *lakou* has gradually changed significance. A *lakou* today could mean a few huts grouped around a yard of stamped earth in the middle of the agricultural plots. This constellation, however, is very remote from the original *lakou*, since it contains none of the social structure associated with the latter. Instead, the nuclear family, consisting of some five to six persons has emerged as the typical family unit of contemporary Haiti.

What were the reasons for the decline of the *lakou* system? To understand this problem it must be kept in mind that land was the property of the individuals and *not* of the extended family. The cohesion of the *lakou* during the first two generations, in spite of the authority exercised by the head of the extended family, was a result of voluntary co-operation rather than of imposed restrictions. Bastien concludes with respect to the situation in the late 1940s:

> To sum up, we find that the social organization of today's *lakou*, even when we are dealing with a small family, is based on the willingness of the individual to co-operate, adhering to certain ethical norms, rather than on the obligation to accept the incontestable authority of a boss.[37]

Bastien's conclusion applies even better to the nineteenth-century *lakou* system. During that period of Haitian history, land was relatively more abundant than in the 1940s and since the inheritance laws state that all children inherit equal amounts, there was of course no reason for those who did not want to participate in the *lakou* system to do so. The system, however, conferred an economic advantage on those who remained. This is what Bastien means when he states that the head of the *lakou* during the first three generations managed to produce something that was of positive economic value in that it allowed for a satisfactory standard of living this period.[38] During the first generation, the *lakou* structure was established and the practice of employing co-operative labor teams was introduced. The system reached its peak during the second generation as a result of the demographic increase. The increase in the labor force allowed for a fuller use of the available land and thereby also for an increase in the standard of living. The third generation continued along the lines laid down by the other two, but at the same time the first signs of decline became visible.

The authority of the head of the *lakou* that had previously been accepted without much question began to disappear, very much as a direct consequence of the increasing subdivision of land. Table 12.1 provides an excellent illustration of the speed with which this took place. The table does not take account of land acquisition by marriage or by purchase. However, doing so would only mean a delay in time. The trends would still remain the same. Sooner or later some of the heirs had to sell out to their relatives or to others and leave the countryside.

Table 12.1: Subdivision of a *Lakou* in the Marbial Valley, 1840-1948

Generation	Area per heir (hectares)
First, one couple, 1840	16
Second, four heirs, 1870	4
Third, 1910	
First heir, 3 descendants	1.33
Second heir, 2 descendants	2
Third heir, 5 descendants	0.80
Fourth heir, 5 descendants	0.80
Fourth, 1940	
Altogether 23 heirs	0.32 on average
Fifth generation, increasing numbers, all descendants under age in 1948	

Source: Bastien (1951), p. 140.

The process whereby some rural inhabitants were forced into seeking urban jobs was not an altogether peaceful one, however. It was accompanied by an increasing number of quarrels and lawsuits over land heritages. Around 1915, according to Bastien's informants, this phase began in which not only lawsuits but also the use of magic was resorted to, in order to force one's adversaries to migrate to towns and cities.[39] During the course of this process, the coherence of the *lakou* was gradually lost. The increasing number of reasons for conflict gradually brought about a disintegration of a *lakou* structure built on mutual assistance and co-operation.

The disintegration process may have been accelerated by the fact that in the 1880s it was already difficult to buy additional land in the neighborhood of that inherited. To solve this problem, the peasants, when they could afford it, took another *plaçée* (woman) who was installed on land not adjacent to the inherited plot. This practice, however, frequently led to an increase in the number of heirs and thus reduced the average size of the plot accruing to each child.[40]

The Problems of Vacuum: Lack of Social Insurance

The traditional co-operative structures represented a kind of informal social insurance system in the rural society. The *lakou* and the employment of co-operative labor teams served to create a sense of unity and mutuality within the extended family. This, in turn, served an important economic purpose in that it contributed to a safe standard of living for the members.

In the first place, the traditional co-operative structures allowed for a high level of production per capita. By resorting to a tightly supervised network of family labor organized in a way which conferred important economies of scale on the methods of production in a situation where land was relatively plentiful and labor was scarce, it allowed more land to be cultivated. This gave rise to a higher average standard of living than would have been the case had the *lakou* members chosen to cultivate the land solely with the aid of the labor resources provided by the nuclear family.

This intensive use of labor in a situation where land was relatively plentiful may appear to be an odd practice, but from the point of view of risk and insurance the procedure had two advantages. In the first place, a fall in average yields due to a harvest failure did not have such a drastic impact on the standard of living if additional hectares had been brought into cultivation. Secondly, the procedure allowed for reserves to be accumulated which could be used in case of need:

> In the past, in case of an emergency, a *grandet* took out one hundred pounds of coffee from his store room and sold it against cash in town or he could borrow twenty or thirty dollars from the coffee 'speculator' . . . being certain of his ability to pay back interest and capital with the sales of his next harvest.[41]

Furthermore the *lakou* system allowed loans to be taken from relatives instead of from outsiders. This was extremely important when funerals, sickness or recurrent voodoo ceremonies required heavy outlays. There would of course always have been the possibility of borrowing the money for meeting this kind of expenditure from non-family members, or of selling the land,[42] but borrowing from relatives as a rule entails much lower interest (if any at all), and the transaction costs involved in buying and selling land may easily be substantial.[43] Transactions limited to the extended family offered maximum security both from the borrower's and from the lender's point of view. The sense of co-operation and solidarity created within the *lakou* system came in handy in these situations.

As we have seen, increasing population pressure has dealt a heavy blow to the *lakou* system. Hence, the Haitian peasants find themselves in a situation that is typical of many traditional societies subjected to the strain of modernization. The following quotation, drawn from the African experience, provides a good summary of some of the problems of transition faced by countries like Haiti:

this dependence upon personal relationships, institutionalized in various fashions . . . is maintained by the hard facts of existence in present day Africa. The African natives are faced with the same problems that beset all people — security of life and property, provision for the nurture and maintenance of their children, assistance in sickness and old age, the mobilization of assistance for economic activities beyond the scope of the individual, and provisions for assistance to handle unforeseen accidents such as entanglement with the law, the necessity to meet a civil claim, or the payment of medical and funerary expenses. In the old day, over much of Africa, men depended for the safety of their lives and property, as they did for meeting their other needs, upon the obligation of kinsmen, or of other associates, to come to their assistance if the need arose. Men were therefore primarily concerned with associating themselves with those who had some diffuse obligation to assist and protect them, and the maintenance of these social ties was a matter which took precedence over other interests . . . Today the various central governments have assumed the obligation of guaranteeing the safety of persons and property throughout the territories over which their mandates run. In general, therefore, throughout Africa the larger groupings such as clans, large lineages, age-sets, guilds, and other bodies which had such political functions are disintegrating and disappearing under the new conditions of public peace. But the central governments have not assumed obligation to provide for the other needs catered to by the old system, and here the African must continue to rely upon the willingness of his fellows to assist and protect him.[44]

The disappearance of the *lakou* is a result of the increasing population pressure. In this sense it represents a rational adaptation to changes in the economic environment. In another sense, it leaves a vacuum. One of the most important functions of the *lakou* was that it served as a primitive insurance, a kind of mutuality organization. This was one of the devices that the Haitian peasant was forced to employ to cope with risks of different kinds.[45] With the gradual demise of the *lakou*, the peasant has been forced into a situation where all risks have to be borne on an individual or nuclear family basis. As a result, there has been a reduction in the efficiency of the rural insurance system.

The risk aversion of the peasant, on the other hand, has increased and the reason is the same as the one underlying the decline of the *lakou*: population growth. Agricultural output per capita of the rural population falls both because of diminishing returns to labor in combination with increasing erosion and because of an increase in the number of people who are to share agricultural incomes. *Ceteris paribus*, this is likely to increase the peasant's aversion to risk. He is facing a situation where his standard of living is separated from the subsistence level by an ever narrower margin. This makes it increasingly important to avoid bad years, since there is a growing likelihood that a harvest failure will force the peasant family into hunger or outright starvation. At the same time the possibility of accumulating reserves to meet the bad years decreases. Finally, the very device that formerly served to increase the standard of living, to reduce risks and to mitigate the impact of bad years once they materialized is in decline.

The main problem that arises from these changes is that the peasants are left entirely on their own. There have not been any serious efforts on the part of the Haitian government to deal with this type of situation by extending some type of modern, more formalized, system of social insurance to rural areas. This would require a much more efficient taxation system than has ever existed in Haiti. This in turn would require a break with the mentality that has characterized Haitian governments since the nineteenth century: i.e. the masses are considered to exist for the benefit of the government and not vice versa. It would also require an efficient administration, not least at the local, rural level. However, Haiti has never at any time possessed such an administration. Down to the middle and lower level cadres the administration is composed of people whose main merits are political. They support the government in power. Any change of government would most probably lead to the installation of another administration with exactly the same goal structure and the same low level of competence.[46]

In this way, the Haitian peasant is worse off than in the past. He is closer to the subsistence level and his traditional defense against risks is no longer functional. Since no efforts have been made by the government to change this situation, the peasant is in a precarious position. Hence, an obvious question is whether new mechanisms could be developed in order to minimize the various risks that confront the peasant. Formal or informal co-operation is a natural response to risk and uncertainty. As we have seen above, co-operative structures have been of use in the past. We will now examine the extent to which these structures have been able to adapt to the changes that rural Haiti has undergone.

The Changing Structure of Co-operative Work

It is not only the *lakou* structure that has changed as a result of changing economic conditions in the countryside; the structure of collective work has also undergone important changes. These changes have, however, been of a more adaptive nature. To understand why the changes have taken place we must recall that an important part of some varieties of co-operative work consisted of the distribution of food, festivities and social activities in general. A *coumbite* proper or the gathering of a *société de travail* did not take place only for the purpose of working the soil. At the same time it provided amusement and relaxation for those participating. In short, it was as much a social event as agricultural work. The more elaborate forms of collective work represented not only a productive effort but bore strong characteristics of *consumption* as well.[47]

This fact is fundamental when it comes to understanding why the character of co-operative work has changed. At the beginning of the century, and in fact until at least as late as the 1940s, the 'proper' way for a peasant of some means to organize a day's collective work was to invite either a *coumbite* or a *société*, feeding the participants lavishly. By doing things correctly, the organizer not only got his field work done but also validated his status so as to gain or maintain prestige in the eyes of his fellow peasants.

This could only be done by showing generosity. It was not enough to feed and entertain those who had actively participated in the work: all the dignitaries of a *société* were entitled to their shares as well, as were all those who showed up when a *coumbite* was held, but without contributing more than to the general social *ambiance* of the occasion – not taking part in any physical work at all. For the day to be complete for the organizer, he had to receive the compliments of those who had participated. His status as a reputable citizen depended on their satisfaction.[48]

This social event retains its popularity in contemporary Haiti. A *coumbite*, for example, does not fail to attract people who are eager to meet, perhaps not so much for the purpose of helping a friend or neighbor, but rather to get a chance to gather to hear news, gossip and have a good time in general.

In spite of the attractiveness of the more elaborate forms of work teams, the *coumbite* and the *société*, both are losing ground to the simpler *escouade* which is more of a pure work effort and does not possess any 'social' characteristics.[49] This is not a new trend but probably one which has been going on for several decades. Alfred Métraux and Rémy Bastien both report that the practice of combining agricultural work and social gatherings was on its way out in the Marbial Valley in the late 1940s.[50] The Marbial Valley is not representative for Haiti as a whole, since this area was in what appeared as an acute state of depression when Métraux and Bastien visited it. Nevertheless, the observation made by these two anthropologists is a very important one, for it is precisely the combination of an economy in decline and the disappearance of the more grandiose forms of work teams that points to the explanation of this process.

When a peasant chose to hire a *coumbite* or a *société* instead of a simple *escouade*, he paid for much more than just the labor effort (although this effort may well have been greater for the first two teams than for the *escouade*). This could only be afforded by the reasonably well off person, not one without financial reserves:

> Not many peasants, even if they have reserves in their own storehouses to draw upon, manage to arrange a big 'coumbite' without some financial outlay. Very often the host is obliged, not only to kill a pig or a goat, but to go to great expense in buying maize meal, beans, fat, and the other foods usually served on such occasions, not to mention drink . . . so a labour team is usually an expensive affair.[51]

Economic events would thus appear to provide an explanation of the changing structure of co-operative labor in Haiti. Real per capita incomes in the Haitian countryside have declined,[52] and the substitution of *escouades* for *coumbites* and *sociétés* is an indication of this fall in living standards. The trend has been away from the more costly forms of co-operative work — those involving not only purely productive efforts but consumption (festivities) as well — towards simple mutual aid among peasants. The peasants have been forced to spend relatively more of their incomes on necessities like food, clothes and shelter and relatively less on social consumption activities. The harsh economic realities of a rural society where the standard of living appears to be falling slowly have thus made the peasants adapt the structure of co-operative work to yield more of the badly needed productive inputs and less of expensive consumption.

Can the Traditional Structures Be Developed?

It is hard to characterize the modern co-operative movement in Haiti as anything other than a failure.[53] At any rate co-operatives based on modern principles have not been able to supersede the traditional structures. The disappearance of these structures is rather a result of marked economic changes which have made adaptation a necessary evil. Would it then not be possible to build on some of the traditional co-operative structures when attempting to introduce modern co-operative ideas as well?

Even if modern co-operatives do not represent a perfect solution to the problem of creating a social insurance system, they could at least serve to pool risks to some extent and also to improve the control of risk factors via the acquisition of better agricultural techniques, i.e. techniques that allow for better control over output.

The problem of whether the traditional co-operative structures can be developed into modern ones has been treated by Marie-Thérèse Vallès and by Michel Laguerre. These authors reach diametrically opposed conclusions. According to Vallès it is not possible to build on the traditional forms of co-operation. As soon as the peasants acquire a fuller awareness of the problems of economic improvement and transformation the traditional structures, exemplified by the *coumbite*, will disappear.[54] The sole purpose of the traditional system is to get a day's work done. The modern system on the other hand has a much more varied goal structure where change and modernization are given considerable weight.

Vallès asked a number of co-operators about the main differences between the *coumbite* and the modern forms of co-operation. The answer was that in the *coumbite*, work was being done for others and that after the harvest nothing was left, whereas in the co-operative 'we work for our children and for our locality which we hope to transform one day by building our houses, our church and schools'.[55] Her respondents claimed not to get anything but a meal and a 'drink' out of *coumbite* work, whereas through the co-operative they saw a possibility of 'being someone and making men of their children'.[56] From this, Vallès concluded that the modern forms of co-operation were much more dynamic than the *coumbite* which would only function in the static setting and not be of any use for implementing change.

Laguerre on the other hand, recommends that the traditional structures, and especially the *escouade*, should be used in rural development projects. The *escouade* has two advantages over other types of collective labor in that it builds on strict reciprocity, with all members performing actual work, and in that its services can be sold to outsiders for cash which allows savings and capital formation to take place.[57] It is efficient in that it does not contain any festive element. The only problem, according to Laguerre, would be to ensure that all members of a given *escouade* are of roughly equal social and economic standing.

On these grounds, Laguerre suggests a confederation at the regional and national level of (stable) *escouades*. These should be legally recognized and development projects in rural areas should be channeled through them. At a later stage the *escouades* could be used to handle such matters as credit and banking, marketing of produce, purchase of inputs and transportation, agricultural education and spread of innovations, and finally measures regarding health, nutrition and hygiene, for their members.

It is doubtful whether either of these two arguments is correct. Vallès is obviously ideologically biased in favor of modern co-operatives. Quite probably, peasants who are not members of a co-operative would come up with a different view of the relative merits of modern and traditional structures. Moreover, if the modern co-operatives had been as dynamic as Vallès seems to think, we would have witnessed a more rapid development of the co-operative movement in Haiti.

Laguerre is right in arguing that the *escouade* seems to be the most functional of the traditional forms of co-operative labor in the contemporary situation. Whether a confederation of *escouades* can be created and whether such a confederation would be able to meet all the objectives envisaged by Laguerre is, however, another matter. Experience from other parts of the developing world indicates that co-operation is no panacea for all kinds of economic and social evils which the government otherwise would not or could not come to grips with. Co-operatives are most likely to succeed in a situation where the problem at hand is limited to only one or two dimensions. Thus, they may provide an excellent means for sharing expensive, otherwise indivisible facilities, 'in irrigation, transport, artificial insemination, storage, refrigeration, common use of threshing or decorticating or dairy machinery'.[58] In Haiti, even such equipment as a plow plus a draft animal qualify under this heading.[59] A second area where co-operation can easily be carried out, since the purpose of it is clear and liable to be understood by everybody involved, is in the marketing of agricultural produce provided that the products follow a given chain to their final destination. This is often the case in the marketing of export crops, when there are a limited number of final buyers (exporters) of the product. Finally, in the case where exploitation of producers or consumers by middlemen is a real danger it does not usually prove too difficult to make the exploited unite on a co-operative basis to get around the intermediaries.[60]

On the other hand, 'ideological' use of co-operatives is often doomed from the outset. To expect co-operation to handle simultaneously all kinds of functions which are better carried out by private (or governmental) specialized agencies does not make much sense. Thus, even if a co-operative is successful in one particular area, it cannot necessarily be expanded to cover any number of purposes. Cases are common

> where a Cooperative, initially successful on a simple scale, has grown overambitious in multipurpose activity, ending up as an Extension Service, a manufacturer, a Credit Bank, and a transportation undertaking. In at least some of these functions a commercial firm is far more likely to work economically than the semi-trained staff of a voluntary organization.[61]

If excessively ambitious projects can be avoided, however, the traditional structures are likely to be useful. In the first place, in the Haitian context, they are the only co-operative structures that have proved to be clearly viable. We already know that the co-operative labor team has been able to adapt to changing circumstances. So, it seems, has the *sangue*. In comparison with modern banks, the *sangue* appears to have several advantages, from the point of view of the average Haitian. In the first place, banks are found neither in the countryside, nor in provincial towns, which means that the peasant does not have easy access to their facilities. Secondly, banks are very formal institutions. Forms have to be filled out, which requires literacy. Thirdly, there is a transportation cost involved in going to the bank. The bus fare is costly and a number of other expenses will have to be paid as well. Furthermore banks are open only at certain times each day, which entails waiting. The peasant has to pay a stamp tax to receive his bank-book. The *sangue* on the other hand has none of these drawbacks.[62] However, a factor of probably even greater importance is that all members of a *sangue* have in turn unconditional right to the *main*. In a modern bank establishment, the creditworthiness of the average peasant is considered to be zero. Thus, the *sangue* corresponds far better to the needs and demands of the peasants than is the case with the modern banks.

From the point of view of the peasants, the *sangue* is also an alternative which is superior to the modern *Caisses Popularies*,[63] in that no funds have to be kept with the president, for example. Instead the money is handed over to the person in turn immediately upon collection from the members. In this way, the risk of embezzlement disappears. In addition, no books have to be kept, since everybody involved is familiar with the principles of operation and participates in the meetings.

The *sangue* would seem to fit contemporary requirements well. Thus, *sangues* are organized by factory-workers in Port-au-Prince as well as by peasants in the countryside. Of even greater interest, however, is the fact that the *sangue* system has been employed to finance emigration and that the structure of the *sangue* in these cases is extended across the national border. Thus, cases are known where an air ticket to New York has been financed by the contributions made by *sangue* members. Upon arrival in New York, the leaving member then starts to send money for the next member to make the trip, etc. Due to the obvious risks of breaking the chain, this type of venture is however confined to very close friends. In this context, it should also be mentioned that *sangues* are known to exist among Haitian *emigrés* in New York. Thus, the *sangue* system has not only made emigration possible in many instances but has followed the emigrants to their new destination as well.

Finally, it is worth noting that even the extended family has been capable of adaptation to some extent. When the *lakou* system began to disappear in the face of the increased population pressure and migration to urban areas began to take place, the extended family played an active role in helping the migrants to make the transition from rural to urban districts. The migrants are received by relatives when they reach their destination and these relatives provide them with living quarters and give them a hand in general and in particular when it comes to looking for a job.

The same principle operates across the national border. Emigration is financed by the extended family.[64] In return for this aid there is a corresponding obligation on the part of the emigrants to care for other relations once they arrive and also to remit money home.[65] Remittance of earnings by emigrants forms a very substantial part of family income for many of those who remain in Haiti. It has been estimated that in 1970 the remittances from Haitians in the United States amounted to some US$16.5 million (corresponding to some 5 per cent of the Haitian GNP that year) and that each employed Haitian in the United States directly or indirectly supports five family members in Haiti.[66] Especially in the case of illness, those remaining in Haiti expect their relatives abroad to contribute to defraying the costs connected with medical treatment.[67] Thus, the extended family remains the most important social insurance device in contemporary Haiti. The principle has not changed, only the mode of its operation.

The conclusions to be drawn from this evidence are that if successful modern co-operatives are to be created in Haiti, use must be made of the traditional structures, especially if they are to provide some social insurance. Vallès is wrong when she contends that there is a conflict between traditional and modern forms of co-operation. At least, the conflict is not one of principles. It should be possible to develop modern structures that incorporate those elements of the traditional forms that the participants in the co-operatives regard as the most valuable ones.

In practice very little has been accomplished along these lines. Recently, however, some experiments have been made. One example is given by the MODECBO (Movement for the Development of the Community of Le Borgne), a project undertaken with aid of the *Institut Diocesain d'Education des Adults* (IDEA), an organization funded by the Inter-American Foundation.[68] In this instance, the underlying philosophy has been that the initiative should not come from outside, but from the grass roots.

IDEA has supported a project in Le Borgne, in the Cap-Haïtien area, which began in 1973. In that year, the priest of Le Borgne agreed to sponsor two persons for a ten-month training course given by IDEA to educate 'not leaders as such, but rather guides and catalysts, helping peasants identify and plan activities'.[69] These two started what eventually became MODECBO. In 1977 a two-year grant of US$63,000 was obtained from the IAF to establish an agricultural pre-co-operative and credit union out of the community groups that were beginning to form. The project aimed at enabling the peasants to control the marketing and processing of their produce. To do so, the pre-co-operative and credit union based on the community groups was to be founded. In this context, community gardens were set up, a savings club was expanded, an intensive educational program was offered and storage and marketing capability was to be developed.

In this, the MODECBO built on the traditional co-operative structure. Each of the community groups, which had been founded to discuss and solve common problems, was divided into agricultural work groups of some 10-15 members who were to lease approximately one acre and farm it communally. Thus, in this case, the traditional *coumbite* was taken one step further, to include common rental of the plot worked. The savings club established clearly derived from the *sangues*. Each time the club met, members made deposits in savings accounts and when the agricultural sub-groups were constituted, these savings accounts were used to create the credit union.

The advantage of the structure represented by the MODECBO is that it does not involve any 'outsiders' to the community. All the staff members are local people who have received some training inside or outside the program. This means that the project is well anchored in the community. No outside advisers have been employed and no outside interests have been able to influence the goals of the project. The whole idea has much in common with Paulo Freire's *conscientização* philosophy.[70] Those affected by the project are to become aware of the reality they are living in and shape the project according to this awareness. The catalysts are not directing the project but only providing assistance. The peasants are to participate, suggest and manage themselves, and the animators are not even always present at the meetings. This represents a radical break with the principle according to which most co-operatives have been run in Haiti, where emphasis has been on the introduction of new structures from the outside and especially on technological change in so far as production has been involved.

The MODECBO program does not emphasize the introduction of new technologies as such. The point of departure is the employment of existing tools, which are made available to the peasants on a rotating basis, and on the more efficient use of the existing technology.

Still, MODECBO is in a sense more far-reaching than most development programs in Haiti, since it launches an attack on some of the existing structures of peasant society. The co-operative and the savings clubs here represent new ideas which the peasants are not used to and for which they have to be educated. They also constitute a challenge to the traditional marketing system and the traditional credit sources in rural Haiti.[71] Interest-free loans are provided via the savings clubs. Literacy courses are held in Creole to facilitate the learning of new skills but also as a means of providing a better understanding of the social system of which the Le Borgne peasants are part. A warehouse has been built to prevent a glut of peasant produce in the market immediately after the harvest.

In undertaking these changes, the MODECBO project, however, is also challenging the existing social and power structure. Building as it does on a *conscientização* type of process, where awareness of the position in a larger, more far-reaching system is to be gained from the common discussion and solution of concrete, specific, everyday problems, the approach is incompatible with the kind of political structure which has been characteristic of Haiti for more than a century. A necessary condition for the success of this type of program is that it must at least be tolerated by those in power. It is possible that isolated efforts may be tolerated, if not supported, but should this kind of co-operative (in a wide sense) effort begin to spread, the chances are that the tolerance will come to an abrupt end. Attempts to change power structures at the same time as economic and social relationships are changed may easily meet with strong resistance from those who dominate these structures.

Thus, there exists a serious contradiction between modern co-operative principles with their stress on democracy and participation and the type of politics that has been sovereign in Haiti at least since the 1840s. The latter builds on clique rule without mass participation, while

> To be a cooperator is to join one's misery, one's intelligence, one's spiritual force, one's moral energy, one's working capacity as a free man in the name of an acting democracy with the aim of transforming the society to which one belongs and to ensure increased economic and social well-being first to the collective and then to oneself. [72]

None of these ideals is likely to have been shared by the governments Haiti has had in the past and continues to have at the present moment. On the contrary, a genuinely co-operative mass movement in Haiti would have to come into existence not with the aid of the government but in opposition to it. The reason is simple. Co-operation would require that the masses are allowed to make decisions in questions concerning their welfare without detrimental interference by the government, and that the government would not permit.

Notes

Thanks are due to Lennart Jörberg for constructive criticism of an earlier draft.
1. Institute Haïtien de Statistique (1973), p. 37.
2. This is one of the leading themes in Lundahl (1979).
3. The word derives from the French *la cour*, yard.
4. Schaedel (1962), p. 25.

5. Cf. e.g. Bastien (1951), *passim*, and especially p. 30; Moral (1961), pp. 169 ff.; and Laguerre (1978:1), note, p. 408.

6. The older *lakous* may have been split into sub-*lakous* once they reached a certain size. (Cf. Bastien, 1951, p. 151.) Such sub-*lakous* would then have fewer houses than the undivided ones.

7. Schaedel (1962), p. 25.

8. This process is analyzed in Lundahl (1979), Chapter 6.

9. One *carreau* equals 1.29 hectares.

10. Lacerte (1975), p. 81.

11. Leyburn (1966), p. 56.

12. Bastien (1951), p. 117; Bastien (1961), pp. 479, 481 ff.

13. Ibid. (1951), pp. 37-40. The system is dealt with in detail by Murray (1977).

14. Bastien (1951), pp. 41 ff.

15. Balanced reciprocity means more or less direct exchange of goods or services. Generalized reciprocity refers to transactions that are of an altruistic nature, of assistance given and, if possible and necessary, returned by the receiving party. For a discussion of these terms, see Sahlins (1972).

16. Bastien (1951), p. 33.

17. This continues to be the case in present-day Haiti.

18. Bastien (1951), p. 133.

19. This was done by means of the co-operative labor teams known as *coumbites* (cf. next section.)

20. Bastient (1951), pp. 133-4. Cf. Bastien (1961), p. 483.

21. The word *coumbite* probably derives from the Spanish verb *convidar* (invite). Other interpretations are given in Laguerre (1975), pp. 3-4. *Coumbite* denotes two different things. On the one hand it is the generic term for all types of collective labor teams in Haiti. On the other, it is a special type of co-operative labor (cf. below).

22. Herskovits (1971), pp. 259-60.

23. Cf. Leyburn (1966), pp. 200-1.

24. Bastien (1951), Chapter 8.

25. Hall (1929), p. 689.

26. This division is due to Laguerre (1975) who gives a detailed description of each type. Cf. also Clerisme (1978).

27. This type of team is also known e.g. as *chaine, ronde* or *colonne*.

28. Murray (1973), p. 12, indicates the lower number and Laguerre (1975), p. 38, gives the higher figure.

29. Bastien (1951), p. 130.

30. The *sangue* is described in Vallès (1967), pp. 124-8 and Laguerre (1978:2).

31. Cf., however, Vallès (1967), pp. 125-6, where an attempt is made to derive the *sangue* from similar African structures.

32. Moral (1961), p. 169.

33. Bastien (1951), p. 30.

34. Moral (1961), p. 170.

35. Schaedel (1962), pp. 25 ff.; Domínguez (1976).

36. Domínguez (1976).

37. Bastien (1951), p. 46.

38. Ibid., p. 128.

39. Ibid., pp. 135-6.

40. Ibid., p. 142.

41. Ibid., p. 144.

42. Today, the necessity of financing voodoo ceremonies is one of the most common reasons for selling land. (See Murray, 1977, Chapter 11, for details.)

43. This is discussed in Lundahl (1979), Chapter 11.
44. Colson (1955), p. 71.
45. See Lundahl (1979), Chapters 11 and 12, for a discussion of risk and risk aversion among the Haitian peasants.
46. Cf. ibid., Chapters 7 and 8, for an overview of these aspects.
47. Hall (1929), p. 692; Herskovits (1971), p. 70; Métraux *et al.* (1951), pp. 69-70; Laguerre (1975), p. 33; Lundahl (1979), pp. 115-18.
48. Métraux *et al.* (1951), p. 70.
49. Laguerre (1975), pp. 37, 39, 49, 65.
50. Métraux *et al.* (1951), pp. 70-1; Bastien (1951), p. 130.
51. Métraux *et al.* (1951), p. 70.
52. For details, see the discussion in Lundahl (1979), Chapter 3.
53. For evidence see e.g. Erasmus (1952); Wood (1955), pp. 351-2, 362-4; Vallès (1967); Laroche (1969); Rotberg with Clague (1971), pp. 289-91; La Gra (1972); Zuevekas (1978), pp. 218-19; Girault (1981), Chapter 10.
54. Vallès (1967), pp. 199 ff.
55. Ibid., p. 202.
56. Ibid.
57. Laguerre (1975), pp. 62 ff.
58. Hunter (1969), pp. 154-5.
59. Lundahl (1979), pp. 590-4.
60. Hunter (1969), pp. 154-5.
61. Ibid., p. 156.
62. Laguerre (1978:2), pp. 16-18.
63. *Caisses Populaires* are co-operative credit unions. These have generally not been successful. See Vallès (1967), pp. 213 ff. and Laroche (1969) for details.
64. Laguerre (1978:1), p. 408.
65. Ibid., p. 438.
66. Segal (1975), note, p. 214.
67. Laguerre (1978:1), p. 438.
68. For a description of the project, see Maguire (1979).
69. Ibid., p. 48.
70. See Freire (1970).
71. The marketing and credit systems may not be the best objects for an attack of this type. See Lundahl (1979), Chapters 4 and 11 for an analysis.
72. Vallès (1967), p. 188.

Bibliography

Bastien, Rémy. *La familia rural haitiana*. México, D.F., 1951
Bastien, Rémy. 'Haitian Rural Family Organization', *Social and Economic Studies*, vol. 10, 1961
Clerisme, Calixte. 'Organisations paysannes dans le développement rural', *Conjonction*, no. 140, 1978
Colson, Elisabeth. 'Native Cultural and Social Patterns in Contemporary Africa', in C. Grove Holmes (ed.). *Africa Today*. Baltimore, 1955
Domínguez, Ramiro. *Comunicación en el contexto rural haitiano*. Mimeo, Institut Interaméricain des Sciences Agricoles (IICA), Port-au-Prince, 1976
Erasmus, Charles John. 'Agricultural Changes in Haiti: Patterns of Resistance and Acceptance', *Human Organization*, vol. 2, 1952
Freire, Paulo. *The Pedagogy of the Oppressed*. New York, 1970
Girault, Christian. *Le commerce du café en Haïti. Habitants, spéculateurs et exportateurs*. Paris, 1981

Hall, Robert Burnett. 'The Société Congo of the Ile à Gonave', *American Anthropologist*, NS, vol. 31, 1929

Herskovits, Melville J. *Life in a Haitian Valley*. New York, 1971

Hunter, Guy. *Modernizing Peasant Societies. A Comparative Study in Asia and Africa*. New York, 1969

Institut Haïtien de Statistique. Département de Finances et des Affaires Economiques. *Résultats préliminaires du recensement général de la population, du logement et de l'agriculture (septembre 1971)*. Port-au-Prince, 1973

Lacerte, Robert K. 'The First Land Reform in Latin America: The Reforms of Alexander Pétion, 1809-1814', *Inter-American Economic Affairs*, vol. 28, 1975

La Gra, Jerry. *Feasibility of Expanding the Integrated Cooperative Project of Bas Boën*. Organization of American States, Port-au-Prince, 1972

Laguerre, Michel. *Las asociaciones tradicionales de trabajo en el campesinado haitiano*. Mimeo, Instituto Interamericano de Ciencias Agrícolas (IICA), Port-au-Prince, 1975

Laguerre, Michel. 'Ticouloute and His Kinsfolk: The Study of a Haitian Extended Family', in Demitri B. Shimkin, Edith M. Shimkin and Dennis A. Frate (eds.). *The Extended Family in Black Societies*. The Hague and Paris, 1978:1

Laguerre, Michel S. *Le sangue haïtien: un système de crédit rotatoire*. Mimeo, Institut Interaméricain des Sciences Agricoles de l'OEA (IICA), Port-au-Prince, 1978:2

Laroche, René. 'Rapport de la Sous-Commission pour la Coopération: La coopérative, moteur du développement rural en Haïti, in Secrétairerie d'Etat des Affaires Sociales. *Actes du Deuxième Congrès National du Travail*. 21-30 avril 1969. Port-au-Prince, 1969

Leyburn, James G. *The Haitian People*. Revised edition. New Haven, 1966

Lundahl, Mats. *Peasants and Poverty: A Study of Haiti*. London and New York, 1979

Maguire, Robert. *Bottom-up Development in Haiti*. Mimeo, The Inter-American Foundation, Rosslyn, 1979

Métraux, Alfred in collaboration with Berrouet, E. and Comhaire-Sylvain, Jean and Suzanne. *Making a Living in the Marbial Valley (Haiti)*. Paris, 1951

Moral, Paul. *Le paysan haïtien (Etude sur la vie rurale en Haïti)*. Paris, 1961

Murray, Gerald, F. 'Aspects de l'actuelle organisation économique et sociale des paysans dans la plaine des Gonaïves', in *Rapport de la Mission Préparatoire de l'IICA dans la zone du projet de développement de la Basse Plaine des Gonaïves*. Institut Interaméricain des Sciences Agricoles de l'OEA (IICA), Port-au-Prince, 1973

Murray, Gerald F. 'The Evolution of Haitian Peasant Land Tenure: A Case Study in Agrarian Adaptation to Population Growth', PhD thesis, Columbia University, New York, 1977

Rotberg, Robert I. with Clague, Christopher K. *Haiti: The Politics of Squalor*. Boston, 1971

Sahlins, Marshall. *Stone Age Economics*. Chicago and New York, 1972

Schaedel, Richard P. *An Essay on the Human Resources of Haiti*. Mimeo, US/AID, Port-au-Prince, 1962

Segal, Aaron Lee. 'Haiti', in Aaron Lee Segal (ed.). *Population Policies in the Caribbean*. Lexington, Mass., 1975

Vallès, Marie-Thérèse. *Les idéologies coopératives et leur applicabilité en Haiti*. Paris, 1967

Wood, Marie V. 'Agricultural Development and Rural Life in Haiti, 1934 to 1953', PhD thesis, The American University, Washington, DC, 1955

Zuvekas, Clarence, Jr. *Land Tenure, Income, and Employment in Rural Haiti: A Survey*. Mimeo, US/AID, Washington, DC, 1978

13 OBSTACLES TO TECHNOLOGICAL CHANGE IN HAITIAN PEASANT AGRICULTURE*

Technological change is perhaps the most efficient way to break the vicious circle of low productivity and insufficient incomes that characterizes most less developed economies. 'Stage' models of economic growth and development often include a radical improvement in technology as one of their most important features. By gradually substituting modern technologies for old-fashioned ones the deadlock is broken and growth is generated in the economy. Leaving the relevance of economic 'stages' aside, few economists today would be prepared to challenge the view that holds technological change to be one of the strongest forces affecting the course and speed of development. Most economic analysis, however, takes technological change as an exogenously given fact, without venturing into the question of what determines whether this change will or will not take place. Yet, it is a universal observation in less developed societies that attempts to change the traditional technologies meet with strong resistance.

Haiti provides a good example of resistance to change. The Haitian economy, and especially its peasant sector, was never technologically dynamic, although from time to time efforts have been made to change this. These efforts go back to the first years of independence when Henry Christophe unsuccessfully attempted to introduce the plow. They continue through the American occupation of the country between 1915 and 1934 when a heavy emphasis was laid on practically and manually oriented education in rural districts, and they still go on today, through international organizations and through domestic agencies.

Yet, these efforts have failed — almost completely. The technology of the peasant is still dominated by a few simple tools — the hoe and the machete — by unimproved seed varieties, by lack of manure and fertilizers, by lack of crop rotation, and by a general lack of knowledge. This picture has not changed since the early days of the past century, and it will presumably continue to dominate the scene for quite some time yet.

The remainder of the present essay will try to identify some of the

*Source: *Conjonction*, no. 135, 1977

most important obstacles to technological change in Haitian peasant agriculture. The discussion concentrates on:

1. the nature of agricultural production,
2. topography,
3. relative factor prices,
4. family size,
5. indivisibilities,
6. risk, and
7. information and education.

The Nature of Agricultural Production

There is a tendency for technological innovation to proceed more slowly in agriculture than in manufacturing, and part of the explanation of this tendency stems from some fundamental differences in the nature of the production processes of the two industries. One such difference is that agricultural production is dealing with developing organic matter while industrial production as a rule is a question of manipulating inorganic substances. All students of biology are familiar with the fact that biology is a science which abounds with astronomically large numbers. A living cell is always infinitely more complicated in its structure than is dead, inorganic matter. Therefore living cells also become infinitely more difficult to handle. One cannot construct a living cell or even organic molecules as one builds a house or a car. There is not very much more for the agriculturalist to do than to imitate nature. Growing, ripening and maturing processes in agriculture and husbandry cannot easily be tampered with by man.

A second difference between manufacturing and agriculture is that the latter in a specific sense is much more time-consuming than the former. The timing of production processes is much easier in manufacturing than in agriculture due to the inherent seasonality of the latter. Production in both manufacturing and agriculture makes use of two different types of production factors: *flows* and *funds*. The latter are the agents of the production process — labor, land and capital — and essentially leave the process intact, while the flow factors, like raw materials, are being used up during production. We will not go into any details regarding flows and funds here. What is of interest to us is mainly that it is not technologically possible to keep all fund factors busy at all times. Tools may have to be used in turn, and both laborers and tools may have to wait at times before work can be continued.

To a certain extent periodical idleness of fund factors is a problem in all production but to reduce idleness is much easier in manufacturing than in agriculture. As long as only one unit of the product has to be made there is no difference, but when more than one unit per production period has to be produced manufacturing has an advantage over agriculture in that it can arrange production processes *in line* while agricultural production has to be arranged *in parallel*. Production in line essentially means that as soon as an operation required to make one unit of a product is finished, the operation is repeated in producing a second unit, etc., and this is repeated for all operations required to complete the product. In agriculture, on the other hand, this is generally not possible, for there it is nature that decides when most operations can be started. As a rule the operations have to be set in parallel when more than one unit of the product is to be made, i.e. each type of operation has to be begun simultaneously for all units of the product. Line production reduces idleness and hence increases the volume of output for a given set of fund factors, while with parallel production idleness is only multiplied by a factor equal to the number of units to be produced.

An example makes it easier to understand the difference. In Haiti the most important determinant of when agricultural processes may be started is the rains. It is in immediate connection with the rain periods that the ground is cleared and prepared and that sowing and planting take place. If the timing is not careful the yield will fall. Irrigation can only partially solve this problem, since the Haitian rivers have a tendency to lose all or most of their water during the dry seasons, when it is most needed. Hence, natural precipitation regulates when planting and sowing may take place. In manufacturing industry, on the other hand, timing requirements are much less severe. In most manufacturing a process can be started at any time without being governed by factors that are outside the influence of the producer.

The relative ease whereby production can be arranged in line naturally affects the possibilities to innovate. Technological progress is often a question of rearranging the operations involved in producing a certain item in such a manner that idleness of the fund factors is reduced. Clearly the scope for such rearrangements is much more limited in agricultural production than in manufacturing.

Topography

The most striking physical feature of Haiti is its topography. Less than 30 per cent of the total area of the country consists of land with a slope not exceeding 10 per cent. The rest is rugged mountains, which in at least three ways may make agricultural innovation difficult. First, some normally superior agricultural practices may become inferior. Plows, draft animals and tractors cannot be used on hillsides that are sometimes so steep that the peasants may have to use ropes or other devices to avoid literally falling off their land.

Topographical ruggedness also increases the amount of time needed for transporting people and equipment from one place to another. Most Haitian peasants do not own a single contiguous plot, but have two or more fields scattered at some (often considerable) distance from each other in hilly terrain. Hence, they have to spend much time traveling (on foot) between the homestead and the fields and going from one field to another, and as the amount of time required for transport goes up the time available for effective work, and consequently also the scope for innovations, is reduced.

The third difficulty emanating from the topography is also connected with communication problems. To transport goods in a mountainous country with a sadly insufficient road quality reduces the extent of the market which is available for peasant products thereby also limiting the extent to which it becomes possible for the peasants to specialize and reap the benefits inherent in specialization. This in turn acts as an obstacle both to the introduction of new products and to adoption of specialized superior tools or other inputs.

Relative Factor Prices

In a certain way investment is the vehicle of technological change. The technical knowledge of a given period of time is embedded in the tools, equipment and other inputs that are produced during the period in question, and technological change is experienced when newer inputs are substituted for older ones. Consequently, an economy or a sector where the rate of gross investment is low will change its technology only slowly.

One of the most important determinants of the speed of this type of technological progress is the relative price of capital and labor. In situations where labor is a factor which is expensive in relation to capital, it will pay to cut labor expenses by using newer inputs instead. As long as labor is the relatively inexpensive production factor it pays to use the old, relatively inefficient material inputs for some more time.

The Haitian peasant is in the position where capital is expensive relative to labor. The price of inputs like fertilizer and irrigation is high in terms of labor, and most peasants do not have access to sufficient external funds at an interest rate which is low enough to make borrowing for investment purposes a profitable venture. In general their only source of credit is the informal credit market, mainly the middlemen in the commercialization of their products, and the going rate of interest on this market is generally very high. Only a very insignificant number of peasants can borrow from government-sponsored credit institutes charging lower interest rates. The high relative cost of capital is translated into technological backwardness. No forces arise to supplant unimproved plant varieties. Simple hand tools continue to dominate, and the old methods of tilling the soil are not abandoned. It becomes impossible for new methods which are more intensive in material inputs to penetrate the Haitian countryside.

Family Size

A second negative influence on capital formation, and hence on technological progress, may come from population growth. When a family gets a new member it also gets an immediate claim on family resources. The new member starts to consume immediately while he cannot contribute to production and incomes until at a later stage. The difference may have to be made up for by a reduction in family savings, which in turn may reduce investment in production capital.

How relevant is such an argument for rural Haiti? This is very hard to know. Childlessness is said to be universally feared among the peasants, and a very commonly heard statement is that *'piti se l'argent'*. On the other hand, the Haitian family is not excessively large — five to six persons on the average — and studies regarding attitudes towards family planning and family size reveal explicit preferences neither for small nor for large families. Birth rates are regarded as being largely beyond human control. Neither do data regarding population growth reveal any definite trends. The Haitian population grew on the average 1.2 per cent per year during the 1824-1922 period, while from the latter year to 1950 the figure was 1.9 per cent. Between 1950 and 1975 migration came to play an important role, which makes demographic statistics difficult to interpret, but there seems to be a fair amount of consensus among observers that the actual *natural* rate of population growth in rural areas lies around 2 per cent. Hence it is possible that dependency ratios are rising.

A high dependency ratio is not a sufficient condition for rural savings and investment to remain low. The hypothesis, as stated, may be an oversimplification of the relevant features of the real world. For one thing, a rise in the dependency ratio may lead to shifts *within* a constant family consumption and hence not affect savings rates. When the new family member arrives more foodstuffs, clothes, etc. and less of other goods may be consumed while savings remain constant. Furthermore, the existence of savings does not guarantee that investment in production capital takes place. The most typical pattern of saving in rural Haiti is one of buying animals or land rather than channeling the funds into purchases of farm capital.

Still, we cannot, strictly speaking, disprove the hypothesis. Studies of a large number of countries seem to indicate that there is a significant negative relationship between dependency ratios and savings rates, and therefore, with due precautions, it may be wise to retain the possibility that this is true for rural Haiti as well until conclusive evidence refuting the hypothesis can be produced.

Indivisibilities

The experience of the Green Revolution has established beyond doubt the fact that indivisibilities are a very important obstacle to technological innovation in agriculture. Very seldom can one type of change be introduced without being accompanied by other changes as well. To be efficient, high-yielding seed varieties need fertilizers and irrigation. By the same token, application of fertilizers or irrigation does not necessarily increase the yield of traditional seed varieties, since the latter have not been selected to take advantage of additional nutrients and water, but rather to do as well as possible in the absence of these.

It is not hard to find examples of indivisibilities in Haiti either. In 1973 an American team identified the Artibonite Valley as the area in Haiti which promised to yield the best immediate results of fertilizer employment, but also found that efficient fertilizer use called for purchase of complementary inputs (most important of which were seeds), for irrigation, for credit and for a delivery system to provide fertilizer and other inputs to the peasants. Another example comes from attempts to introduce improved varieties of sorghum, which proved difficult since the superior seeds were of limited storability, so that investment in new types of storage would be called for.

The most important obstacle to innovations stemming from indivisibilities is the difficulty of financing investment. When no indivisibilities are present the peasants can gradually substitute new technologies for old ones. Investment can proceed in infinitesimally small steps. With indivisibilities this is no longer possible. Large sums are required, and since the Haitian peasant is poor he would have to borrow the money. Saving may be out of the question, since saving means postponing consumption and if the amount needed is large, and no loans can be obtained, the consumption of the peasant household may fall short of the bare subsistence requirements. External finance is not without problems for the peasant. He generally has access only to short-term credit at interest rates which are so high that borrowing large amounts at those rates would render investment unprofitable. As long as the peasant borrows only small amounts for shorter periods, the normal surplus from peasant production is enough to enable him to repay his loans, but when it comes to long-term borrowing of larger sums there is a limit to the rate of interest that the peasant can afford to pay, and that limit is lower than the rate of interest that e.g. a middleman would ask.

The plow presents an especially interesting case of indivisibilities. We have already seen why the plow cannot be used in mountainous terrain, but we still have to explain why it is not commonly used in the plains either. The plow is essentially a labor-saving device, which saves a number of man-days for each hectare plowed. Hence, by plowing a field instead of tilling it with hoes or machetes, the wage bill can be reduced. Now, it is generally not possible for a peasant to rent a plow in Haiti. He has to buy it, and this leads him into some complications. The relevant cost for the peasant to compare to the wage-bill saved by plowing is the annual cost over the life of the plow. When this cost equals the savings in the wage-bill the peasant is indifferent between using the traditional hoe and machete technology and buying a plow. Whether the wage-bill savings that can be made from buying the plow are large enough to warrant the purchase is heavily dependent on how large the area to be plowed is. The wage-bill saved which is equal to the annual cost of the plow defines a threshold farm size. If the land at the disposal of the peasant falls short of this size the savings in labor costs made by plowing will be lower than the annual cost of having a plow. The threshold size is dependent not only on how much labor per unit of plowed land can be saved, but also on the relative cost of capital (the plow) and labor. The higher the former in relation to the latter the larger must the farm be to make plowing a profitable business.

The indivisibility of the plow increases even more when we take into account that a plow needs traction. Either bullocks or tractors have to be used, and this raises the threshold farm size unless bullocks or tractors can be rented when needed, which is, however, not generally possible. In addition, there are strong reasons to believe that the labor-saving effects of the plow in Haiti are small. The peasants generally diversify their cultivations, growing a number of different products. Furthermore, the same field contains more than one crop at each point in time, and this in turn makes plowing such fields a very cumbersome affair. Great care must be taken not to destroy growing, not yet harvested, crops.

The other side of the threshold size problem is that the size of most Haitian farms is very small indeed, not very much more than a hectare on the average, and all of this land is usually not flat enough to be suitable for plowing. Weighing the small size against the small labor-saving effects of plowing and against the large indivisibility represented by plow-cum-traction, and finally against the high relative cost of capital, the rejection of the plow by the Haitian peasant even on flat land, does not come as a surprise.

Indivisibilities can be overcome by co-operative efforts. Instead of, for example, buying individual plows and bullocks, the peasants in a region could get together and buy the necessary equipment and thereafter share its use. Rural Haiti has a long and strong tradition of co-operative work, as manifested in the *coumbite*, the Haitian working-bee, but the organized co-operative movement cannot by any reasonable meaning of the term be said to have been successful. Most efforts have failed. The most important reason for this is that most co-operatives have been imposed on the peasants from above. The approach has been very *dirigiste*, and has consequently been viewed with great scepticism by the peasants. There have been other obstacles as well to a successful co-operative movement. One such factor is the high incidence of illiteracy in rural areas. The 1950 census indicated that 93 per cent of the rural population could not read and write, and while in 1971 according to that year's census the incidence had fallen to 85 per cent, the figure is still far too high. Forming a co-operative means that books and accounts of various kinds have to be kept, which requires literacy and arithmetical skills. In addition, it is not enough that only the people keeping the books are literate. When money is to be handled temptations may become too big. The ordinary members of the co-operative must be able to supervise the use of their funds.

Also, contacts and leadership appear to be a problem in rural Haiti. The population in general is not concentrated in villages but is extremely dispersed. The well-defined social network and information structure of the village is lacking, and with that community leaders. The *houngan* and the representative of the Catholic or Protestant clergy are the natural leaders, and neither of them is in general an active agent of community change, although a few co-operatives reportedly have been formed by Protestant pastors. Spontaneous formation of peasant co-operatives may also be looked upon with resentment by the local rural political officers, who are used to having the last word in important community decisions.

Risk

Peasants in less developed countries typically have to face four kinds of risks or uncertainties, which furthermore are inter-related. First, there is the production risk. Droughts, floods, hurricanes, parasitic diseases, etc., are all recurrent phenomena which may reduce production drastically. The second risk is that the price of peasant output may fall. Following good harvests markets are frequently glutted. Prices fall, and with them peasant incomes. Especially where peasants are involved in export production, as is the case with Haitian coffee, or otherwise, if they are competing with producers in other regions, this kind of risk is important, since a local harvest failure may be accompanied by a bumper crop in competing districts, so that the peasants whose output is reduced also suffer from falling prices. This type of risk becomes more pronounced if the peasants concentrate on one or a few crops.

Concentration of cultivation on other crops than food crops also makes the peasants vulnerable to a third type of risk: that of an increase in the price of food. This, as well as a decline in the price of the commodities produced by the peasants, in a situation where food has to be purchased in the market may hit the non-food-producing households severely. Finally, for such inputs that are rented or purchased and for which it is hard to substitute, a price increase may reduce output and incomes or reduce consumption (if production is not to fall). Perhaps the best illustration of this risk is the rise in fertilizer prices during the early seventies.

In varying degrees all the above risks apply to the Haitian peasant, and what makes risk such an important problem is that the peasants are desperately poor and that they have no satisfactory arrangements to protect them against risks. Perhaps the best indicator of the poverty can be found in the nutrition standard which indicates a calorie deficit range from 25 to 30 per cent and a protein deficit of around 25 per cent. This has to be contrasted with the fact that Haiti does not possess a social security system which can cope with sudden decreases of peasant incomes. All risks in principle have to be born by the peasant himself. The number of protective devices at his disposal is limited.

The combination of risks, poverty and inadequate protection makes the peasant a strong risk averter, adopting a 'survival strategy' in his actions, where the alternatives at hand are first and foremost evaluated in terms of their relative capability of maximizing the probability of survival for the peasant and his family. Adoption of such a strategy, in turn, has very definite consequences for the rate at which technological progress can penetrate the countryside.

All innovative activity in tropical or subtropical agriculture represents potential risks. It is never possible to tell *a priori* whether a new technique or product will be successful under local conditions. Many new techniques that increase yields also increase the variability of the volume of output. Traditional seeds, for example, may yield less but are more resistant to drought, insects, etc., than new, high-yielding varieties. Therefore, for a strong risk averter to accept new practices or products, the benefits of the latter must be established beyond doubt. A profit-maximizing peasant would base his judgement on whether the expected benefits from adopting the novelty exceed the expected costs, while a risk averter would be much more concerned with the possibility of a bad outcome in an individual year. The Haitian peasant cannot afford to have a satisfactory standard of living four years out of five, with a drastic fall in income during the fifth year, since his possibilities of saving anything are small, and hence he will not have any reserves to back him up should his income fall short of subsistence requirements during the fifth year.

One of the mechanisms that the peasants may use to protect themselves against the vagaries of nature and against those of the market is to keep whatever assets they may have in a comparatively liquid form. A peasant who concentrates his portfolio on production capital, not holding cash or other liquid assets, does not have any buffer against unforeseen events. Let us assume, for example, that there is a possibility that the harvest may fail. If the harvest failure materializes the peasant has to borrow *ex post*. This, in turn gives a positive return to holding cash or other liquid assets *ex ante*, since by doing so the peasant will decrease the expected cost of illiquidity (i.e. interest payments on *ex post* loans). Hence, part of his portfolio will not be production capital but liquid assets, like animals perhaps, which can be sold when the need arises.

We have already mentioned that indivisibilities constitute one of the main obstacles to innovation in rural Haiti. The lumpiness of superior technologies in combination with high interest rates which preclude long-term borrowing of large sums prevent the peasants from reaping the benefits of technological change. Let us assume, however, that the indivisibilities are not large enough to require outside finance, but that the peasant has enough savings to buy what he needs for making the technological transition. Assume, furthermore, that the new technology entails some indivisibilities and that it not only increases expected returns but also variability of yields, as in the above-mentioned case of superior seeds. The profit-maximizing peasant would always maximize expected returns and adopt the new technology provided that he had funds enough to overcome the indivisibilities. The risk averter would not necessarily do the same thing, however, since adoption of the new technology might force him to part with more liquidity than he is willing to. Instead of acquiring the superior technology and higher expected income by putting a larger share of his assets into production capital and less into liquid assets he may prefer the lower expected income from traditional technology for the latter is connected with a higher degree of security since a larger cash buffer may be kept.

A special and presumably very important case of risks is the comparative insecurity of peasant landholdings. In most statistical descriptions of the landownership system in Haiti it is stated that the overwhelming majority of the peasants own their land, but it is also a well-known fact that very few of them can present any written deeds. Theoretically 20 years of uninterrupted possession without titles establishes an undisputed right to the land in question. In practice, however, things are not so easy. Haitian history is full of examples where the peasants have undertaken to improve the quality of their land, where the value of it has increased, and where somebody from the outside has immediately moved in to dispute the rights of the peasants. We only have to think of the realization of the irrigation works in the lower Artibonite Valley around 1950, where eviction of peasants by 'legally founded' interests went so far that a commission of inquiry had to be appointed to straighten out the situation. The situation for tenant farmers is of course even worse. There is not very much a sharecropper or a tenant can do if the landowner wants to increase the rent or evict the tenant if the value of the land increases.

Naturally, the relative insecurity of ownership constitutes another important obstacle to innovations. One cannot reasonably expect the peasants to undertake measures that will increase their incomes and the value of their land unless they can be sure to reap the benefits of their efforts themselves without outside interference.

Information and Education

In the foregoing we have tacitly assumed that the peasants have had at their disposal enough information to be able to make a decision on substituting new technologies for traditional ones. This assumption was made only to focus the attention on the factors discussed. In practice the assumption is not very likely to hold. The peasant often does not have the proper knowledge of the alternatives open to him, nor does he know how to handle new products and technologies properly.

The amount of search for innovations going on in a society like rural Haiti is typically very insignificant. Unless demonstration farms or experiment stations have been established in the immediate neighborhood the peasants are not likely to search actively for novelties. Efforts to spread extension knowledge to the peasants are constantly being made by the Department of Agriculture and by other government and non-government bodies. The number of peasants affected has not been too high, however, and extension efforts have to fight several difficulties resulting from the general lack of education among the peasants.

One of the main problems when it comes to reaching the Haitian peasant with appropriate information stems from the fact that the peasant is illiterate. In general he has not gone to school at all or has gone only for one or two years, during which, with frequent interruptions due to illness, malnutrition, the need to stay at home and help on the farm, etc., he has received a low-quality education. The amount of useful knowledge absorbed is usually small. It is also soon forgotten. Little printed material finds its way into rural areas, so there is not very much to be read once school has been finished. In addition he has been taught how to read and write in French, which is a language utterly foreign to him and which he will have very few opportunities of using. If he has gone to adult literacy classes he has been taught literacy in

Creole, but the scarcity of printed matter in that language may soon make him lapse back into illiteracy again.

To reach uneducated, illiterate peasants for demonstrations of new techniques requires a large and well-qualified staff, which for the time being is not available in Haiti. It also requires repeated demonstrations for several reasons. The peasants cannot take notes. Nor is it possible to distribute *aide-mémoires* which they can go back to when the demonstrations are over. Also the capacity for complex reasoning is lowered among uneducated people. Risks may not be correctly assessed, etc. There is, finally, an important psychological aspect of the problem. Uneducated people tend to have narrower horizons and to be less receptive to change and novelty than educated persons. All this the extension agents and *animateurs* have to cope with.

Conclusions

Against the background of the foregoing discussion the fact that the Haitian peasants resist technological change becomes logical. In fact, there are very few factors in the rural environment that are conducive to propelling and spreading innovations and change among the cultivators. The analysis in the present essay indicates some of the areas where outside assistance is needed. Credit must be advanced to overcome indivisibilities. Arrangements must be made to help the peasants protect themselves against risks. Education and information are needed to increase the knowledge of available alternatives. New techniques must be mastered, etc.

Whatever prosperity there has ever been in Haiti has been based upon agriculture. More than any other Latin American nation Haiti has been a peasant country. On the other hand, very little has been done to help the peasants to solve their problems. Throughout the history of Haiti runs the abysmal gap between the urban elite and the rural masses. This situation cannot continue to exist in the long run. The capacity of the agricultural sector to feed the population is clearly insufficient, as indicated by the high incidence of malnutrition. Without technological change, agricultural production will continue to lag behind population growth, and in the end a Malthusian situation will arise. Technological change does not, however, come out of nowhere. It will have to be deliberately introduced and promoted, and this is largely a government responsibility. Recent years have seen some budding efforts at rural development and change. These efforts will have to be continued and pushed beyond the embryonic stage before too long, or the Malthusian specter will materialize.

14 PEASANTS, GOVERNMENT AND TECHNOLOGICAL CHANGE IN HAITIAN AGRICULTURE*

Introduction

Haiti is the poorest country in the Western Hemisphere: a small peasant nation where some 80 per cent of the population desperately attempt to squeeze a living out of a shrinking natural resource base with the aid of a technology which at best remains at the same level as 100 or 150 years ago. It is even probable that this level in certain respects is lower than it was during the French colonial period and very little is being done to change this sad fact. Hardly anywhere in the agricultural sector does one find any examples of technological progress. For several reasons the Haitian peasant resists technological change when it is introduced from the outside. At the same time, there are few incentives to spontaneous innovations in the agricultural sector. The capacity of the peasant economy to generate the necessary changes remains low with the result that the per capita income is falling in rural areas — a trend that is likely to continue at least in the immediate future.

In the present essay we will deal with some aspects of the problem of technological change in rural Haiti. We will then pay special attention to the inability of the peasants themselves to create technological development, to the lack of assistance from the government and to the possibility of designing development strategies which involve a minimum of government efforts. As a necessary background to the discussion of these matters we must, however, trace the historical origins of the Haitian peasantry and its separation from political decision-making and government and also find out which is the most important economic problem facing today's peasants.

The Rise of a Peasantry

The French colony of Saint-Domingue was characterized by large landholdings producing mainly for export. The most important crop

*Source: Hans F. Illy (ed.). *Politics, Public Administration and Rural Development in the Caribbean* (Munich, Weltforum, forthcoming)

of the colony was sugarcane which for technical and economic reasons required large-scale plantations, ranging from 150 to 300 hectares. Other important crops, notably coffee, which at the outbreak of the French Revolution in 1789 represented an export value almost equal to that of sugar, could be produced on smaller estates, ranging from 10 to 20 hectares in the case of cocoa to perhaps 100 hectares for coffee and indigo.[1] These plantations were based on slave labor. In 1789 452,000 slaves were at the disposal of 40,000 whites and 28,000 *affranchis* (freed slaves and their offspring).[2]

With the uprising of the slaves in 1791 and the ensuing wars of liberation, which did not end until 1804, the plantation system was subjected to an enormous strain but nevertheless survived in a form which was essentially the same as the colonial one. The population could not be brought back into slavery. This was utterly unthinkable. But slave work could be disguised under other names. The first Haitian rulers, Toussaint, Dessalines, Christophe and, during his first years in office, Pétion also, decided to keep the large estates as intact as possible and preserve *la grande culture*. The plantations were distributed to the members of the new elite as property or leasehold and each plantation was assigned a labor force of former slaves who were attached to the soil in a *fermage* system where the necessary work discipline was upheld by means of military supervision.[3]

Military supervision notwithstanding, the plantation system started to break down a mere five years after the liberation of the country from the French when Alexandre Pétion started to redistribute government land in the southern part of the country.[4] Hereby Pétion set the pattern which was to continue during the entire nineteenth century and until the beginning of the American occupation in 1915. The existing estates were divided time after time until Haiti had become a peasant country with smallholdings dominating. This structure has proved able to resist virtually all attempts to reintroduce large estates during the twentieth century. Today smallholdings still dominate the picture — the only difference being that the average size of today's holdings is far smaller (less than 1.5 hectares) than that of a century ago.

Pétion's land reform was the decisive event in the creation of the Haitian peasantry but long before 1809 tendencies were at work which had prepared the average Haitian for the transition from slavery to peasant agriculture. In fact, during the colonial period a small-scale agriculture which worked 'in parallel' with *la grande culture* and part of which interacted with the latter, had been created. In the first place slaves had escaped from the plantations (*marrons*) and set themselves up as squatters in remote areas where the authority of the colonial government could not be enforced.[5] Secondly, in an attempt to put an end to or at least minimize the extent of *marronage*, many plantation owners had taken out provision plots for the slaves, i.e. practically private, individual plots where each slave could raise crops which could be consumed or sold in the market. The proceeds from such transactions could be kept by the slave in question.[6]

These provision plots were to assume increased importance during the revolutionary wars since, when the exports from the large estates were lost, importing food became extremely difficult. It is unlikely that at any time during the 1791-1804 period more than 30 per cent of the adult male population of fighting age ever formed part of any organized fighting force.[7] Everyone else continued peaceful activities in a mainly agricultural context. More people ran off to form new *marron* communities but many stayed on the plantations and continued to work and consolidate the old provision plots, expanding the extent of their activities since by then the marketed surplus from these plots had become critical for the provision of the entire nation.[8]

These two groups, the *marrons* and, even more so, those who have remained on the plantations working the provision plots (and the land allotted to production of export crops) were fully prepared to take over the land of the estates as soon as the possibility of a takeover arose. This possibility emerged in 1809 when the retreat of the landed elite from rural to urban living began. Not only was government land redistributed but for reasons that I have dealt with in some detail elsewhere[9] the entire plantation system, whether based on government or on private property, slowly crumbled and dissolved.

During this dissolution process the ex-slaves acquired land in three different ways. In the first place, they simply squatted on available land. Most interpretations of Haiti's nineteenth-century history hold this to be the common way.[10] A second avenue to gain access to land was by means of sharecropping arrangements between those who remained in the countryside and those who moved to urban areas. Finally, land was purchased in cash transactions by ex-slaves who had earned money by working their provision plots and selling in the internal market system. (Gerald Murray has insisted that the latter was the most common method.[11]) Since the ruling groups were not able administratively to wrest a large enough surplus out of the peasants by simply resorting to taxation or rent collection, alienation of landed property became an important supplementary measure. The future peasants responded eagerly. Land was plentiful in relation to the population. Land prices were low.

The Separation of the Peasantry from the Government

The creation of a peasantry was not only a decisive event in the history of land tenure in Haiti but it was of equal importance in the field of politics since it led to a separation of the masses from the tiny elite, and it was the elite and those who aspired to an elite position who were to govern the country up to the present time.

When the land redistribution took place and the Haitian peasantry was firmly established during the nineteenth century, the peasants were simultaneously removed from contemporary and future political events.[12] The most fundamental cause behind this alienation was that the priorities of the mass of ex-slaves differed widely from those of the elite. When Toussaint L'Ouverture reverted to the colonial mode of production and once more put the laborers back to compulsory work, the latter had had but a small taste of freedom, but this was enough. Intent at all costs on shaping their own destinies, also in the economic field, the peasants valued obtaining a plot of land which could be cultivated without intervention from the outside above everything else. From their point of view the less they had to do with *autorités*, the better.

For their part, the elite and near-elite did not cherish any ardent desire to draw the masses into politics. For them, the peasants were an object of taxation rather than anything else. When the plantation system collapsed the elite retired to urban districts. Many went into commerce, sometimes attempting to keep their estates,[13] but the most lucrative of all economic pursuits was politics which turned into an activity where the rewards sought were mainly of the pecuniary variety. The peasantry formed the productive base on which large parts of the extreme Haitian spoils system was built. By taxing products bought or sold by the peasantry, substantial incomes could be ensured for those who held power.[14]

In the political field, the peasants were basically of no interest to the cliques competing for power. At the time of Pétion's death, politics concerned no more than 600 or 700 people directly.[15] I have in another context stressed the 'kleptocracy' features which so strongly pervade virtually every single Haitian government at least since the death of Christophe in 1820.[16] This undoubtedly was the most important

driving force in Haitian politics all the way up to the American occupation in 1915. When the American forces left in 1934 these tendencies
were again allowed to take precedence and continue to do so in present-
day politics.

In a recent historical study of Haitian politics and ideologies,[17]
David Nicholls has stressed the importance of color as a dividing line
between political parties and factions. Nicholls's research conclusively
points to the subordinate role of the peasantry in politics. The peasants were never allowed to have any positive word in political decisions, although from time to time black politicians bidding for power
posed as champions of the masses. The best example here is perhaps
that of Lysius Salomon, president between 1879 and 1888. He came
from a family of wealthy landowners in the south but nevertheless
managed to fall back on peasant support, persuading the masses that
the real enemy was the mulatto group, using the color question to
obscure the far more important differences between elite (of whatever
color) and peasants in the economic field.[18] Salomon was typical of
the black politicians of the nineteenth century in his use of the color
issue.

The peasants only frequently played any direct role in politics, and
when they did, it was mainly a negative one:

> In nineteenth-century Haiti the two main parties which were con-
> tending for power, distinguished broadly by colour, did not, then,
> represent the interests of two distinct social classes, but are more
> properly to be seen as representing two factions of a single class.
> For most of the time the great mass of rural workers and small
> peasants was politically inactive, though at crucial stages peasant
> groups did intervene either on the initiative of one of the political
> parties, or under the effective leadership of a man from their own
> class. These sporadic actions frequently served to bring down govern-
> ments or to rectify particular grievances but rarely had any signifi-
> cant effect upon the general policy pursued by the succeeding
> regime. They are thus to be seen as rebellions rather than as revolu-
> tionary movements. Important in these uprisings was a class of
> independent peasants large enough to be self-supporting and to make
> small loans to their neighbours, but small enough to be excluded
> from the ruling elite groups. These peasants also maintained links
> with the small towns and regional capitals. It was from this social
> class that the piquets and cacos bands were organised and manned
> from the time of Jean-Jacques Acaau to the rising against the American

occupation under Charlemagne Péralte.[19]

François Duvalier in the fifties and sixties was to build some of his support on the same group,[20] projecting himself as extending and completing the populist policies of Dumarsais Estimé who was 'un fils authentique des masses paysannes'.[21] In both cases, however, the main popular connection was one with the rising urban middle class rather than with the peasantry.

The Shrinking Natural Resource Base

The most important economic problem for today's Haitian peasant is how to make a sufficient living on a shrinking natural resource base. The per capita income appears to be falling in the Haitian countryside and the most important reason for this is that as the rural population increases, the soil is destroyed — and it seems at an increasing rate. The easiest way to convey an idea of the magnitude of the problem is perhaps by means of the map in Figure 14.1, where the shaded area shows the steep hillsides under cultivation. (More than 50 per cent of the total land area consists of hills and mountains with a slope exceeding 40 per cent.[22]) With the cultivation techniques currently employed this entire area is either threatened or already subject to erosion. It has been estimated that by 1973, 1.2 million hectares had already been lost, that another 1.2 million were subject to erosion, and that the remaining 0.4 million hectares (out of a total of 2.8 million) were threatened in one way or another.[23] These figures presumably are too high, but must still be taken seriously. We can allow for a very high margin of error but Haiti is still facing a rate of soil destruction which may eventually have fatal consequences.

What makes the erosion process particularly dangerous is not only the tendency for soil destruction to proceed at an increasing rate but also the fact that the peasants already live close to or at the subsistence level, i.e. that the average calorie intake is insufficient in rural areas.[24] This sets the stage for recurrent famines, locally or regionally (especially in the dry northwest area which is one of the poorest in the country), e.g. when a drought occurs.[25]

Figure 14.1

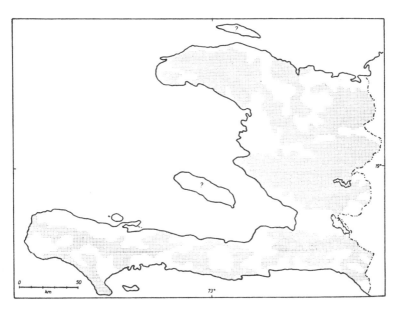

Source: Donner (1980), p. 198.

The Need for Innovations

The Haitian population presently grows at a natural rate of at least 2 per cent per annum.[26] Had no emigration taken place, an additional 100,000 mouths would have had to be fed in 1981. (The 1980 population figure was estimated to be 5 million.[27]) Emigration brings this figure down to some 65,000 (or maybe a little less),[28] but this increase has to be seen against a yearly loss of perhaps 10,000 hectares of agricultural land.[29] (Should this trend continue, which of course is impossible, no agricultural land would be left around the year 2000.[30])

This represents one side of the agricultural problem. The other side is that, according to official figures, the availability of jobs outside agriculture increased by only some 11,000 per year between 1950 and 1971 (the last two census years).[31] These figures are, however, known to be too high, since they hide the fact that a large share of the 127,000 women who were reclassified from 'agriculture' to 'commerce' did the same type of job (entailing both agricultural and commercial activities) in 1971 as in 1950.[32] Discounting these altogether brings the yearly increase in the availability of non-agricultural jobs down to a mere 1,200 per annum,[33] while at the same time the active population grew by an average of almost 23,000 people per year.[34]

Needless to say, the growth of the population and the difficulty of obtaining urban employment puts a tremendous burden on agriculture – both in terms of feeding the population and in terms of providing employment. Innovations – technological change – are badly needed. One way or another, agricultural production must be made to increase, both per hectare of cultivated land and per person employed in agriculture.

Technological progress is, however, sadly lacking in Haitian agriculture.[35] The techniques employed by today's peasant very closely resemble those employed in the nineteenth century or by the slaves working their provision plots during the colonial period. It is even likely that Haitian agriculture underwent a process of technological retrogression during the nineteenth century. In contemporary Haiti, innovations are almost nowhere to be seen.[36] In particular, innovations which have been consciously introduced from the outside are extremely difficult to find.[37]

In economic theory innovations are frequently introduced as exogenous events, in the same manner as manna from heaven. Only their effects are analyzed and not their causes. In the case of Haiti it is the causal aspect which is paramount, but causation cannot be isolated from the likely effects, since if the latter are deemed undesirable by the peasants, innovations will be rejected. Then, the question arises as to which type of innovations are needed in Haitian agriculture.

Bruce Johnston and Peter Kilby make a distinction between two kinds of agricultural development strategies; *bimodal* and *unimodal*.[38] The former 'entails a . . . rapid adoption of a wide range of modern technologies and . . . resources are concentrated within a subsector of large, capital-intensive units' while the latter strategy 'seeks to encourage a more progressive and wider diffusion of technical innovations adapted to the factor proportions of the sector as a whole. The . . . unimodal strategy emphasizes sequences of innovations that are highly divisible and largely scale-neutral. These are innovations that can be used efficiently by small-scale farmers and adopted progressively.'[39]

For obvious reasons – Haiti is a country with very few large-scale units and no concentration of landholdings – the unimodal strategy is the only one that is compatible with the agrarian structure of Haiti. It is also a strategy which fits the country's needs relatively well. Most important here is the stress on small scale and divisibility of innovations, since lack of these features is likely to act as a strong obstacle to technological progress in the context of small farms.[40] Concentration on divisible innovations, on the other hand, is likely to have favorable consequences:

> If purchased inputs are primarily divisible inputs such as seed and fertilizer, the new technologies can be widely adopted in spite of the purchasing power constraint.[41] Spread of such inputs coupled with changes in farming practices and growth of farm cash income will generate demands for improved equipment to increase the precision as well as reduce the time required for various farming operations; but with progressive modernization this demand will be directed towards simple and inexpensive implements. And if output expansion results from widespread increases in productivity among the small farm units which necessarily predominate when the farm labor force is large relative to the total cultivated area, capital requirements for investment in labor-saving farm equipment will be limited . . . electric- or diesel-powered pumpsets in India and Pakistan have represented an innovation that has been essentially complementary to the internal resources of labor and land.[42]

In general, the problem with pursuing a unimodal strategy appears to be that such a strategy does not necessarily lead to an increase in the output per worker employed in agriculture. This is due to the high rate of growth of the agricultural labor force and the comparatively low rate of growth of the effective demand for agricultural products. The latter, according to Johnston and Kilby, is unlikely to surpass 4 per cent per year.[43] In the Haitian context, this means that a minimum increase of per capita income in the order of 3 per cent per annum is needed. This is easy to see. At given prices, the growth of the domestic demand for agricultural products is given by

$$D = p + \eta g \qquad (1)$$

where p represents the rate of population growth, η the income elasticity of demand for agricultural products and g the rate of growth of real per capita income. We know that p = 1.6, and that the upper limit of D is 4. According to John Mellor, the typical income elasticity of demand for *food* in low-income countries equals 0.8.[44] For lack of appropriate Haitian data we may use this as a proxy for the income elasticity of demand for *all* agricultural products. Given these assumptions, g will equal 3.0.

In practice, however, the growth of demand will be lower. Clarence Zuvekas has suggested 0.5 as a more appropriate value of η (for food). The growth of per capita income appears to be approximately 1.6 per cent per annum (or at most 1.9 per cent according to official figures from the *Institut Haïtien de Statistique*). These figures produce a mere 2.4 per cent growth for foodstuffs. To this we must add that the prospects for most of Haiti's agricultural exports do not look too good.[45] (In the early seventies, export crops accounted for a mere 10 per cent of the value of agricultural output, however.[46]) Thus, the purchasing power constraint should presumably be put somewhere in the 2 to 2.5 per cent interval.

In the case of Haiti, the purchasing power constraint is unlikely to be binding, however. As Table 14.1 shows, imports of foodstuffs increased rapidly during the first half of the seventies. The agricultural sector simply failed to keep pace with the expansion in demand which came from the increases in population and per capita incomes. The shrinking natural resource base more than outweighed the addition of labor to agriculture. Diminishing returns to labor were reinforced by the erosion process.

Table 14.1: Imports of Food Products, 1970-6 (million US dollars)

Year	Food imports
1970	8.1
1971	10.5
1972	15.5
1973	16.2
1974	20.8
1975	30.7
1976	43.5

Source: Zuvekas (1978), p. 22.

This gives land-augmenting innovations the highest priority. These will raise yields per hectare and counteract the diminishing returns to labor. It is not too difficult to think of examples of such innovations. First of all we have techniques for maintaining and improving soil fertility. Such techniques are not at all widespread in Haiti, but Ernest

Charles Palmer in a study of the Belladère region found that a majority of farmers there were using a quite elaborate battery of soil conservation practices:

> The disappearance of the fallow has tied the farmer to his small parcel of land; once his farm is no longer productive, he has no place to go. He has been compelled, therefore, to develop a system by which he can conserve his land and maintain continuous production without a fallow period. This system includes such conservation techniques as interplanting, terracing, contour cultivation, composting and mulching . . .
>
> An increasing number of . . . farmers construct hillside terraces with brush, banana stalks, or on a more elaborate scale, with limestone rocks . . . Ninety per cent of the farmers interviewed claimed to practice some form of terracing . . .
>
> Most . . . farmers who cultivate hill slopes follow the contour as they hoe or spade in order to build up ridges to prevent soil erosion. Contour tillage is practiced even in very slightly inclined areas, but it is most in evidence on the steep slopes, and when viewed from a distance it gives the impression of elaborate terracing.
>
> Rather than burning dried grass in the fields, most farmers turn the sod with a hoe or spade. [The] . . . farmers are also familiar with composting and often spade decaying plant material into their cultivated fields. Some farmers, particularly in the highlands, construct compost pits. Others practice mulching, utilizing the refuse from sugar cane. In the coffee zone, farmers carefully pile up decaying vegetation around the base of coffee trees to enrich the soil . . .
>
> Although their system of interplanting is not highly developed compared to some (in parts of Africa or the Philippines, for example), they understand the importance of a mixture of crops for maintaining permanent production without a fallow. Through experience they have found that by interplanting their entire parcels, the total yields, although small in terms of unit area, are more secure and the long-term effects on the soil are less harmful than if they practiced a rotating fallow system and planted only a portion of their land at a time. An indication of the success of the system is the fact that many farmers in the region have maintained their terraced and inter-cropped fields in continuous production without fallow for thirty years or more.[47]

A second example of a type of innovation that is potentially of interest in the Haitian context is given by relatively simple machines which do not require large investments and which may be shared by a few peasants. In *The Economics of Insurgency in the Mekong Delta of Vietnam*, Robert Sansom reports on the invention of a simple motor pump which had exactly these features of complementarity with land and labor. The invention process is worth quoting at some length:[48]

> Mr. Van Nam, who rented one hectare of rice land, was also a part-time mechanic, servicing motor-bicycle engines in his village area . . . he had trained at a French vocational school in Saigon and . . . had worked for twelve years as a mechanic for a French dredging company in Saigon.
>
> In 1962 Nam invented the motor pump. While searching for an alternative method to obtain fresh water, he recalled that the French dredges he repaired in Saigon operated on an impeller principle, using a propeller to inject water and river-bed sediment into a large pipe, and he sought to devise a new type of pump based on this principle.
>
> . . . he faced three basic problems. First, he had to find an adequate source of power; second, he had to apply the operating principle of the French dredge to a workable tin sleeve arrangement enclosing the shaft and impeller of the pump and allowing water pushed by the impeller to traverse this sleeve; and third, he had to design an impeller, since the existing sampan propellers, even when reversed, would not impel water.
>
> He began with [an] . . . engine from a French-built motor-bicycle; it was available in his workshop and inexpensive. His first impeller was a modification of a copper propeller, which involved trimming the blades at their extremities, cutting them at their base, changing their pitch, and rewelding them to the base at the new angle. Since this impeller was 10 centimeters in diameter, fitting it at its upper end . . . with a boxlike chamber through which the water was expelled. This exit chamber was a direct imitation of the French dredge; in later models it proved unnecessary and was dropped.
>
> Nam's first model failed; the . . . engine was too weak to transport an appreciable quantity of water through the sleeve. After two months of unsuccessful testing, he purchased a . . . 4.0 horsepower engine for 2,000 piasters and used it to build a second model. On this model he began with the standard diameter propeller, changing the pitch but not trimming the blades. This impeller proved too large for the engine, and its blades were progressively trimmed in several

steps . . . After nearly four months of testing at a cost of 6,000 piasters, Nam was successful. On the basis of his success he was able to borrow 4,300 piasters from a relative to purchase a 4.5-horsepower . . . engine that, running at a higher speed (revolutions per minute), proved an ideal source of power for the motor pump. By September 1962 he was renting the pump to neighboring . . . village residents for 40 piasters per hour.

Nam's invention received the immediate attention of other nearby residents, and the innovation spread rapidly as motor dealers, acting on descriptions from farmers, built similar models.[49]

The attractiveness of the pump was at least fourfold. 1962 was a year of serious drought which compelled the Mekong Delta peasants to undertake canal work to save their crops, but this in turn made some kind of pumping device necessary. Thus, the pump enabled the peasants to survive in a difficult moment. Second, the pump was a profitable investment for those who purchased it. The monetary outlay involved was not large by the standards of the area: roughly comparable to the price of a pig, and the pump paid for itself in a single year. Third, the practice of renting the pump made the innovation a divisible one. Finally, the pump was *not* a labor-saving device, in fact, it raised the inputs of labor in relation to land because it allowed land to be double-cropped and hence eliminated a lot of the seasonal unemployment previously prevailing in the area. (The pump was a good example of what Amartya Sen has termed 'landesque' capital, i.e. capital which acts as a substitute for land without replacing labor.[50])

Population Growth and Innovative Activity

In her study of agrarian change under population pressure Ester Boserup has shown that population pressure in agrarian societies may act as a powerful incentive for technological change.[51] As the population grows, the cultivation of a given plot of land is intensified and this, according to Boserup, is not a mere movement along a given production isoquant in response to a change in the relative price of labor and land but entails genuine shifts in the production function. As the man-land ratio increases the fallow system changes in the direction of ever shorter fallows, but new inputs also appear in the process: new kinds of tools, draft animals, manure and fertilizer, irrigation, etc.

Population growth may, however, also act as a deterrent to technological change. We stated above that economic theory often treats technological change as an exogenous variable. In reality, innovations require inputs of various kinds. Production functions frequently contain shift parameters to allow for technological progress, but the latter should in turn be viewed as a production process which requires labor, capital and other inputs in the same way as all other productive activities.

Limiting our attention to agriculture, such a view enables us to divide all farming activities into two types: one that is required to produce agricultural goods in the present period with a given technology and one that has no influence on today's output but which encompasses all activities aiming at improving the technology so that more can be produced with a given factor endowment in the future. Assuming, for the moment, that all labor efforts are expended at the same time (i.e. that no seasonality exists) the agricultural workers could conceptually be divided into two groups according to which of the two types of activities they take part in. We then find that the innovative workers cannot work independently of those responsible for current agricultural production. The former group must be fed even though it does not contribute to today's output. In addition, it is likely that some inputs in the innovation process (e.g. tools) must be purchased from outside the agricultural sector. In other words, for an agrarian economy to be able to carry out technological transformations (receiving no gifts from the outside), the economy must produce a surplus above that which is consumed by those who are responsible for current production.

This surplus may have to grow as the population pressure on the land increases:

> With a given rate of population growth in a given territory the amount of investment per head is likely to become larger and larger the more densely populated the territory becomes, because the land improvements with lowest investment cost are likely to be chosen before the less remunerative ones. Moreover, the increasing intensity of land use reduces the off-season leisure periods with the result that the ability to carry an additional work burden becomes smaller and smaller, when the burden becomes larger. Since the size of the burden is dependent also on the rate of population growth, the conclusion is that the rate of population growth which a given rural community can sustain by its own efforts becomes smaller the more densely populated its territory becomes.[52]

The failure to produce or correctly use a surplus above the customary standard of living may hamper innovative activities. Let us assume that the agrarian economy at the outset produces a surplus which is being used at least partly to provide inputs in the innovative process: material inputs like tools on the one hand and improvements of the human capital in the form of education on the other (which we assume not to be free but to have an opportunity cost). This creates a flow of innovations which counteracts the diminishing returns to labor as the population and the agricultural labor force grow. Assume now, however, that this flow of innovations turns out to be insufficient to preclude the per capita income from decreasing over time.[53] In this situation obviously either the surplus must be increased by increasing the number of hours worked or the share of the surplus going into innovative inputs must rise. Alternatively, if the entire surplus is already being absorbed by the innovation process and additional work with a given technology is unable to stop the process, per capita consumption must be reduced yet further to allow for more material inputs to be purchased or for more knowledge pertinent to the innovation process to be amassed. If the economy fails to undertake this *voluntary* reduction of present per capita consumption, the tendency for the per capita income to fall and hence for per capita consumption to fall secularly and *in*voluntarily will continue.[54] When people see their standard of living fall, attempts will be made to cut corners by refraining from what is perceived as 'unnecessary' expenditures, on the one hand, and to use whatever family labor that is disposable for increasing *current* production of agricultural goods, on the other. This means, for example, that school attendance will become more irregular, if going to school entails costs — in the form of direct costs for books, uniforms, food, etc., and in terms of output foregone in agriculture or income foregone on outside jobs.

In this way the agrarian economy may easily fall into a downwards cumulative spiral where the failure to maintain a high enough rate of innovations leads to a lower agricultural production per person employed in the agricultural sector and, thereby, also to lower incomes. The latter in turn leads to attempts to reduce unnecessary outlays and if the rate of time preference is high in the economy, as it probably often is in rural areas of less developed countries, preferences for present consumption will be so strong as to preclude the necessary investment in physical or human capital from taking place. This, in turn lowers the rate of innovations still further. A 'Gresham's law of innovations' will be at work whereby current production and consumption tend to drive the important activities designed to increase productivity in the future 'out of the market'.[55]

Unless something is done to stop this 'law' from operating, an 'iron law of innovations' may take over. At very low per capita incomes, the very calorie intake may act as a deterrent to technological change. An economy where the population pressure (but not necessarily the rate of population growth)[56] is high, may be in the situation where insufficient attention is devoted to innovative activities because the calorie supply at the disposal of the economy is too low. This may be true also in the case where we allow for important seasonal variations in the agricultural production process so that most of the labor effort takes place during the sowing, planting and harvesting periods, as is usually the case. In an investigation of Asian agriculture, Harry Oshima found that for the necessary amount of calories to be available during these peak periods of heavy labor requirements, the post-harvest calorie intake had to be considerably lower. Weeding was absent. The energy required for planting more crops was lacking. Few people sought outside jobs, etc.[57] This type of economy which is incapable of producing any surplus, may be caught in some type of low-income trap where small additions to current incomes must be used for consumption and where a non-marginal surplus over current consumption may be required to get the innovation process underway again.

A process which resembles the one just described appears to be at work in Haiti. Quite probably the rate of time preference is high in rural areas.[58] With an average standard of living that is not too much above the subsistence level — with the *average* rural calorie intake being 35 per cent below the recommended standard in 1975[59] — additions to present income and consumption are regarded as much more important than possible future increases. This in itself tends to make that part of agricultural output which goes into education and purchase of material inputs very low. The average Haitian peasant is illiterate and works his land with the aid of a single tool — a hoe or a machete only — without employing either fertilizer, manure, irrigation or improved seed varieties.[60]

In many instances the situation described by Oshima has presumably been reached as well. As a rule in Haiti, very few cultivation activities take place between sowing or planting and harvesting. Once the seeds or the plants are in the ground the rest is left to nature. This, in a situation where labor is the relatively cheap production factor, could very well be the result of a lack of working capacity during the off-seasons.[61] This could help to explain the observed underemployment during these seasons on the one hand and failure to perform erosion control on the other. Terracing, for example, requires 'a laborious effort'[62] and although something like 320 idle man-days may be available each year on the average Haitian farm[63] which could be devoted to this type of work, there is no guarantee that such work will be undertaken. It has been estimated that erosion control projects require up to 200 work-days per hectare on steep eroded hillsides,[64] which means that the entire farm could be saved in a year, but still this effort is not forthcoming, in certain cases no doubt because the energy to expend the effort is lacking.

In other cases, however, the knowledge of how to carry out the proper changes may be missing. Both formal and informal instruction of agricultural practices is deficient in Haiti. The rural primary school curriculum does not offer much scope for agricultural training, and during the seventies the country possessed a mere 750 extension agents[65] — a figure which should be compared to that of some 600,000 farms during the same period.[66]

Palmer's investigation of the Belladère area lends some indirect support to our views. One way of interpreting Palmer's data is that the Belladère peasants appear to have been better off than the Haitian peasant in general and that it was because of this that they were able to produce a large enough surplus which when devoted to innovative activities could bring about the transition to higher yielding methods. In Belladère the average size of farm in 1974 was 3.43 hectares,[67] while the average for Haiti as a whole around the same time was estimated to be 1.4 hectares (1971).[68] In addition, Palmer states that the Belladère peasants 'are able to provide adequate food for their families. Examples of extreme malnutrition are rare.'[69] This must be contrasted with the observation we quoted above of a 35 per cent average calorie deficit in rural Haiti in 1975. Thus, there presumably was no calorie constraint to preclude innovations in the Belladère case.

Nor was the high rate of time preference able to hinder change. The Belladère peasants did not have to indulge in a costly search for relevant methods with which to carry out the innovations. The knowledge which was applied appears to have been introduced via two short-lived development schemes which operated in the area in the late forties and between 1959 and 1962, respectively.[70] Neither scheme left any lasting direct impact,[71] but still, viewed in a long-term perspective, both of them in retrospect appear as crucial determinants of the innovation process, since some peasants learned how to construct terraces and undertake other soil conservation work in these schemes and it was precisely this knowledge which was put to productive use later.[72]

The Government as an Obstacle to Innovations

Presumably, one of the crucial factors behind the comparative ease with which the Belladère peasants were able to transform their technology was that no, or extremely little, surplus needed to be produced to gather the necessary knowledge. The latter was available *at virtually no cost* to the peasants. This is generally not the case in Haiti where formal education in agriculture is practically absent in rural areas and where, as we have seen, extension activities are undertaken on a ridiculously small scale.

In such a situation search for relevant knowledge is likely to be both costly and inefficient. Unless experiment farms and plots which the peasants can visit are available in the neighborhood and from which they feel that they can imitate or adopt methods and techniques with *confidence*, only other farming communities can assist in providing the necessary knowledge. For reasons that we will come to soon, the peasants' confidence in government officials is likely to be low, however, and as we have already seen, examples of successfully innovating farming communities are hard to come by in Haiti.

Both these factors make search difficult. In addition, the lack of education may hamper search in several ways.[73] The less educated a peasant is, the less likely is he to search for innovations. His inquisitiveness and his perception of problems are likely to be better developed if he possesses some education than if he does not. If he is not literate, an important means of communication, especially outside the local area, is lost. Received knowledge is likely to be forgotten faster (especially if not used immediately) if no notes can be made. The interpretation of cause-effect relationships may easily be severely biased. Haitian peasants are often prone to blame supernatural forces when something goes wrong, instead of producing an explanation along rational grounds, i.e. they 'search' in a completely wrong direction. Long time horizons and the ability to understand complex explanations are both likely to be better developed among trained peasants. This is important both in situations like the invention of the Vietnamese pump referred to above[74] and when it comes to understanding changes which do not yield any immediate benefits but which are operative only in the longer run. Education is also likely to spill over to peasants who are not educated themselves but who know and have confidence in fellow farmers who may then be active in introducing new ideas. Lastly, lack of education is likely to make peasants judge risks to be higher than they really are. They may not be able to analyze risks accurately for lack of proper knowledge and when this is the case, they are quite likely to err (subjectively) on the 'high' side.

It is obvious that peasant search for technological change in Haiti is unlikely to be successful if left on its own. Some outside help is badly needed, and there is only one body that can possibly successfully carry out or at least co-ordinate assistance on the scale that is needed presently and that is the Haitian government. For various reasons, however, the gulf between the government and the peasant masses, the creation of which we described at the beginning of this essay, is likely to prove too wide to be spanned in the foreseeable future. The government acts as an obstacle to change (both technological and other) rather than as an agent for it and the peasants do not have this kind of confidence in government agencies and officials that is needed if government-directed change is to prove successful.

If we begin with the former aspect, two facts in particular need to be emphasized. In our analysis of the two 'laws' of innovation, the ability of the agricultural sector to produce a surplus and the uses to which this surplus was put emerged as central features in the reasoning. In that analysis, however, we abstracted completely from the existence of any outside power – in the present case the government – which was able to divert this surplus or part of it from the agricultural sector. But in peasant economies the existence of outside groups that appropriate some of the surplus is a central feature; so central, in fact, that anthropologists, notably Eric Wolf,[75] tie the very definition of peasants and peasant economies to it.

The appropriation of the surplus of the peasant economy in Haiti takes place mainly via taxation of the goods the peasants buy and sell. This surplus is thereafter redistributed and transformed in various ways. Haitian taxation displays strongly regressive features. Income taxes, for example, are hardly used. In 1970-1 only some 1,100 people actually paid any income taxes at all, and no more than 1 per cent of GNP at the time was declared liable for personal income taxes when calculations showed that the 'true' figure should lie somewhere in the neighborhood of 20 per cent. Those who *did* pay any income tax got away with paying an average of US$ 118 per person.[76]

The heaviest tax burden instead falls on the peasants, mainly via taxes on exported and imported goods. Among the latter, items like kerosene, cotton textiles and soap accounted for the larger share of the import duties a few decades ago. When domestic production of certain items, like flour and cigarettes, which are mass consumption goods, was begun, excise duties were substituted instead. Luxury foods on the other hand, to cite just one example, have been subject to very moderate duties. The incidence of export taxes has also rested in the main on the peasants. Here, the most important product is coffee, where most of the burden is shifted backwards to the producers. It has been estimated that some 40 per cent of the peasants' potential incomes from coffee production was appropriated in this way around 1970.[77]

Little of the surplus finds its way back to the Haitian countryside after being transformed into government expenditures. Virtually all Haitian governments have neglected the agricultural sector. On average, less than 10 per cent of the government expenditures have been allocated to agriculture.[78] Scarce resources have instead been squandered on repayment of a foreign debt which was contracted during the nineteenth century mainly to fill the pockets of the Haitian politicians, on military and police forces kept largely for political reasons, and on wage and salary payments to a bureaucracy which has been recruited mainly on political merits.[79] It is, of course, not necessary that a strategy for economic development should spend what is taken from the agricultural sector (in the form of taxes) in the same sector. Industrial development could, for example, receive priority over agriculture. Still, in a country like Haiti, where some 80 per cent of the population are directly dependent on agriculture and where simultaneously the natural resource base of that sector is very severely threatened, it makes eminent sense to make strong efforts to promote technological change there by channeling a large portion of the resources back as assistance of various kinds. This, the Haitian governments have failed to do.

The second way in which the government acts as an obstacle to change in agriculture is in its educational policies.[80] During the period after the American occupation at least up to the early 1970s, rural education presented a stationary picture in Haiti. Approximately 90 per cent of the rural population was illiterate at the beginning of the seventies, and it is very doubtful whether any progress has taken place since then. Rural education has remained devoid of the necessary financial resources with the inevitable result that both teachers and equipment have been lacking.

Worse yet is that the system of rural education has not served as a means of enhancing the human capital in the countryside, but rather as a means whereby the ruling cliques have managed to *prevent* the peasants from increasing their knowledge. In the mid-seventies less than 2 per cent of all rural children managed to pass through the entire primary cycle. This dismal performance is a direct outcome of the construction of a system where French, a foreign language, is used as the medium of instruction instead of the vernacular Creole. (Few peasant children have had any contact with French before they enter school.) This difficulty is compounded by the fact that due to the financial starvation of the rural school system, teachers and equipment are as a rule of very low quality. Add to these two obstacles the fact that great stress has been placed on examinations held at the end of each school year to determine whether or not the pupils will be promoted from one class to the next one, and it is easily understood that peasant children do not get a fair chance to acquire even a primary education. The rural school system works as a filter, but not in any positive sense of the word. It rather operates so as to prevent large numbers of pupils who, with a school system better adapted to their needs and qualifications, would have had no difficulties in passing the grades, from receiving even an elementary education. This naturally is of great importance when it comes to explaining the failure to innovate in agriculture.

Against the failure of the government to promote technological change in the countryside we must set the suspiciousness with which the peasants view government agencies and officials. The government is for the peasants a very distant entity. Contacts between peasants and government representatives as a rule take place only at the local level.[81] Data on peasant attitudes towards the government are scarce but a series of interviews conducted in rural districts in the late 1960s showed that the peasants knew very little about the president and the central government. What they *did* know were the local political figures: deputies, *tonton macoutes*[82] and the *chef de section*.[83] The latter is a most important person in rural life. For the peasants the *chef de section* not only represents the government but he *is* the government. Being the local sheriff, tax collector, etc., he wields a considerable amount of power — much more than anybody else in the local area.[84]

The Haitian countryside has always been governed in an authoritarian, or rather autocratic, fashion where the peasant has seldom if ever had any voice:

Haitians know from childhood that authority is rarely responsive and that deviance is dangerous; only obedience is rewarded. They lack the self-assertiveness 'to take the sustained action necessary to reorder their social situation'. *Au fond*, what at present is totally absent among Haitians is an awareness that their relative deprivation is capable of being assuaged,

concludes Robert Rotberg in his study of the political history of Haiti up to the late sixties.[85] Today, the situation is exactly the same. The peasants are taxed but have no political voice. President Jean-Claude Duvalier in a 'historical message' in 1978 promised a more equitable sharing of the burden of raising government revenues,[86] but the entire history of Haiti as a free nation contradicts him on this point. Such a measure would be nothing short of sensational. The likelihood that it will ever be implemented is extremely low.

Consequently, the peasants have no confidence in government-directed efforts. Since the presence of government officials in rural areas has brought few blessings, it is not so simple to make a distinction between tax collectors and *chefs de section* on the one hand and extension agents and *animateurs* on the other. They are too easily confused and a risk-minimizing peasant, living close to the subsistence level, may have perfectly valid reasons for not getting involved more than he has to with the local or national government.

In a 'soft' state like Haiti, where corruption is ubiquitous and sanctioned at the highest levels of the administration, government-sponsored attempts to change may easily backfire because interests other than the unselfish ones take over. An example of HACHO (Haitian American Community Help Organization) activities in the poor northwest region explains this point:

In 1975-76, individual community councils in the northwest began to request specific assistance from HACHO. After a year of involvement, however, HACHO felt that the community council-identified activities were not successful primarily because the councils were unable to set priorities and establish cohesive work plans. HACHO addressed this by providing trained animation agents to the councils . . .

The problem with the animators is that, although they frequently come from the bottom sector of society, for various reasons they often wind up supporting the local elite. This happens sometimes because the animators, not being from the community in which they work, seek economic and personal security, which the local power brokers can most easily grant . . . Some of them even become land-owners, and rent their land to those with whom they are supposed to be working. Their ineffectiveness as change agents becomes complete when they reach the point where they defend the status quo instead of seek to challenge social relationships.[87]

Getting Around the Government

If the mountain does not come to Mohammed, Mohammed must go to the mountain. If the Haitian government is an obstacle to change, and in particular to technological change, is there any way of getting around this obstacle if it cannot be removed? Hardly a single author writing on the economy of Haiti has failed to make the observation that the lack of government commitment to the agricultural sector constitutes one of the major constraints to development in Haiti but the strategies suggested for coping with this problem differ from author to author.

Among the first (post-1950) writers to stress the importance of the separation of elite interests from those of the peasants was John Friedmann, who in a critique of the report of the 1948 United Nations' mission to Haiti put strong emphasis on the selection of a peasant-oriented strategy for development (in contrast to the mission report which departed from an assumption of consensus of interests between the two groups):

> Inevitably, development will call for sacrifices, and these sacrifices are borne more readily when they are seen as contributing to some 'common good'. But in peasant society, the 'common good' finds expression first of all through local improvement rather than through improvement elsewhere. It is through local change that changes on the larger national scene come to be accepted. If the Haitian peasant comes to be drawn into some worthwhile activity that will accrue to his own benefit, he will be more likely to become 'progress-oriented'.[88]

Local understanding, leadership and co-operation are stressed as prerequisites for development. Still, at the end of his article, Friedmann goes on to point towards the government (which at the time without doubt was an elite government) as the ultimate agent for change: 'It is quite obvious that the Haitian government is in no position to carry out more than a small number of . . . projects simultaneously.'[89] He thus fails to design a strategy which takes full account of the conflicting interests.

Writing from a Marxist standpoint, Gérard Pierre-Charles ten years later in 1965 saw the need to substitute a new form of government for the contemporary one where a minority governed the masses without taking the interests of the latter into account in planning the future of the economy:

> Those who benefit from the present economic structure are not those envisaged to act as protagonists in the Haitian development. Essentially, the real interests are those of the poor and middle level peasants who constitute the most numerous productive classes in the country. They are those of the workers who want to improve their living conditions and liberate themselves from the spectre of un-employment, of the national sector of the local bourgeoisie who want to enlarge the local market and create the conditions for maximum profits permitting the accumulation of capital, of the petite bourgeoisie and the radical intellectuals, of the thousands of young and old who have never received any wages and who consider employment as their prime demand.[90]

If these groups could take over the leadership of the nation, a new philosophy of power would *automatically* spring into existence, according to Pierre-Charles. In his opinion, the experience of countries like Cuba provides an example of how rural, illiterate populations can be made to participate in the political process as soon as their education has started. It is the mobilization of the peasant population that appears as the main guarantee of a rapid transformation of the rural world and the national economy towards continuous progress. Mobilization, in turn, will be ensured by the political cadres of the revolutionary party, who by their work or origin are those who live closest to the rural world: the peasant leaders themselves and the urban militant groups who are moved by their class consciousness and unselfishness.[91]

This may sound neat but the problem is that the very group which is to initiate the mobilization of the masses, which in turn will lead to a change of government, did not exist in Haiti at the time Pierre-Charles wrote his study. Nor does it exist today. Thus, the solution indicated is utopian. No revolutionary change of government is imminent.

A third type of solution has been proposed by Christopher Clague. He explicitly points to the lack of government interest in rural development schemes and focuses on the role that international organizations might play:

> If, as seems sensible, we assume that only moderate improvements in

political mobilization and administrative capacity are possible in the short term, then even if international agencies can persuade Haitian governments to employ economic assistance for rural betterment most conceivable regimes are apt to be uninterested and to lack the administrative capacity to make such peasant-directed schemes prosper. For these and other reasons, we suggest that external assistance will have a greater chance of promoting the welfare of all Haitians if it is aimed at the elite as well as the peasants.

Since the prospects for development in Haiti — even given a more promising political environment — must be regarded as bleak, modest goals are the only ones worth setting. International agencies should avoid the most difficult problems and devise a simple, gradually ameliorative strategy within the capabilities of any likely Haitian government. The alternative, an all-or-nothing approach based on the promise that substantial economic advance is necessary if acceptable governments are to emerge, presumes the dubious existence of a sharp discontinuity in the favorable effects of economic progress on political development and population control . . .

We argue that some economic development is possible despite exceedingly dour political prospects. Only by proposing a modest strategy which neither depends upon nor institutes radical social alteration can we maximize the present possibilities for economic progress.[92]

Clague goes on to propose some 'tactics' for economic development which, it is stated, are based on the above philosophy. Surprisingly enough, he starts with education — an area where the government plays a most important role — and concludes that the benefit-cost ratio of primary school education is higher in urban areas than in the countryside so that 'Haiti should continue to concentrate its educational dollars on the towns until such time as the proportion of urban children in school increases markedly'.[93] In the light of our previous remarks regarding government educational policy, this appears to be a strange recommendation. Continued concentration on urban schools would only contribute to maintaining the opportunity gap and would definitely not make innovations easier in the countryside.

Improvements in the transport sector are rightly stressed. This should contribute to making search more efficient for the peasants. But here as well, government participation could not possibly be avoided. Little is, however, proposed with respect to the agricultural sector proper, although it is suggested that reafforestation should not be spread too thinly but rather be concentrated in specific areas where chances of success are high. Small innovations, like reconstruction of dikes and irrigation channels, are recommended and international agencies are told to maintain a close supervision of projects to prevent them from collapsing.

Although Clague is right in stressing gradualism instead of large projects which require a highly capable administration of a kind which is not available in Haiti, it is still very hard to see how his strategy could be made to work. There is very little a foreign aid donor can do to implement a program, no matter how desirable it may be, if the government refuses to co-operate. Erosion control provides a good example. Jack Ewel, in a report on erosion and soil conservation measures, has suggested that the *goals* of soil conservation assistance programs, which basically aim at assisting poor peasants, may not be at all compatible with working via government agencies.[94] But if this is correct, and it probably is, how could an international organization manage to get around the government? After all, Haiti is a sovereign state and even though refusing co-operation in matters of technical assistance to agriculture would not be favorably received by international agencies, there is very little the latter can do about it. Haiti is a politically stable country which is firmly governed, at least in some respects. What the government says goes, even in cases where outside organizations may hold other views. This was amply demonstrated by Papa Doc. Even as powerful an organization as the World Bank has for more than a decade insisted that the accounts of the *Régie du Tabac*, whose funds are used e.g. for paying the *tonton macoutes* and for other purely political purposes,[95] be opened to public inspection without any trace of success. If the government chooses not to go along with a project, it has the power to stop it.

A populistic approach to rural change in Haiti has been suggested by Robert Maguire. His point of departure is that development schemes in Haiti in most cases fail to involve local people in the effort:

On the road to Belladare in the north of Haiti — a road once paved as part of some long-forgotten development effort and now mostly potholes — high on a knoll overlooking the countryside, sits a relatively large, abandoned, cement building, the remains of a school built in the 1950s by a non-Haitian development assistance organization. Despite the obvious need for improved formal education in the area, this building stands empty, rapidly deteriorating in the tropical climate . . . The school . . . stands empty because the people in the area did not feel part of the physical mutation that simply appeared in their midst. Perhaps they would not have identified this building as a first priority. They were probably never consulted.[96]

Maguire points out that participation and involvement by the people affected by a development project is essential for its success. This principle is, however, all too often violated. Instead, a top-down approach is pursued where the intended beneficiaries play a passive role and where the impulse to change comes from the outside.

To get away from this type of *dirigiste* scheme, Maguire suggests that international agencies should work via *local private* development organizations — 'facilitators' — as the most efficient means to reach the peasants in their environment and effect change from the grass-root level. By choosing a bottom-up approach, a better correspondence between the needs perceived by the peasants and the contents of development projects could be obtained. Quoting evidence from the activities of a facilitator organization in northern Haiti, Maguire points to the general lack of peasant leadership at the base and calls for a 'conscientization' of the peasantry.[97] In this particular instance such conscientization was arrived at by selecting and training animators among the local population. The idea is not to produce leaders as such but rather to educate 'catalysts' who may help the peasants in identifying problems and urge them to establish cause-effect relationships which can thereafter be used for finding a solution. No outside supervision is to take place, but all team members in a project are to come directly from the local area, since 'skills existing in the community, and adaptions of local technical knowledge, are sufficient to enable animators to begin the development process'.[98]

Maguire's scheme is no more watertight than any of the preceding three. The actual experience in Haiti of programs of the type suggested by Maguire has shown that at least four important factors may impair the efficiency of these schemes.[99] The animators are selected by a community sponsor in the area, often a cleric or a community development group, before they undergo the necessary training. When returning to their local district to start working, the animators, however, have often found that the sponsors are no longer willing to offer much support — materially or morally — or that the sponsors have been trying to impose their own ideas on the animators. Second, the animators do not possess any specific skills. This is not a problem in so far as the animators work only as catalysts to make the peasants discuss their problems, but as soon as practical solutions are to be undertaken, a point is eventually reached when concrete knowledge, for example, of how to control soil erosion is needed, and this calls for special skills. Third, outside organizations working via the local facilitator organizations cannot be relied upon not to impose their own outside views. It appears that the most important problem in this area has been that of trying to impose infrastructural changes before the peasants are ready for them. Technology has often taken precedence over social consciousness. Most important of all the difficulties, however, is that local facilitators and animators can no more work without the tolerance of the government than can international organizations. Social and technological change always threatens to upset the prevailing power structure. To make people at the bottom of the social scale conscious of their situation while simultaneously stimulating change may be impossible in the situation where those who are invested with the ultimate power attempt to maintain the status quo.

None of these four strategies for coping with government unwillingness to change looks very promising. While all of them contain elements that are highly desirable in any attempt to achieve technological change they all fail to solve the basic problem: that of neutralizing a government which is an obstacle rather than an agent for change. I am afraid that the reason for this failure is simple. It is *not possible* to devise a strategy which does not encompass government action. Schemes that entail a minimum of administrative capacity can be invented, but it is hard to see how anybody could possibly avoid running into government resistance when proposing changes that run counter to the interests of the center of political power.

Nor should we expect any change of government accompanied by a shift in the attitude towards rural development. No political mass movement capable of challenging government passivity in development matters exists in Haiti and if any opposition exists within the top echelons of the power structure which in the future may form a new government, there is no reason to expect that the latter will be more prone to implement change than any other government Haiti has had since 1820.

Conclusions

Some 80 per cent of all Haitians are peasants. These peasants find themselves in an utterly precarious situation — a situation which becomes worse every year. The population grows at a steady rate while at the same time that natural resource which constitutes the base of all agricultural production — the land — is shrinking, quite probably at an increasing rate.

In this situation technological change is badly needed. If the rural per capita income is not to continue its present downwards trend, new technologies that are capable of yielding a higher output with given resources must be introduced. Yet it is difficult to find examples of successful innovations in the agricultural sector and especially of innovations which have been consciously introduced from the outside. The peasants cannot be relied upon to solve their problem spontaneously. Yet, for various reasons they tend to reject attempts to introduce methods which have proved to be efficient in other parts of the world.

It is not difficult to find examples of the type of innovations suited to Haiti's needs. Given the agrarian structure, where small family holdings dominate, a unimodal development strategy aiming at a gradual transformation of the sector as a whole is to be recommended. Within such a strategy simple soil conservation methods and other techniques that increase both yields per hectare and output per person employed in agriculture should play a strategic role. These improvements can be complemented with simple machinery which does not act as a substitute but as a complement to labor.

In peasant societies that are subject to population pressure technological change usually takes place in the long run but population pressure may also act as a deterrent to change. If the agrarian economy is not capable of producing a surplus which can be used to sustain innovative activities or if too little of the surplus is used to this end, the rural per capita income will tend to fall, as it does in Haiti. Then, for reasons explained in the present essay, current production of agricultural goods tends to take precedence over innovative activities and a downwards circular and cumulative process which depresses incomes even further is set in motion. This process could very well end in a situation where technological change is precluded because of a deficiency of calorific intake.

The natural agent for change when the peasants cannot innovate themselves is the government, but in Haiti the government has acted instead as an obstacle. The peasants are taxed, thereby losing a large part of their surplus, but very little of these taxes finds its way back to rural areas in the form of government assistance. Likewise, the governments of Haiti have managed to create a system of rural education which, by and large, serves to preserve the status quo.

Different strategies have been suggested to cope with the problem of initiating change without involving an unwilling government. These suggestions range from revolutionary takeover to modest changes at the grass-root level, but none of the strategies presently reviewed offer any solution to a problem where no solution seems to exist. The Haitian government must be considered a fairly stable one. The Duvalier dynasty has ruled the nation autocratically since 1957 and as it will probably continue to do so for some time the government definitely has the power to stop all changes which it deems undesirable — for whatever reasons. Regardless of whether one likes it or not, this is a fact that must be taken into account when discussing the possibilities of implementing change — technological and other — in rural areas. This government — and virtually all others that have ever held power in Haiti for that matter — constitutes an excellent example of what Colin Leys meant when he stated that 'if there are sacred cows in politics, general economic development is very rarely one of them, *least of all in poor countries*; and the basic importance of this paradox is so great that one is tempted to speak of politics, not economic, as somehow "primary"'.[100] Haiti continues to be ruled by cliques who 'seldom hesitate to subordinate economic development to . . . other ends'.[101] Prospects for economic development in Haiti, and rural development in particular, appear bleak indeed.

Notes

1. See Lundahl (1979), pp. 256-9, for details.
2. Moreau de Saint-Méry (1958), p. 28.
3. Cf. Lundahl (1979), pp. 259-63, for more details.
4. Ibid., pp. 263 ff.
5. *Marronage* is dealt with in detail by Gabriel Debien (see Debien, 1966). Cf. also Debbasch (1961-2) and Fouchard (1972).
6. Murray (1977), pp. 47-53.
7. Ibid., pp. 55-7.
8. Ibid., pp. 57-63.
9. Lundahl (1979), Chapter 6.
10. Cf. the references given in ibid.
11. Murray (1977), p. 102.
12. See Lundahl (1979), Chapter 7, for a discussion.
13. Joachim (1970), p. 456.
14. Lundahl (1979), Chapters 7 and 8.
15. Lepkowski (1968), p. 139.
16. Lundahl (1979), Chapters 7 and 8.
17. Nicholls (1979:2).
18. Ibid., p. 87.
19. Ibid., pp. 9-10. A short account of peasant uprisings during the nineteenth century up to 1869 is given in Nicholls (1979:1).

20. Ibid., pp. 210-11.
21. Denis and Duvalier (1948), p. 357.
22. Lundahl (1979), p. 58.
23. Gill (1973), p. 4. Donner (1980), pp. 180-215 gives an excellent overview of different estimates.
24. See the discussion in Lundahl (1979), pp. 106-10, and Chapter 9. Cf. also Beghin, Fougère and King (1970) for more details.
25. Cf. Lundahl (1979), pp. 446-7.
26. Lundahl (1979), p. 193. Cf. Donner (1980), p. 230. Population problems are discussed in detail in Segal (1975).
27. Lundahl (1979), p. 193.
28. Segal (1975), p. 199.
29. Donner (1980), p. 206.
30. Ibid.
31. Lundahl (1979), p. 634.
32. Ibid., pp. 633-4.
33. This probably is too low a figure, however.
34. Lundahl (1979), p. 634. The number of new non-agricultural jobs provided every year appears higher today. Between 1971 and 1979 the small-scale export assembly industries are said to have provided 18,000 new jobs (Donner, 1980, p. 234).
35. See Lundahl (1977) and (1979), Chapter 12 for a discussion.
36. Cf., however, Erasmsus (1952) and Palmer (1976), pp. 167 ff., for exceptions to this rule.
37. Cf. Rotberg with Clague (1971), p. 331.
38. Johnston and Kilby (1975).
39. Johnston (1972), p. 594.
40. Cf. Lundahl (1979), pp. 585 ff.
41. '. . . the sectorwide expansion in the use of external inputs (i.e. purchased from nonfarm sectors or imported) is subject to a purchasing power constraint that derives from the limited size of the commercial market for farm products relative to the number of farm households. Given that the demand for farm products is price inelastic, expansion of production for market at a faster rate than the secular increase in commercial demand would mean a reduction in farm cash receipts' (Johnston and Kilby, 1975, pp. 141-2).
42. Ibid., pp. 148-9.
43. Ibid., p. 145.
44. Mellor (1966), p. 57.
45. Zuvekas (1978), pp. 199-202. A projection of the world market demand for coffee and cocoa is found in Singh *et al.* (1977).
46. Zuvekas (1978), p. 16.
47. Palmer (1976), pp. 167, 168, 170, 171.
48. I am not arguing that pumps of the Vietnamese type could solve Haiti's problems. The pump is only offered as an example of a simple innovation process which yielded a product suited to a labor-intensive, small-scale economy.
49. Sansom (1970), pp. 166-7.
50. Sen (1962), pp. 90-7.
51. Boserup (1965). An attempt to formalize certain aspects of Boserup's argument has been made by Darity (1980).
52. Boserup (1965), pp. 103-4.
53. In an article on technological progress in agrarian communities, Fei and Ranis state that 'we believe a facet of economic life in the agrarian economy is the emergence and utilization of "slacks" in the dominant agricultural production sector. Such slacks are of two kinds, agricultural goods not required for the

maintenance of traditional consumption levels and manpower not needed for agricultural production . . . If . . . the economy is not capable of generating either type of slack . . . the analysis of such an economy which cannot even maintain its initial consumption standard is not very interesting from the long-run point of view – though at times undoubtedly of historical relevance' (Fei and Ranis, 1966, pp. 9-10, note, p. 11). To me, this appears to be a very strange position. An analysis which assumes that the necessary slack is automatically forthcoming, at the same time assumes away an important problem, especially when one thinks in terms of the long run.

54. Ester Boserup points to one such instance: 'The capacity of work of the labour and peasant families set an upper limit to the process of adaptation by means of additional toil. When the stage is reached where all able-bodied members of the rural communities, males and females, young and old, are labouring from sunrise to sunset all the year, the community has reached the point where additional investment can be undertaken only if current work is reduced and *per capita* food consumption declines' (Boserup, 1965, p. 104). This is an extreme example, however, since it assumes that it is not possible to increase the amount of work simply because no more time is available. Our reasoning above suggests that the situation where per capita consumption may have to be reduced could arise at a far earlier stage where it would be possible to work more.

55. This may be viewed as being parallel to, but with much more fatal consequences than, 'Gresham's law of planning', according to which current routine activities tend to take precedence over long-term planning in organizations in developed countries (cf. March and Simon, 1958, p. 185).

56. Cf. the quotation from Boserup above.

57. Oshima (1967), p. 390. Cf. Herskovits (1952), pp. 290-4 and Turnham and Jaeger (1971), note, p. 83.

58. Cf. the analysis of erosion control and rural credit respectively in Lundahl (1979), Chapters 5 and 11.

59. Ibid., pp. 418-19.

60. Ibid., Chapters 10 (education) and 2 (use of material inputs).

61. Cf. ibid., p. 606.

62. Palmer (1976), p. 172. Cf. Zuvekas (1978) p. 341, where a figure of 230 man-days per hectare is mentioned.

63. Zuvekas (1978), p. 144. Note, however, that the 320 man-days figure has been calculated on the assumption that the only activities taking place are crop production activities. Thus, the figure must be revised downwards to an unknown extent. Still, Zuvekas is no doubt correct in concluding that 'there is reason to believe that a substantial amount of labor time is idle' (ibid.).

64. Ibid., p. 341.

65. Lundahl (1979), p. 615.

66. Ibid., p. 154.

67. Palmer (1976), p. 209.

68. Lundahl (1979), p. 51.

69. Palmer (1976), pp. 176-7.

70. One was a border development project initiated by president Estimé, and the other was the US-backed 'Watershed' program: 'an integrated natural resource conservation project which focused on the drainage basin of Lake Péligre. Activities included reforestation and teaching of contour plowing, terracing, strip cropping and gully control' (ibid., note, p. 170).

71. At least the border development project in the forties turned out to be a more or less complete flop: 'The short-lived development of Belladere . . . was a classic example of lack of continuity in policy. The plan . . . might have had a long-term impact, but presidents succeeding Estimé had other development

priorities and increasingly neglected the frontier region. The development of Belladère had been too much the project of a single individual. It never had the full backing of other factions of government which might have carried such a project through after the end of the Estimé regime. A few farmers continued to use the new techniques learned from government extension agents but, in general, this Haitian development scheme left little imprint' (ibid., pp. 119-20).

72. The factor which triggered off the changes in the area was no other than the mounting population pressure and the concomitant destruction of the soil. Palmer compared the Belladère region with the Elías Piña area on the Dominican side of the border where the Haitian techniques were known but not used. Since the destruction of the natural resources base had not yet proceeded to the same stage as the one found on the Haitian side, the step into using the more labor-intensive technology found on the Haitian side had not yet been taken when Palmer carried out his field study in 1974-5 (ibid., pp. 171-5).

73. Lundahl (1979), pp. 606-10.

74. Inventions of this type, requiring technical knowledge, are not very likely to take place in Haiti. Remember that Mr Van Nam – a farmer – had a vocational education plus twelve years of experience in the mechanical field.

75. See Wolf (1966), Chapter 1.

76. Lundahl (1979), pp. 391-2. (The owner of one of the more well-known hotels in Port-au-Prince once told me that 'I got here in 1947, and I haven't paid any taxes since then'. He is not atypical.)

77. Ibid., p. 397.

78. See ibid., Chapter 7, for an extensive discussion.

79. Ibid., Chapter 8. Some of these aspects are also dealt with e.g. in Pierre-Charles (1969), and (1973).

80. See Lundahl (1979), Chapter 10.

81. An overview of government on various levels is given in Donner (1980), pp. 72-83.

82. Duvalier's notorious paramilitary bogeymen.

83. Rotberg with Clague (1971), pp. 362-5.

84. Surprisingly little has been written about the *chef de section*. Cf., however, Comhaire (1955); Lahav (1975); and Murray (1977), pp. 155-76.

85. Rotberg with Clague (1971), p. 366. The quotation is from Martin C. Needler: *Political Development in Latin America: Instability, Violence, and Evolutionary Change.* New York, 1968, p. 57.

86. Duvalier (1978).

87. Maguire (1979), pp. 28-9.

88. Friedmann (1955), p. 47.

89. Ibid., p. 52.

90. Pierre-Charles (1965), pp. 280-1.

91. Ibid., p. 282.

92. Rotberg with Clague (1971), pp. 318, 322.

93. Ibid., p. 330.

94. Ewel (1977).

95. Cf. Lundahl (1979), pp. 380-3. A thorough analysis of *Régie* revenues, based on indirectly available material, is made in IBRD (1974), Technical note 2.

96. Maguire (1979), p. 5.

97. Presumably along the lines indicated by Freire (1970).

98. Maguire (1979), p. 59.

99. Maguire quotes evidence from the activities of the *Institut Diocesain d'Education des Adults* – funded by the Inter-American Foundation – in northern Haiti. (See ibid., pp. 45-61.)

100. Leys (1971), p. 111.
101. Ibid.

Bibliography

Beghin, Ivan, Fougère, William and King, Kendall W. *L'alimentation et la nutrition en Haïti*. Paris, 1970

Boserup, Ester. *The Conditions of Agricultural Growth. The Economics of Agrarian Change under Population Pressure*. London, 1965

Comhaire, Jean. 'The Haitian "Chef de Section" ', *American Anthropologist*, vol. 57, 1955

Darity, William A, Jr. 'The Boserup Model of Agricultural Growth. A Model for Anthropological Economics', *Journal of Development Economics*, vol. 7, 1980

Debbasch, Yvan. 'Le marronage: Essai sur la désertion de l'esclave antillais', *L'Année Sociologique*, vol. 3, 1961, 1962

Debien, Gabriel. 'Le marronage aux Antilles Françaises au XVIIIe siècle', *Caribbean Studies*, vol. 6, 1966

Denis, Lorimer and Duvalier, François. *Le problème de classes à travers l'histoire d'Haïti*. Port-au-Prince, 1948. Reprinted in François Duvalier. *Oeuvres essentielles. Tome I. Eléments d'une doctrine*. Third edition, Port-au-Prince, 1968

Donner, Wolf. *Haiti – Naturraumpotential und Entwicklung*. Tübingen, 1980

Duvalier, Jean-Claude. 'Creation du CONAJEC. L'historique message du 13 Avril', *L'Assault. Organe du Jean-Claudisme*, vol. 1, 1978

Erasmus, Charles John. 'Agricultural Changes in Haiti: Patterns of Resistance and Acceptance', *Human Organization*, vol. 2, 1952

Ewel, Jack. 'A Report on Soil Erosion and Prospects for Land Restoration', Mimeo, US/AID, Port-au-Prince, 1977

Fei, John C.M. and Ranis, Gustav. 'Agrarianism, Dualism, and Economic Development', in Irma Adelman and Erik Thorbecke (eds.). *The Theory and Design of Economic Development*. Baltimore, 1966

Fouchard, Jean. *Les marrons de la liberté*. Paris, 1972

Freire, Paulo. *Pedagogy of the Oppressed*. New York, 1970

Friedmann, John R.P. 'Development Planning in Haiti: A Critique of the UN Report', *Economic Development and Cultural Change*, vol. 4, 1955

Gill, Tejpal S. 'An Evaluation of Soil Resources in Relation to the Agricultural Potential of Haiti', Mimeo, US/AID, Washington, DC, 1973

Herskovits, Melville J. *Economic Anthropology. The Economic Life of Primitive Peoples*. New York, 1952

IBRD (International Bank for Reconstruction and Development). *Current Economic Position and Prospects of Haiti. April 18, 1974*. Washington, DC, 1974

Joachim, Benoit. 'La structure sociale en Haïti et le mouvement d'indépendence au dix-neuvième siècle', *Cahiers d'Histoire Mondiale*, vol. 12, 1970

Johnston, Bruce F. 'Criteria for the Design of Agricultural Development Strategies', *Food Research Institute Studies*, vol. 11, 1972. Reprinted in Gerald M. Meier (ed.), *Leading Issues in Economic Development*. Third edition, New York, 1976

Johnston, Bruce F. and Kilby, Peter. *Agriculture and Structural Transformation. Economic Strategies in Late-Developing Countries*, New York, 1975

Lahav, Pnina. 'The Chef de Section: Structure and Functions of Haiti's Basic Administrative Institution', in Sidney W. Mintz (ed.). *Working Papers in Haitian Society and Culture*. New Haven, 1975

Lepkowski, Tadeusz. *Haití, Tomo II*. La Habana, 1968
Leys, Colin. 'Political Perspectives', in Dudley Seers and Leonard Joy (eds.). *Development in a Divided World*. Harmondsworth, 1971
Lundahl, Mats. 'Les obstacles au changement technologique dans l'agriculture haïtienne', *Conjonction*, no. 135, 1977
Lundahl, Mats. *Peasants and Poverty: A Study of Haiti*. London, 1979
Maguire, Robert. 'Bottom-up Development in Haiti', Mimeo, The Inter-American Foundation, Rosslyn, 1979
March, James G. and Simon, Herbert A., with the collaboration of Guetzkow, Harold. *Organizations*. New York, 1958
Mellor, John W. *The Economics of Agricultural Development*. Ithaca, 1966
Moreau de Saint-Méry, Médéric-Louis-Elie. *Description topographique, physique, civile, politique et historique de la partie Française de l'isle Saint-Domingue*. New edition, Paris, 1958
Murray, Gerald F. 'The Evolution of Haitian Peasant Land Tenure: A Case Study in Agrarian Adaptation to Population Growth', PhD thesis, Columbia University, New York, 1977
Nicholls, David. 'Rural Protest and Peasant Revolt in Haiti (1804-1869)', in Malcolm Cross and Arnaud Marks (eds.). *Peasants, Plantations and Rural Communities in the Caribbean*. Guildford and Leiden, 1979:1
Nicholls, David. *From Dessalines to Duvalier. Race, Colour and National Independence in Haiti*. Cambridge, 1979:2
Oshima, Harry T. 'Food Consumption, Nutrition, and Economic Development in Asian Countries', *Economic Development and Cultural Change*. vol. 15, 1967
Palmer, Ernest Charles. 'Land Use and Landscape Change along the Dominican-Haitian Border', PhD thesis, University of Florida, Gainesville, 1976
Pierre-Charles, Gérard. *La economía haïtiana y su vía de desarrollo*. México, D.F., 1965
Pierre-Charles, Gérard. *Haití: radiografía de una dictadura – Haití bajo el régimen del doctor Duvalier*. México, D.F., 1969
Pierre-Charles, Gérard. *Para una sociología de la opresión (El caso de Haití)*. Santiago de Chile, 1973
Rotberg, Robert I. with Clague, Christopher K. *Haiti: The Politics of Squalor*. Boston, 1971
Sansom, Robert L. *The Economics of Insurgency in the Mekong Delta of Vietnam*. Cambridge, Mass., 1970
Segal, Aaron Lee. 'Haiti', in Aaron Lee Segal (ed.). *Population Policies in the Caribbean*. Lexington, Mass., 1975
Sen, Amartya K. *Choice of Techniques. An Aspect of the Theory of Planned Economic Development*. Second edition, Oxford, 1962
Singh, Shamsher, de Vries, Jos, Hulley, John C.L. and Yeung, Patrick. *Coffee, Tea, and Cocoa: Market Prospects and Development Lending*. Baltimore, 1977
Turnham, David assisted by Jaeger, Ingelies. *The Employment Problem in Less Developed Countries. A Review of Evidence*. Paris, 1971
Wolf, Eric R. *Peasants*. Englewood Cliffs, 1966
Zuvekas, Clarence, Jr. *Agricultural Development in Haiti: An Assessment of Sector Problems, Policies, and Prospects under Conditions of Severe Soil Erosion*. US/AID, Washington, DC, 1978

INDEX

'ATE